Usability Testing for Survey Research

Usability Testing for Survey Research

Emily Geisen

Jennifer Romano Bergstrom

MORGAN KAUFMANN PUBLISHERS

AN IMPRINT OF ELSEVIER

elsevier.com

Morgan Kaufmann is an imprint of Elsevier
50 Hampshire Street, 5th Floor, Cambridge, MA 02139, United States

Notices
Knowledge and best practice in this field are constantly changing. As new research and experience broaden
our understanding, changes in research methods, professional practices, or medical treatment may become
necessary.

Practitioners and researchers must always rely on their own experience and knowledge in evaluating and
using any information, methods, compounds, or experiments described herein. In using such information or
methods they should be mindful of their own safety and the safety of others, including parties for whom
they have a professional responsibility.

To the fullest extent of the law, neither the Publisher nor the authors, contributors, or editors, assume any
liability for any injury and/or damage to persons or property as a matter of products liability, negligence or
otherwise, or from any use or operation of any methods, products, instructions, or ideas contained in the
material herein.

British Library Cataloguing-in-Publication Data
A catalogue record for this book is available from the British Library

Library of Congress Cataloging-in-Publication Data
A catalog record for this book is available from the Library of Congress

ISBN: 978-0-12-803656-3

For Information on all Morgan Kaufmann publications
visit our website at https://www.elsevier.com/books-and-journals

  Working together
to grow libraries in
developing countries

www.elsevier.com • www.bookaid.org

Publisher: Todd Green
Acquisition Editor: Todd Green
Editorial Project Manager: Lindsay Lawrence
Production Project Manager: Punithavathy Govindaradjane
Designer: Victoria Pearson

Typeset by MPS Limited, Chennai, India

To my loving family—Pete, Andrew, and Bradley.

—Emily

To Hadley, for your endless support and inspiration, and for providing calm in an otherwise chaotic life.

—Jen

Contents

About the Authors

Emily Geisen is the manager of RTI's cognitive/usability laboratory and specializes in designing and evaluating survey instruments to improve data quality and reduce respondent burden. In addition, Ms. Geisen teaches a graduate course on Questionnaire Design at the University of North Carolina (UNC), Chapel Hill. In her tenure at RTI, she had conducted hundreds of usability tests on a variety of projects from the Survey of Graduate Students and Postdoctorates to the 2020 Census questionnaires. She was the 2010 conference chair for the Southern Association for Public Opinion Research (SAPOR) and the 2009–11 secretary of the Survey Research Methods Section of the American Statistical Association. She is the 2016–18 American Association for Public Opinion Research (AAPOR) Membership and Chapter Relations Communications subchair. Ms. Geisen developed a short course on *Usability Testing for Survey Researchers* that was taught at the 2011 annual SAPOR conference; the 2016 AAPOR annual conference; the 2016 International Conference on Questionnaire, Design, Development, Evaluation and Testing; and UNC's Odum Institute. Ms. Geisen also teaches an *Introduction to Focus Groups* course at the Odum Institute. Ms. Geisen received her BA in Psychology and Statistics at Mount Holyoke College, and received her MS in Survey Methodology in 2004 from the University of Michigan's Program in Survey Methodology where she was an Angus Campbell fellow. While attending the University of Michigan, she also worked at the Institute for Social Research.

Jennifer Romano Bergstrom has over a decade of experience planning, conducting, and managing user-centered research projects. At Instagram, she leads user experience (UX) research in emerging markets. She leads, conducts, and manages UX studies across multiple teams simultaneously and collaborates across disciplines to understand the user experience. Jen specializes in experimental design, implicit learning, and eye tracking. Jen coauthored *Eye Tracking in User Experience Design* (Elsevier, 2014) and has published peer-reviewed articles in *Applied Cognitive Psychology, Memory, Annals of the New York Academy of Sciences, Journal of Health Communication, Computers in*

Human Behavior, Survey Practice, International Journal of Human-Computer Interaction, Social Science Computer Review, Universal Access in the Information Society, and *Journal of Usability Studies.* Jen frequently presents research and conducts workshops at local, national, and international events and conferences. Prior to Instagram, Jen led UX research at Facebook for Privacy, Safety Check, Facebook Lite, and Videos. Jen previously formed the UX Division at Fors Marsh Group, in the Washington DC area, where she designed a state-of-the-art laboratory and recruited, trained, and led a team of UX researchers. She also taught a team of researchers at the US Census Bureau how to use eye-tracking data in usability research to impact design change for website, surveys, and forms. Jen is the President of the User Experience Professionals Association (UXPA), and she is past President of the DC Chapter of the Usability Professionals Association (UPA) and the DC Chapter of the American Association for Public Opinion Research (AAPOR). Jen received her BA in Psychology from Central Connecticut State University, and her MA and PhD in Applied/Experimental Psychology from The Catholic University of America.

Acknowledgments

The idea for this book came from a friend and colleague, Sarah Cook, who asked for some resources she could use to learn more about conducting usability testing on surveys. The information available was limited, so we sought to change that. It started with a short course, which morphed into this book.

We would like to acknowledge the support of RTI International, and in particular Murrey Olmsted, for not only allowing time away from important project work to write this book, but actively encouraging and supporting this process.

We would like thank the following illustrators for their wonderful contributions to the visual design of this book:

- Christina Lall: Figures 4.8, 4.9, 4.10, and 4.11
- Grace Oliver: Figures 2.13, 4.12, and 4.13
- Sarah Spencer: Figures 1.1, 2.4, and 3.8

We would like to thank Ecotonos and Emma Craig, who allowed us to use an image from usability testing of early mobile prototypes (Figure 3.5).

We would like to thank the following people who reviewed early drafts of the manuscript:

- Emilia Peytcheva (RTI International): whose feedback helped in shaping the idea for the Model of Usability Testing.
- Merrie Aiken (RTI International): who helped clarify the language used and gave us the idea for the key concept call-outs used in each chapter.
- Gordon Willis (National Cancer Institute): who provided an extraordinarily helpful review of early drafts and whose book *Cognitive Interviewing* was a source of inspiration for this book.
- Donna Tedesco (Facebook): who reviewed early chapters and provided valuable insight on in-lab and remote testing.

We would like to thank our peers and colleagues who allowed us to discuss some of their work with designing and testing surveys in this volume, including Don D. Dillman, Leah M. Christian, Jolene D. Smyth, Mick P. Couper, Gordon B. Willis, Caroline Jarrett, Elizabeth M. Nichols, Erica Olmsted-Hawala, and Jeff Sauro.

We would like to thank Lindsay Lawrence at Morgan Kaufmann for her patience and editorial assistance.

We are indebted to Ronnie Lipton, our editor, who reviewed the final version of this draft and made this book about usability testing more usable.

Introduction

Usability testing of surveys is essential yet often overlooked. We often spend time to ensure our questions are created properly and are understood well, but we forget the crucial step of ensuring that interviewers and respondents can record responses easily and accurately. This is especially critical for surveys conducted via the web or mobile applications. Technology is constantly changing, allowing for innovation and advancements in the way we conduct surveys in these modes. We are not always going to know what the best design is or what the best approach should be. And when surveys are self-administered, it is even more crucial to conduct usability testing on them—there is no interviewer present to correct or assist respondents who have difficulty recording responses.

Much of our focus in this book is on usability testing of web- and application-based surveys, which we refer to as web-based surveys. This includes self-administered web and mobile surveys as well as interviewer-administered surveys conducted on computers or mobile devices. The methods and approaches we discuss can be also be applied to paper surveys, but our focus is predominantly on web-based surveys.

The goal of this book is to blend usability theory and survey research best practices in an effort to provide a method for developing better surveys. Although this is NOT a book about designing surveys, we cannot help but discuss certain aspects of design and how design affects usability. In fact, good survey design is an integral part of the user-centered experience. However the focus of this book is on the mechanics of usability testing, which is used to evaluate surveys.

Throughout this book, we provide case studies that demonstrate the ideal way to conduct usability testing and analysis. However, we recognize that many organizations are moving to an agile product development process for surveys, where survey applications are developed incrementally and tested iteratively with only a few participants. This process values working solutions over detailed documentation. Where applicable, we present considerations that can be applied when developing and testing surveys in an agile environment.

WHO SHOULD READ THIS BOOK?

Our goal is to provide readers with a basic understanding of how respondents interact with surveys, as well as practical tools for conducting usability testing on surveys.

This book is designed for:

- Those who conduct surveys but have no formal training in survey methods or usability testing
- Those who are familiar with survey methods but not usability testing
- Those who are familiar with usability testing, but not how to tailor it to surveys

HOW IS THIS BOOK ORGANIZED?

This book contains eight chapters, with a table of contents, a glossary of terms, a list of evidence-based references at the end of each chapter, and an index to help you find topics by terms you may already know. The chapters will guide you through the background of surveys and usability, and then planning, conducting, and analyzing usability studies. Each chapter includes real-world examples from our own work and other cited work to give the reader insight into usability problems and testing techniques that have been discovered and used.

Chapter 1: Usability and Usability Testing

Chapter 1, Usability and Usability Testing, provides a brief history of usability and explains the key components of usability testing—the product, the users of the product, users' goals, the context of use, and the metrics of evaluation. We explain what these usability components mean when evaluating the usability of surveys. We discuss the importance of usability testing as a pretesting method, but note that it does not replace good questionnaire design. We conclude with a brief overview of the usability testing process as applied to survey research.

Chapter 2: Respondent—Survey Interaction

Chapter 2, Respondent—Survey Interaction, introduces the concept of survey error, which consists of errors of nonobservation and errors of observation (measurement error). We discuss how measurement error in particular affects the quality of data we collect from surveys, and how survey researchers are interested in preventing or reducing error. We describe the four cognitive processes respondents use to answer survey questions: comprehension, retrieval, judgement, and response. We then describe the key components of the respondent–survey interaction: interpreting the design, completing actions, and navigating and processing feedback. We show how understanding the way that respondents comprehend survey questions and interact with the survey instruments can be used to identify and reduce potential sources of error.

Chapter 3: Adding Usability Testing to the Survey Process

Chapter 3, Adding Usability Testing to the Survey Process, describes how to apply usability principles to survey research to identify and reduce survey errors. We start by explaining that usability testing does not replace good questionnaire design but instead is designed to build off of existing literature. We discuss how to build iterative design and testing into the survey development cycle. We discuss the three primary types of testing that can be conducted depending on the goals of the study: exploratory testing, assessment testing, and verification testing. We then provide guidance on what aspects of a survey or survey design can be tested, from a survey concept to a wireframe to an early interactive prototype to a finished product. We include key considerations for integrating testing on mobile devices into the process as well. We conclude the chapter by introducing the concept of the usability testing continuum that explains what situations require more intensive usability testing with repeated rounds or more participants and what situations require less testing.

Chapter 4: Planning for Usability Testing

Chapter 4, Planning for Usability Testing, describes the necessary steps to take when planning usability testing. We discuss considerations for participant selection and recruitment as well as sample size. We then discuss testing equipment including software such as screen recorders and hardware such as mobile sleds that can be used for testing on mobile devices. We then discuss the differences between laboratory testing, in-the-field testing, and remote testing. Finally, we provide guidance on practical considerations to keep in mind when planning.

Chapter 5: Developing the Usability Testing Protocol

Chapter 5, Developing the Usability Testing Protocol, details the necessary components of the usability testing protocol, also known as the moderator's guide or script. This begins with identifying the scope of the project—i.e., the main concerns that the usability test aims to identify. We then introduce the three types of usability measures that can be collected—self-report, observational, and implicit—and why they may be needed for your study. We then discuss how to develop scenarios and tasks.

Chapter 6: Think Aloud and Verbal-Probing Techniques

Chapter 6, Think Aloud and Verbal-Probing Techniques, describes the think-aloud approach and why it is used for moderating usability testing. We discuss variations of the approach, such as concurrent and retrospective think aloud. We also discuss verbal-probing techniques and variations of this approach, such as concurrent and retrospective verbal probing, and scripted versus spontaneous probing. We provide guidance on how to develop and administer unbiased verbal probes. We then discuss how to choose a moderating technique depending on your pretesting goals and objectives. We discuss methods for combining usability testing with other pretesting methodologies, such as cognitive interviewing.

Chapter 7: Conducting Usability Sessions

Chapter 7, Conducting Usability Sessions, describes the process for setting up and conducting a usability session. The focus starts with the "day before" testing, which includes preparing the equipment and organizing the materials. We then provide guidance on how to moderate the session in an unbiased manner, with special consideration for remote moderating. We provide tips on dealing with common situations as well as moderating challenges. We then discuss the roles of the moderator compared with note-takers and other observers and how to involve stakeholders in the usability testing process. The chapter ends with a discussion of how to collect and record data during the session and how to log observations.

Chapter 8: Analyzing and Reporting Results

Chapter 8, Analyzing and Reporting Results, focuses on analyzing and reporting the findings from usability studies. We begin by outlining the approach for analyzing data, which includes compiling the data, summarizing the data, and interpreting the data. We provide guidance and examples for completing each step in the process, including both a detailed version as well as a simplified version for surveys conducted in an agile environment. We then discuss approaches for revising usability problems. Finally, we describe the key components to include when reporting the results of your study.

Glossary of Terms

At the end of the book, we provide a glossary of key terms.

While we each have over a decade of experience conducting usability tests of surveys and teaching others how to use this technique, we recognize that much is still to be learned. Many of the examples in this book are from our own research, as well as from colleagues who present as conferences and publish in peer-reviewed journals. We hope that this book inspires others to publish their techniques and findings. While usability testing has made its way into the pretesting stages for many surveys, many others still miss this crucial step. In order for usability testing to become a standard pretesting methodology, those of us in this field need to share methods, theories, and results with each other. You can be part of this too, by presenting your usability work at conferences, publishing in peer-reviewed journals, and documenting your approach and findings in final reports.

We hope you enjoy the book!

Emily and Jen

CHAPTER 1

Usability and Usability Testing

When I (Emily) was attending graduate school, I met an engineer who worked at Ford Motor Company. He explained that it was his job to take artists' concept drawings and use them to engineer a working car. He noted that while the designs were usually beautiful, modern, and stylish, they were not always usable. As a result, his conversations usually went something like this (Fig. 1.1):

> ENGINEER: "This is a lovely design, but a car really must have wheels to function."
> ARTIST: "Oh, but wheels are so ugly!"

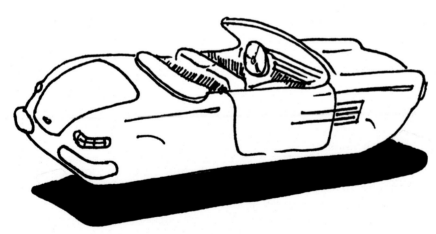

FIGURE 1.1
A car without wheels might have a nice design, but people cannot use it.

Usability Testing for Survey Research. DOI: http://dx.doi.org/10.1016/B978-0-12-803656-3.00001-4

While it is obvious that cars need wheels to work, many aspects of what makes a design usable are not clear, which necessitates usability testing. In his ground-breaking book, *The Design of Everyday Things*, Norman (2002) demonstrated that design—and consequently, usability—affects things that people use, from teapots to airplanes to surveys.

In this chapter, we provide a brief history of *usability*, make the case for why usability is needed for evaluating surveys, explain what it means—generally and specifically for survey research—and conclude with an overview of the *usability testing* process.

A BRIEF HISTORY

The concept of usability, which stems from the discipline of Human Factors, is grounded in industrial efficiency and has been around for centuries. Intuitive design, ease of use, and error reduction have long been used in war scenarios, such as in training soldiers and in designing airplane cockpits.

The concept has been used for survey research for decades. Beginning in the late 1970s, a significant body of research evaluated how respondents completed paper surveys and forms, identifying designs and layouts that made surveys easier to use (Dillman, 1978, 1991, 1995; Dillman, Sinclair, & Clark, 1993; Jenkins & Dillman, 1997; Marquis, Nichols, & Tedesco, 1998).

The terms "usability engineering" and "usability" were first used in 1979 to discuss how people interacted with computers (Bennett, 1979). In the 1980s, as personal computers became more affordable, there was value in designing intuitive computer interfaces.

With the emergence and rise of *computer-assisted interviewing* in the 1990s, researchers began to assess not only the feasibility of computer-based surveys (i.e., how likely it was that the new technology would work), but also their usability (Couper, 2000; Hansen, Fuchs, & Couper, 1997).

Couper (2000) predicted that usability testing would become a standard questionnaire-pretesting technique. Although usability testing has become significantly more prominent, it has not yet become standard in many organizations. Of those organizations that regularly conduct usability testing, few have documented their process. To become a standard, practitioners must first share their methods and theories, so the field can reach a consensus on best practices. The primary purpose of this book is to fill that gap and present a model for incorporating usability testing as a standard pretesting technique for surveys and to share knowledge about best practices.

DEFINING MODERN USABILITY

The International Organization for Standardization (9241-11, 1988) defines usability in this way:

> The extent to which a product can be used by specified users to achieve specified goals with effectiveness, efficiency, and satisfaction, in a specified context of use.

We start by breaking apart that definition into the five key components.

1. The product
2. The specified users of the product
3. The goals of the users
4. The context of use
5. Metrics of evaluation (effectiveness, efficiency, and satisfaction)

To relate these concepts to a more traditional situation, let us imagine that we will usability-test a desk chair (the product). We would test how well teachers (the specified users in this example) can use the test chair at their desk in the classroom (the context of use). We would give them tasks that are identical to how they normally would use the chair. For example, the teachers' task might be to sit in the chair and adjust it to their preferred height (the goals of the users). We would measure usability by evaluating (metrics) if and how well they can adjust the height (effectiveness), how quickly they can adjust the height (efficiency), and how satisfied they are with the height they adjusted the chair to (satisfaction).

Additionally, we would conduct *iterative usability testing*, in which changes would be made to the chair based on the usability testing findings, and then we would test the chair again with a new set of participants, using the same tasks and metrics. We would compare metrics in each round of testing to the previous round, and if usability improves, so would our metrics. This iterative process would continue until optimal usability is achieved.

DEFINING USABILITY FOR SURVEYS

Usability testing of surveys is really no different—we give realistic tasks to participants who represent the real survey respondents. Then we assess how well participants can use the survey to complete tasks, which often include entering responses, navigating, and finding information.

The Product

Survey *products* include anything from paper surveys to web-based surveys, and *self-administered surveys* to *interviewer-administered surveys*. In addition to surveys, usability testing also can be helpful for evaluating forms and other products related to surveys, such as supplementary items, like showcards needed during interviews, project and data dissemination websites, data collection monitoring systems or dashboards, and custom control systems.

We test self-administered surveys because they are very prone to usability errors, regardless of the mode of administration (e.g., paper or web-based: desktop computer, laptop, tablet, smartphone). This is largely because of the absence of an interviewer to help navigate the survey, provide additional information, or resolve consistency errors. Consequently, a respondent may provide inaccurate data or become frustrated and break off the survey. Usability testing is one method that can be used to identify, evaluate, and ultimately resolve some of these issues.

Interviewer-administered surveys have an advantage over self-administered surveys because interviewers are usually trained on how to administer the survey correctly, they practice using the survey, and they conduct the survey multiple times. Therefore it may seem that these survey products need less testing. Although the presence of an interviewer reduces the likelihood of certain types of usability errors, a poorly designed interviewer-administered survey can still affect data quality, burden interviewers, or unnecessarily lengthen interview times.

For example, when an interviewer asks a respondent, "What is your date of birth?," the respondent could give a variety of valid responses, such as August 28th 1975, or 8-28-1975, or 1975-8-28, or 28-8-1975. However the interviewer may be able to enter responses in only one format, such as 8/28/1975. Requiring interviewers to convert the name of a month to a numeric format in their head during the interview could introduce error. This extra step could also add burden.

Usability testing is likely to detect these types of errors in interviewer-administered surveys by observing a long pause or an error as interviewers convert a verbal response to a numeric response. Alternately, the interviewer may suggest how the survey could be revised to fix a problem that they experienced during the test. In this example, a good practice is validating date of birth by having the interviewer repeat it to the respondent; it is always better to prevent errors rather than correct them.

Another reason to test interviewer-administered surveys is to evaluate the navigation strategies that are the most intuitive for interviewers to use, which can decrease survey-administration times. Let us look at an example.

Fig. 1.2 is a screenshot from an interviewer-administered survey on a tablet. The purpose of Question 5 is to determine whether the property contains additional living quarters or households. The *red*, ALL-CAPS text is meant for interviewers to read to themselves. It instructs them to ask about additional households only if the property is a "regular housing unit." If the property is an apartment or a condo, the interviewer can simply touch the appropriate button and skip to the next question.

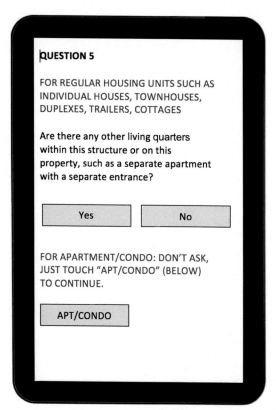

FIGURE 1.2

Some interviewers overlooked the *red*, ALL-CAPS text and read the survey question to respondents in apartments and condos as well as "regular housing units."

Researchers found that interviewers sometimes asked about additional households when interviewing at apartments and condos because interviewers missed the red ALL-CAPS instructions. To address this usability problem, the survey was revised to automatically determine the households that are apartments or condos, based on the information provided on the sampling frame. As a result, interviewers did not have to decide whether to ask the question because they saw it only when it applied.

If residence information had not been available beforehand, the questions could have been revised, as shown in Fig. 1.3. Only if the answer is no (not an apartment or condo) would the interviewer receive the follow-up question about potentially missed housing units on the property (Question 5b). If the answer to Question 5a is yes, the survey program would skip Question 5b and the interviewer would not see it.

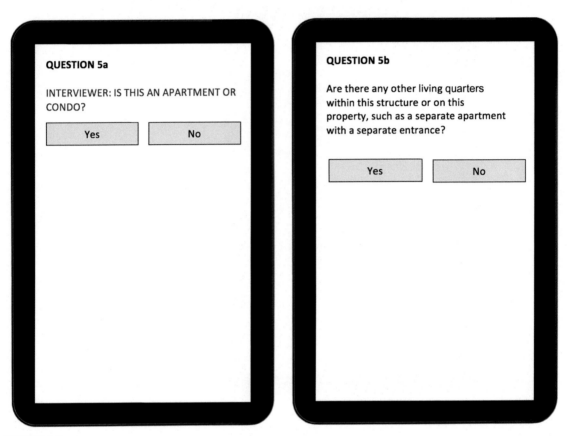

FIGURE 1.3
The question could be split into two separate questions. Interviewers are first asked if they are at an apartment or condo. If no, they see the next item and ask respondents Question 5b. If yes, the survey program skips Question 5b.

The Specified Users of the Product

In summary, usability testing is simply watching a typical *user* try to achieve specific goals, such as answer survey questions.

Who is a typical user?

- For self-administered surveys, the participants in the usability study should be potential survey respondents.

- For an interviewer-administered survey, the participants should be interviewers attempting to administer a survey to a respondent.

- For other survey-related products, participants might be the public, data analysts, or project staff.

Surveys often use *question branching* to ask different questions for different respondents. For example, a survey on drug use might have different questions for respondents who use drugs than for respondents who do not. To ensure accurate estimates of drug use within a population, the survey must make sense to respondents in both groups. Even for respondents who receive the same questions, differences in education, computer literacy, or other factors may affect the usability of the survey. Researchers must carefully consider how usability concerns may differ by respondent characteristics when choosing study participants.

The Goals of the Users

When we assess the usability of a survey, we assess whether survey users (respondents or interviewers) can achieve specified goals—the users' goals, NOT the product team's. This is an important distinction. Researchers often focus on the goal of the product, company, or agency and forget to assess whether the users can use the product and what difficulties they face trying to do so. For example, a team's goal might be to measure the prevalence of marijuana use in the past 12 months in the United States. The goal is for the respondent to provide accurate opinions, stories, facts, or predictions. However the respondent may simply want to finish the survey as quickly as possible to receive the offered incentive. Understanding respondents' goals and motivations can help you to develop surveys that apply user-centered design principles that ultimately work well for the respondent and lead to accurate data collection.

> Important distinction: Specified goals are the user's goals, NOT the product team's goals.

The Context of Use

A specified *context of use* means that the product needs to be evaluated for usability in the context in which it will actually be used. You need to think about where users will complete the surveys and how users will complete them. Will users be in their homes? ...in their offices? ...on the train? ...in the library? Was the survey designed to be completed on a desktop computer, yet people complete it on a mobile device?

For example, *establishment surveys* should be tested at respondents' workplaces to allow them access to any records necessary to complete the survey.

Similarly, to test a survey that appears after consumers complete a website purchase, you should simulate the shopping experience prior to testing the survey. At the very least, the test should ask usability-study participants to pretend they have just made a purchase in a given scenario.

Although laboratory testing is commonly used for early rounds of testing, later ones can benefit from being conducted in the field. An example is the usability testing of the US Navy's performance-management system (Dean, Aspinwall, Schwerin, Kendrick, & Bourne, 2009), which consisted of electronic forms that staff had to complete while on duty. The Navy wanted to make sure that its staff members could actually use the forms on the job, not just in a laboratory. Therefore several rounds of usability testing were conducted with active-duty personnel on a Navy ship off the coast of Japan.

This does not mean that surveys need to be tested in all possible contexts, such as with respondents in their home while they are watching three children and cooking dinner. However, it does mean that, to the extent a product can be tested in the primary and most likely contexts, the better the product will be. This is especially true when the context will have a significant effect on how the user interacts with the product.

For example, a survey that respondents complete on a mobile device provides unique challenges: the smaller screen size, the touch screen, and the fact that users are likely to be "out and about." For most surveys, it is critical to design for mobile devices and conduct usability testing on them.

But conducting usability testing in the actual context may not always be feasible. For one thing, it is costly to fly staff around the world to test a product. However, you should factor the survey context into your usability-testing considerations, budget, and schedule. Not all products require that level of testing, but if yours does and you do not have a travel budget, you may be able to conduct *remote usability testing*. In this case, researchers use the phone, web, and other tools to talk and interact with participants wherever they might be. We discuss remote testing further in Chapter 4.

Metrics of Evaluation

Here, we focus on the three most common *metrics for evaluation*: effectiveness, efficiency, and satisfaction:

- *Effectiveness*—whether users are successfully able to complete specific tasks (e.g., finding the Frequently Asked Questions).
- *Efficiency*—the time or the number of steps it takes to complete a task.
- *Satisfaction*—often self-rated measures or qualitative comments elicited from the user during usability testing.

Depending on your needs, you might collect other metrics as well, such as whether and to what extent the interface is engaging, error tolerant, or easy to learn (Quesenbery, 2003). If *eye-tracking data* are collected, you might evaluate participants' attention or gaze to determine the parts of the screen that participants focused on or how quickly they noticed a relevant button.

To evaluate a survey's usability, you must understand that the focus of testing surveys differs from testing other products, such as websites or software, and this plays a factor when determining how to measure effectiveness. For example, Google evaluated 41 shades of blue to identify the shade that users clicked on more (Holson, 2009). The more times that a Google link is clicked, the more revenue Google makes: effectiveness = clicks = revenue. As is true of survey testing, web testing can also support varying goals. For example, if the American Association for Public Opinion Research (AAPOR) conducted usability testing of its website, it might measure effectiveness as the percentage of users who were able to find a specific standard (effectiveness = clicks = information finding), renew their membership (effectiveness = clicks = membership), or sponsor the annual conference (effectiveness = clicks = revenue).

When testing surveys, on the other hand, the three main measures of evaluation (effectiveness, efficiency, and satisfaction) equate to two primary goals of pretesting:

- Improving data quality by reducing error
- Preventing item or unit nonresponse (e.g., skipping items) by reducing respondent burden

Evaluating the effectiveness of a survey means evaluating the accuracy and validity of the survey data that is collected. For example, does the design cause bias or variance in the survey estimates being collected? Are respondents able to answer the survey questions as the designer intended?

Measuring effectiveness is unique to each survey. A question that performs well in one survey may not perform well in another, depending on the mode, respondents, and context. For example, think again about a date-of-birth question. In an interviewer-administered survey, a response category that gives both the verbal and numeric description of the month (e.g., "August—08") may improve accuracy by keeping interviewers from having to match the name to the number.

However, on a self-administered form that asks for a credit card's expiration date, it is more efficient for users when the format on the survey or form matches the format on the credit card, that is, a two-digit month (e.g., "08") and two-digit year (e.g., "19") (Holst, 2012). This format also makes it easier for people who speak different languages or are accustomed to different formats to find the month and year more easily. This consistency allows users to transcribe the number from the card to the survey easily. Users may not know the text equivalent for the month, and including that requirement is likely to confuse and delay them.

Improving efficiency and satisfaction is associated with reducing respondent burden. When you reduce respondent burden, you may also reduce skipped questions, *break-offs*, and *satisficing*. Examples include reducing the time it takes to answer a question and avoiding cognitively complex demands, such as converting a date into a specific format. Another example is providing a "calculate" button rather than asking respondents to add individual values—likely to increase satisfaction as well.

In general, reduce respondent burden by allowing respondents to answer surveys without having to think too hard about interacting with the instrument. Respondents should not wonder how to select a response, where to go next, or what a specific link or button does. This ease of use can (1) prevent users from accidentally or intentionally skipping questions, (2) reduce the number of respondents who break off a survey, and (3) generally encourage participation.

In addition to encouraging participation and preventing nonresponse, reducing respondent burden can often lead to improved accuracy. For example, a too-long survey may cause fatigue, which affects the quality of answers provided. Sometimes though, survey designers have to choose between improving accuracy and increasing efficiency or satisfaction, as this next example illustrates.

In a usability test that included slider questions, such as those shown in Fig. 1.4, participants found the sliders to be novel and often commented that they were interesting and fun to use. Participants were able to use the sliders easily and quickly to select their response.

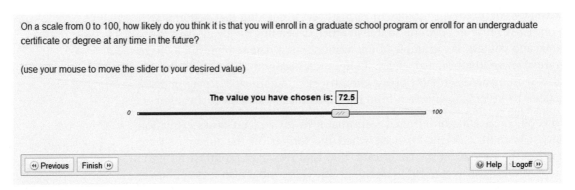

FIGURE 1.4

Slider questions, including this one, on a survey of recent college graduates are enjoyable for respondents, but they do not always result in accurate answers.

During usability testing, some participants provided specific—unrounded—responses to the questions, such as 72.5. When this occurred, participants were asked about it, "You answered 72.5. How did you come up with your answer to this question?"

Participants said they found it difficult to move the slider to an intended value such as 75, so they would often pick a value that was "close enough." Although satisfaction was high, use of the sliders would lead to increased variance and lower precision in the survey estimates. Due to the limitations of the software, it was not feasible to make the slider movements more fluid. Instead, the sliders were replaced with traditional *Likert-scale questions* to assess satisfaction.

This study, along with others, demonstrated that respondents perceive questionnaires using sliders as engaging (Downes-Le Guin, Baker, Mechling, & Ruylea, 2012; Sikkel, Steenbergen, & Gras, 2014; Stanley & Jenkins, 2007; Thomas, 2011). However, Sikkel et al. (2014) found that the positive feelings diminish over subsequent waves of the study; and Couper, Tourangeau, Conrad, and Singer (2006) found that sliders were considered no more engaging than radio buttons or text input. The effects of sliders on data quality are mixed, with most studies showing that sliders are no different or worse in data quality compared to more traditional methods (Couper et al., 2006; Roster, Lucianetti, & Albaum, 2015; Sellers, 2013).

IMPORTANCE OF USABILITY TESTING AS A PRETESTING METHODOLOGY

Pretesting a questionnaire before conducting a survey is common practice for identifying potential errors in the questionnaire. The three most common *pretesting methodologies* are *expert review*, *cognitive interviewing*, and *pilot testing*.

Traditionally, pretesting begins with an expert review by survey methodologists and subject-matter specialists. An expert review can identify common pitfalls in survey questions (e.g., double-barreled questions, inappropriate assumptions, missing reference periods) and ensure that the questions are measuring the intended constructs. Cognitive testing, which identifies potential problems in survey questions by evaluating the cognitive processes respondents use to answer survey questions, often follows. Once questionnaire content and study design have been finalized, a pilot test is usually conducted. The pilot test is used to evaluate how well the survey will work in the "real world" by testing the procedures with a small number of respondents.

Although these traditional pretesting methods have provided great insight into many types of survey errors, they are not ideally suited for detecting usability concerns, especially for web-based surveys. Increasingly, respondents complete surveys on touch-screen mobile devices, such as tablets and smartphones (Lugtig, Toepoel, & Amin, 2016; Saunders, 2015), and interviewers use mobile apps to administer screening surveys on household doorsteps. Yet, existing pretesting methodologies do not fully account for the way that respondents interact with these modes and how that interaction affects the way that respondents answer survey questions. With the pace of change in survey administration, we need to look into newer methods that can be used to evaluate the unique challenges associated with web-based surveys.

Usability testing is intended to complement, not replace, other pretesting methods. Pilot testing focuses on the logistics and procedures of conducting a survey, whereas cognitive testing emphasizes understanding and answering survey questions, and usability testing targets use and interaction. These pretesting methodologies are not mutually exclusive in the sources of error identified, and they often overlap, as shown in Fig. 1.5. By combining pretesting methods, we can improve the overall quality of data obtained from our surveys.

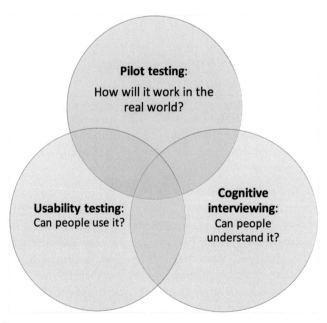

FIGURE 1.5

Combining multiple methods of survey pretesting can identify more potential survey errors than a method can.

USABILITY TESTING DOES NOT REPLACE GOOD DESIGN

Designing high-quality surveys is no easy task. And although usability testing surveys is essential, it is no substitute for good survey design. The key to user-centered evaluation is starting with best practices or secondary-research findings. Survey designers first should ensure that they are using standard web or survey conventions (e.g., radio buttons for single choice, check boxes for multiple choice) and avoiding designs that are known to cause frustration or errors for respondents. Then the designs should be tested to ensure the chosen designs work as intended for the respondents.

> Reviewing and incorporating best practices can reduce the number of testing iterations required and save time and money developing and evaluating a survey.

Reviewing and incorporating best practices can reduce the number of testing iterations required and save time and money developing and evaluating a survey. For example, a best practice in self-administered surveys (both mail and web-based) is to list response options in one column. That format generates more accurate and reliable responses than options displayed in two or three columns, as shown in Fig. 1.6 (Christian & Dillman, 2004).

Respondents do not process two- or three-column response categories in a consistent manner. Some respondents move from right to left and then down, while others move from top to bottom then right to left.

However, we must keep in mind that a question format that worked well on one type of survey may not necessarily work well on another type. Dillman, Tortora, and Bowker (1999) advise using multiple columns when all responses cannot be displayed on the screen in one column without scrolling. Romano and Chen (2011) confirmed this recommendation in an eye-tracking study. They tested two versions of a survey with a long list of response options. Eye-tracking data from the study revealed that when the response options were split into two columns, participants were more likely to look at the second half of the list, and they looked at the list longer, than in the version that required them to scroll one long column (Fig. 1.7).

Usability testing results are primarily qualitative, conducted with small samples, and used for exploratory analysis; results typically are not generalizable to the population. Consequently, usability testing will not identify certain types of issues that can be found with large, probability-based methodological design experiments. For example, numerous studies have found that a check-all-that-apply format (e.g., Question 1 in Fig. 1.8) yields fewer "Yes"

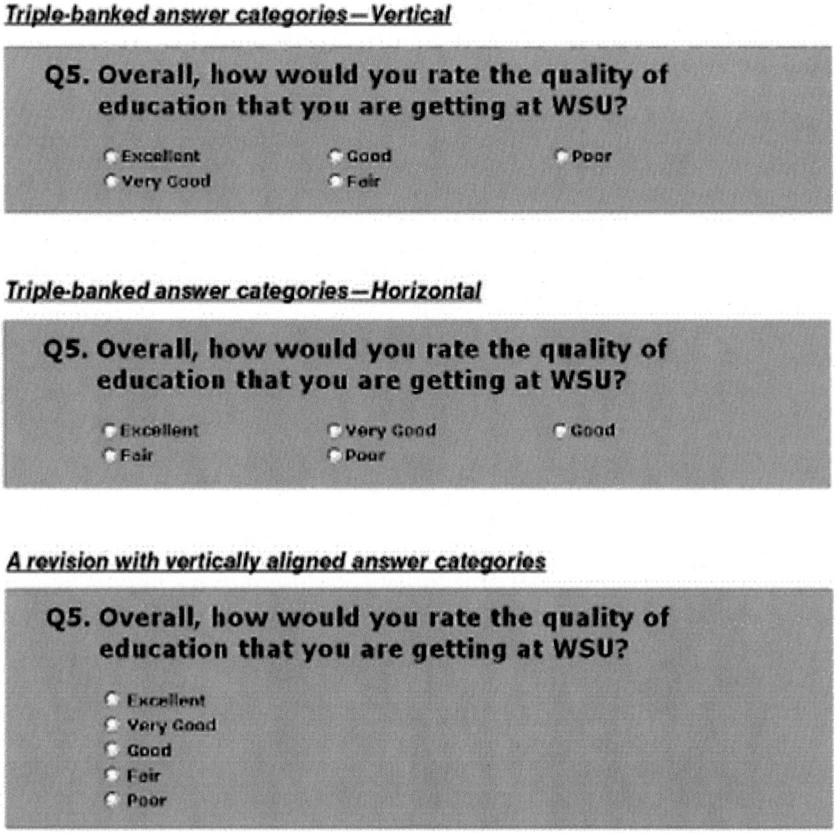

Triple-banked answer categories—Vertical

Q5. Overall, how would you rate the quality of
education that you are getting at WSU?

    Excellent   Good   Poor
    Very Good   Fair

Triple-banked answer categories—Horizontal

Q5. Overall, how would you rate the quality of
education that you are getting at WSU?

    Excellent   Very Good   Good
    Fair   Poor

A revision with vertically aligned answer categories

Q5. Overall, how would you rate the quality of
education that you are getting at WSU?

    Excellent
    Very Good
    Good
    Fair
    Poor

FIGURE 1.6

Response options should be listed in one column. *Reproduced with permission from: Christian, L. M., & Dillman, D. A. (2004). The influence of graphical and symbolic language manipulations on resources to self-administered questions. Public Opinion Quarterly, 68(1), 58—81.*

responses than the same question asked with the use of a forced-choice format (Question 2 in Fig. 1.8) (Callegaro, Lozar-Manfreda, & Vehovar, 2015; Dykema, Schaeffer, Beach, Lein, & Day, 2011; Smyth, Christian, & Dillman, 2008; Smyth, Dillman, & Stern, 2006; Thomas & Klein, 2006). It is not likely that usability testing would identify this type of finding, which often requires a much larger sample size and quantitative comparisons between approaches.

Reviewing and building on the literature before conducting usability testing will improve the overall quality of your survey for two reasons. First, usability testing is unlikely to uncover all potential issues with a survey. Second, the literature will prevent you from wasting time finding the

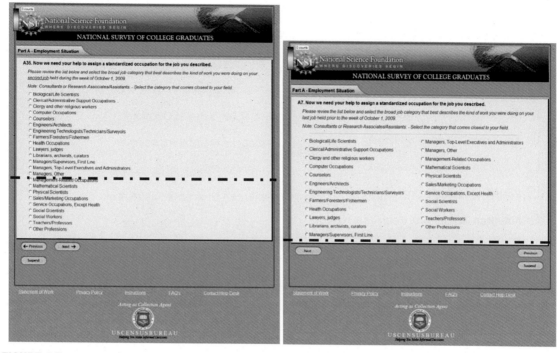

FIGURE 1.7

A long scrolling list (left) and a double-banked list (right). The *dotted line* denotes the "fold" of the page; users had to scroll to see what was below the fold. *Reproduced with permission from Romano, J. C., & Chen, J. M. (2011). A usability and eye-tracking evaluation of four versions of the online National Survey for College Graduates (NSCG): Iteration 2. Statistical Research Division (Study Series SSM2011-01). U.S. Census Bureau. Retrieved from https://www.census.gov/srd/papers/pdf/ssm2011-01.pdf.*

problems that others have already found. Although we provide some examples of design best practices throughout this book, we recommend the following texts for a more extensive discussion and recommendations for good design of web-based surveys.

SURVEY DESIGN RECOMMENDATIONS

Callegaro, M., Lozar-Manfreda, K., & Vehovar, V. (2015). *Web survey methodology.* London: Sage.

Couper, M. P. (2008). *Designing effective web surveys.* New York, NY: Cambridge University Press.

Dillman, D. A., Smyth, J. D., & Christian, L. M. (2014). *Internet, phone, mail and mixed-mode surveys: The tailored design method* (4th ed.). Hoboken, NJ: Wiley.

Tourangeau, R., Conrad, F. G., & Couper, M. P. (2013). *The science of web surveys.* Oxford: Oxford University Press.

1. Are you currently a member of the following professional associations?

- ☐ American Society of Clinical Oncology
- ☐ Society of Surgical Oncology
- ☐ American Medical Association
- ☐ American College of Surgeons
- ☐ American Urological Association
- ☐ Society of Urologic Oncology
- ☐ American Academy of Pediatrics

Next

2. Are you currently a member of the following professional associations?

	Yes	No
American Society of Clinical Oncology	○	○
Society of Surgical Oncology	○	○
American Medical Association	○	○
American College of Surgeons	○	○
American Urological Association	○	○
Society of Urologic Oncology	○	○
American Academy of Pediatrics	○	○

Back   Next

FIGURE 1.8
Check-all-that-apply questions (left) often yield fewer "Yes" responses than forced-choice question formats (right).

Usability testing is particularly advantageous when there are no best practices available or the current literature is not appropriate for your study population (potential respondents). The field of survey research, particularly for web-based surveys, is constantly changing and new best practices are always emerging (e.g., images, videos, maps and GPS, interactive features, and mobile devices). For example, there may be best practices for how to handle certain designs for desktop and laptop surveys, but not for web surveys. Or there may be relevant literature about a particular survey design tested with college students, but your survey is for retirees.

There is an interaction between how respondents cognitively process survey questions and how they interact with surveys. Therefore a design best practice in one context may be very different in another context. Usability testing can verify whether the design applied works well in the new context too. For example, the best format for collecting month and year is different depending on whether you are asking for someone's date of birth versus a credit card expiration date. Usability of this question is affected not only by survey mode (e.g., interviewer-administered vs self-administered), but also by how the respondent retrieves and formats a response. This is because date of birth is autobiographical information that is easy for a respondent to retrieve.

On the other hand, the respondent may not remember the credit card expiration date and have to look it up. When you map their response to the survey, you will find that accuracy is improved when the format of the response matches how the information is retrieved.

In some cases, you will find that the experts simply disagree, and you may decide to conduct a study to figure out the best practices for the survey you are evaluating. For example, some researchers argue that the Next navigation button should be placed on the left side of the screen because it is the most-used button, and the mouse is closest to the left when responding to questions that are aligned to the left side of the screen (Couper, Baker, & Mechling, 2011; Dillman, Smyth, & Christian, 2009). Others argue that the Next button should be placed to the right of the Previous button as this is the standard convention used on most Web browsers and popular websites. Given the inconclusive findings, Romano and Chen (2011) and Romano Bergstrom, Lakhe, and Erdman (2016), conducted usability studies with eye tracking to determine what attracted people's attention while they completed surveys and what they preferred.

Read the literature, follow best practices for questionnaire design and web conventions (for web-based surveys), do all due diligence, but know that not everything works for every case. Usability testing provides an additional tool for determining whether a specific design will work well for your survey.

OVERVIEW OF THE USABILITY TESTING PROCESS

Although most usability studies for surveys follow these general steps, their implementation may vary based on the survey's specifics.

1. Decide what aspect of the survey to test.
2. Review survey for potential usability problems.
3. Identify testing focus and concerns.
4. Determine where to conduct tests and what equipment to use.
5. Determine number and type of participants.
6. Choose testing approach and develop testing protocol.
7. Identify measurements to collect.
8. Recruit and schedule participants.
9. Conduct usability tests.
10. Record observations, participant comments, and usability metrics.
11. Debrief with observers.
12. Interpret data and diagnose problems.

13. Determine what to fix and how to fix it.

14. Report or present findings to stakeholders.

15. Repeat as needed!

The next chapters explain each step in detail and the factors to consider in designing each usability study.

References

Bennett, J. L. (1979). The commercial impact of usability in interactive systemsIn B. Shackel (Ed.), *Infotech state of the art report: Man/computer communication* (2, pp. 1−17). Maidenhead: Infotech International.

Callegaro, M., Lozar-Manfreda, K., & Vehovar, V. (2015). *Web survey methodology*. London: Sage.

Christian, L. M., & Dillman, D. A. (2004). The influence of graphical and symbolic language manipulations on resources to self-administered questions. *Public Opinion Quarterly, 68*(1), 58−81.

Couper, M. (2000). Usability evaluation of computer-assisted survey instruments. *Social Science Computer Review, 18*(4), 384−396.

Couper, M. P. (2008). *Designing effective web surveys*. New York, NY: Cambridge University Press.

Couper, M. P., Baker, R., & Mechling, J. (2011). Placement and design of navigation buttons in web surveys. *Survey Practice, 4*(1). <http://surveypractice.org>.

Couper, M. P., Tourangeau, R., Conrad, F. G., & Singer, E. (2006). Evaluating the effectiveness of visual analog scales. *Social Science Computer Review, 24*(2), 227−245.

Dean, E., Aspinwall, K. R., Schwerin, M. J., Kendrick, D. E., & Bourne, M. J. (2009). Multi-iteration usability testing of the US Navy's performance management system. *Military Psychology, 21*(1), 126−138.

Dillman, D. A. (1978). *Mail and telephone surveys: The total design method*. New York, NY: Wiley-Interscience.

Dillman, D. A. (1991). The design and administration of mail surveys. *Annual Review of Sociology, 17*, 225−249.

Dillman, D. A. (1995). Progress in the design of respondent-friendly self-administered questionnaires. *Survey Statistician*, 3−4.

Dillman, D. A., Sinclair, M. D., & Clark, J. R. (1993). Effects of questionnaire length, respondent-friendly design, and a difficult question on response rates for occupant-addressed census mail surveys. *Public Opinion Quarterly, 57*, 289−304.

Dillman, D. A., Smyth, J. D., & Christian, L. M. (2009). *Internet, mail, and mixed-mode surveys: The tailored design method*. New York, NY: Wiley.

Dillman, D. A., Smyth, J. D., & Christian, L. M. (2014). *Internet, phone, mail and mixed-mode surveys: The tailored design method* (4th ed.). Hoboken, NJ: Wiley.

Dillman, D.A., Tortora, R., & Bowker, D. (1999). *Principles for constructing web surveys*. <http://claudiaflowers.net/rsch8140/PrinciplesforConstructingWebSurveys.pdf>.

Downes-Le Guin, T., Baker, R., Mechling, J., & Ruylea, E. (2012). Myths and realities of respondent engagement in online surveys. *International Journal of Market Research, 54*(5), 1−21.

Dykema, J., Schaeffer, N., Beach, J., Lein, V., & Day, B. (2011). Designing questions for web surveys: Effects of check-list, check-all, and stand-alone response formats on survey reports and data quality. In *Paper presented at the annual meeting of the American Association for Public Opinion Research, Phoenix, AZ, USA.*

Hansen, S. E., Fuchs, M., & Couper, M. P. (1997). CAI instrument and system usability testing. In *Paper presented at the annual conference of the American Association for Public Opinion Research, Norfolk, VA.*

Holson, L. M. (February 28, 2009). Putting a bolder face on Google. *New York Times* (Business Day online section). Retrieved from <http://www.nytimes.com/2009/03/01/business/01marissa.html?pagewanted = all&_r = 0>.

Holst, C. (2012). Retrieved from <http://baymard.com/blog/how-to-format-expiration-date-fields>.

International Organization for Standardization (9241-11, 1988). *Ergonomic requirements for office work with visual display terminals (VDTs)—Part11: Guidance on usability.*

Jenkins, C. R., & Dillman, D. A. (1997). Chapter 7: Towards a theory of self-administered questionnaire design. In L. Lyberg, P. Biemer, et al. *Survey Measurement and Process Quality* (pp. 165–196). New York, NY: Wiley-Interscience.

Lugtig, P., Toepoel, V., & Amin, A. (2016). Mobile-only web survey respondents. *Survey Practice, 9*(4).

Marquis, K., Nichols, E., & Tedesco, H. (1998). Human-computer interface usability in a survey organization: Getting started at the census bureau. Proceedings of the Survey Research Methods Section, American Statistical Association.

Norman, D. (2002). *The design of everyday things.* New York, NY: Basic Books.

Quesenbery, W. (2003). The five dimensions of usability. In M. A. Bers, & M. B. Mazur (Eds.), *Content and complexity:* Information design in technical communication (p. 81). Mahwah, NJ: Lawrence Erlbaum.

Romano, J. C., & Chen, J. M. (2011). *A usability and eye-tracking evaluation of four versions of the online National Survey for College Graduates (NSCG): Iteration 2.* Statistical Research Division (Study Series SSM2011-01). U.S. Census Bureau. Retrieved from <https://www.census.gov/srd/papers/pdf/ssm2011-01.pdf>.

Romano Bergstrom, J. C., Lakhe, S., & Erdman, C. (2016). *Next* belongs to the right of *Previous* in web-based surveys: An experimental usability study. *Survey Practice, 9,* 1.

Roster, F., Lucianetti, L., & Albaum, G. (2015). Exploring slider vs. categorical response formats in web-based surveys. *Journal of Research Practice, 11*(1), Article D1.

Saunders. (2015). *Improving the survey experience for mobile respondents.* Retrieved from <http://www.marketingresearch.org/article/improving-survey-experience-mobile-respondents>.

Sellers, R. (2013). How sliders bias survey data. *Alert!, 53*(3), 56–57.

Sikkel, D., Steenbergen, R., & Gras, S. (2014). Clicking vs. dragging: Different uses of the mouse and their implications for online surveys. *Public Opinion Quarterly, 78*(1), 177–190.

Smyth, J., Christian, L., & Dillman, D. (2008). Does "yes" or "no" on the telephone mean the same as "checkall-that-apply" on the web. *Public Opinion Quarterly, 72*(1), 103–113.

Smyth, J., Dillman, D., Christian, L., & Stern, M. (2006). Comparing check-all and forced-choice question for- mats in web surveys. *Public Opinion Quarterly, 70*(1), 66–77.

Stanley, N., & Jenkins, S. (2007). Watch what I do: Using graphical input controls in web surveys. In *Proceedings of the fifth international conference of the Association for Survey Computing* (pp. 81–92). Southampton, UK.

Thomas, R. K. (2011). A comparison of visual analog and graphic rating scales in web-based surveys. In *Paper presented at the FedCASIC 2011 Workshop, Washington, DC, March 22–24, 2011.*

Thomas, R. K., & Klein, J. D. (2006). Merely incidental? Effect on response format on self-reported behavior. *Journal of Official Statistics, 22*(2), 221–244.

Tourangeau, R., Conrad, F. G., & Couper, M. P. (2013). *The science of web surveys.* Oxford: Oxford University Press.

CHAPTER 2

Respondent—Survey Interaction

Usability testing allows for an in-depth evaluation of how respondents interact with surveys and how this interaction affects the quality of a survey. For example, a respondent may understand the survey question and response options but may have difficulty selecting an answer accurately on a smartphone's small screen.

To begin to understand how usability testing can be used to identify potential problems with surveys and improve the overall quality of data collected, we consider the different types of error that can occur in the survey process.

SOURCES OF POTENTIAL ERRORS IN SURVEYS

The two major categories of survey errors, as shown in Table 2.1, are *errors of nonobservation* and *errors of observation* (Groves, 1989). We will look at them one at a time.

Table 2.1 Sources of Error in Surveys

I. Errors of nonobservation
- Coverage
- Sampling
- Nonresponse

II. Errors of observation
- Interviewer
- Instrument
- Respondent
- Mode

21

Usability Testing for Survey Research. DOI: http://dx.doi.org/10.1016/B978-0-12-803656-3.00002-6

Errors of Nonobservation

As the name suggests, errors of nonobservation occur when certain members of the target population are not included in the survey. These errors further group into: coverage, sampling, and nonresponse. *Coverage error* occurs when members of the population of interest in are not in the sampling frame—the list of individuals, businesses, or households used to select the sample. *Sampling error* occurs because our survey estimates are produced from only a subset of the population of interest.

In usability testing, we are not concerned with coverage error or sampling error. We are concerned to some extent, though, with *nonresponse error*.

Nonresponse error occurs when survey responders are systematically different than nonresponders on the key concepts the survey is measuring. For example, if a survey intends to measure customer satisfaction, and only unhappy customers respond to the survey, the results will not reflect the opinions of all customers.

When surveys are difficult to use, respondents may break off, which will lead to nonresponse error if those who break off are different from those who complete the survey. Because usability testing focuses on respondents' experiences interacting with the survey, we are interested in learning about issues that might cause people to quit the survey. However, break-offs are just one type of nonresponse error. Usability testing will not identify other reasons people have for not responding to a survey.

Errors of Observation

Although we strive to reduce break offs, we are primarily concerned with reducing errors of observation, also known as *measurement error*. This occurs when the true value is different from the value reported by the respondent. For example, the question, "In the past 12 months, how many times have you seen a doctor?" may not provide us with an accurate account. First, a respondent may not be able to recall every time they saw a doctor. Second, the respondent's understanding of "seen a doctor" may be different from the researcher's. For example, do nurses or other types of healthcare professionals count? Does it count if the respondent spoke with the doctor on the phone?

Measurement error in surveys can come from any of these sources: interviewer, respondent, instrument, and mode of administration (Biemer, 2010; Groves, 1989).

- *Interviewer error* (for interviewer-administered surveys) occurs when respondents' answers differ due to the ways that interviewers read and administer the survey. This may be for any number of reasons related to the interviewers' performance or the interviewers themselves. For example, an interviewer might misread a question or record a response incorrectly. Respondents' answers also can be affected by the interviewer's manner and appearance, tone, feedback, and behavior. For example, young people may answer differently when the interviewer is close to their age compared to older (Davis & Scott, 1995).

- *Instrument error* arises from a problem with the wording and ordering of the survey questions or the layout of the survey instrument. For example, small question-wording changes—such as asking about "Obamacare" instead of the "Affordable Care Act"—can affect how respondents answer questions: a 2013 CNBC poll found that when "Obamacare" was used in the question, 46% of respondents opposed the law, compared with 37% who opposed the "Affordable Care Act." Similarly, visual design features, such as listing response options horizontally instead of vertically, can affect the distribution of responses to identically worded questions (Toepoel, Das, & van Soest, 2009).

- *Respondent error* occurs when differences in respondents' experiences, cognitive ability, and motivation affect responses. For example, some respondents may be better able than others to recall how many times they have been to a doctor. Some respondents may interpret "doctor" to include nurses and other healthcare professionals, and other respondents may not. Finally, some respondents may not want to report the true number of times they went to the doctor.

- *Mode effects error* occurs when the mode of the survey (e.g., mail, telephone, web) introduces differences in survey results. For example, telephone surveys often suffer from recency effects, where participants are more likely to recall the last response options read to them, while mail surveys often suffer from primacy effects, where participants are more likely to select the first response options (Krosnick, 1991). Mode error can also occur when respondents complete a survey on different devices. For example, Stapleton (2013) compared surveys administered on laptops and mobile devices. They found that when only some of the response options were visible on a mobile device without scrolling, respondents were significantly more likely to choose response options on the visible part of the screen.

When evaluating the usability of a survey, we are concerned with instrument, respondent, and mode effects types of measurement error and some types of interviewer error. Usability testing *can* and *should* be conducted with interviewer-administered surveys, but in these situations, the interviewers are our users. Even though they are not formulating an answer to the survey question the way a respondent would, interviewers are the ones using and interacting with the survey to record respondents' answers. Usability issues in the survey that affect some interviewers more than others could introduce interviewer error.

Usability testing allows us to identify potential issues in the usability of the survey that may lead to measurement or nonresponse error. The goal is then to reduce these errors through iterative usability testing. To do this, we evaluate how well respondents can use and interact with the survey instrument to provide their responses. We observe and evaluate what works well and what does not. Then the survey is revised and tested again to see if we have resolved the issues.

This error-reduction process hinges on our ability to (1) identify potential sources of errors in surveys and (2) understand why these errors occurred, so we can revise our surveys to correct for them. We next explore how respondents answer and respond to survey questions, particularly self-administered survey questions.

> The goal is to identify and reduce potential sources of error through iterative usability testing.

HOW RESPONDENTS ANSWER SURVEY QUESTIONS

To evaluate surveys well, we must examine both how respondents understand and answer survey questions and how they interact with surveys. Let us start with an overview of the response processes respondents use to answer survey questions.

The *response formation model* (Tourangeau, 1984; Tourangeau, Rips, & Rasinski, 2000; also see Willis, 2005 for more discussion) is a conceptual model that shows the four steps and associated cognitive processes that respondents follow when answering survey questions.

- *Comprehension*
  - Question focus: Determining the intent and meaning of the question and instructions.
  - Context: Assigning meaning to specific words used in a question.
- *Retrieval*
  - Strategy: Deciding on retrieval strategies, such as episodic enumeration (listing and counting individual events), estimating (e.g., about twice a week), or inferring (e.g., less often than I go to the store).
  - Attitude recall: Consulting memory for relevant information.
  - Factual recall: Recalling specific or general memories.

- *Judgment*
  - Compile: Compiling information retrieved to generate a relevant answer.
  - Motivation: Deciding how much cognitive effort to expend to retrieve an answer.
  - Sensitivity: Determining whether to tell the truth or present a more socially desirable answer.
- *Response*
  - Response selection: Selecting a response category that best represents the respondent-derived answer.

A respondent will not necessarily go through these steps in order and may not go through them all when answering a question. For certain questions, the necessary cognitive processes are automatic. The premise of the model, though, is that each specific process must be successful to prevent error. Therefore a breakdown in any one of these cognitive processes could introduce measurement error.

But, a question can be problematic even if a respondent follows the four-step process. For example, Chepp and Gray (2014) acknowledge that how a respondent answers questions is also informed by their "social experiences and cultural contexts." Researchers have observed differences in response style based on respondents' cultural background (Harzing, 2006). Differences include *acquiescence* (the tendency to agree with survey questions) and extreme response (selecting the endpoints on the scale).

The more we understand how respondents answer survey questions, the better we will be at designing usable surveys that yield high-quality data and accurately address our research objectives. In fact, many textbooks and courses on survey-research methods rely on this model as the theoretical foundation for questionnaire-design principles (e.g., Fowler, 2014; Groves et al., 2004; Tourangeau et al., 2000).

HOW RESPONDENTS INTERACT WITH SURVEYS

How respondents use and navigate a survey also affects the data collected from surveys. Fig. 2.1 shows a series of slider questions that were included on a web survey (Romano Bergstrom & Strohl, 2013). These questions were usability tested to evaluate how well people were able to complete the survey. Testing revealed a problem related to how participants used the slider to indicate their selected response. When a participant's answer to a question was "Never," he or she often left the cursor in its "start" position on the far left of the slider. However, to accurately reflect an answer of "Never," the survey tool required that respondents actively move the cursor to the middle of the "Never" box. If the cursor was not moved, no response was registered, and it was treated as missing data.

	1 Never	2	3	4	5 All of the time
Teach others about something you have learned					
	1 Never	2	3	4	5 All of the time
Get better at doing something					
	1 Never	2	3	4	5 All of the time
Give updates throughout the day					
	1 Never	2	3	4	5 All of the time
Have fun					
	1 Never	2	3	4	5 All of the time
See/hear something entertaining					

FIGURE 2.1
Respondents did not understand that they had to move the cursor to indicate a response of "Never." Unmoved cursors registered as missing data. *Adapted from Romano Bergstrom, J. C., & Strohl, J. (2013). Improving government websites and surveys with usability testing: A comparison of methodologies. In* Proceedings from the Federal Committee on Statistical Methodology (FCSM) conference, November 2013, Washington, DC.

This potential source of error in the survey was not with any of the four stages of cognitive processing described in Tourangeau's (1984) response formation model. The participants did not have trouble mapping their internally generated answers to the response category "Never." The reason they did not input their response correctly is that they did not correctly interpret the screen functionality. If the survey had been fielded without usability testing to identify this error, it would have been impossible to tell if respondents selected Never or simply did not respond.

Groves et al. (2004) noted that, beyond the cognitive processes described in the response formation model, additional aspects of the question-and-answer process occur with self-administered surveys, such as navigating the survey and interpreting instructions about how to complete it. In addition, web-based survey respondents and interviewers who use computer-assisted interviewing (CAI) must also understand various computer features and functions.

Hansen and Couper (2004) describe additional considerations for visual design and usability evaluation that come into play with surveys administered on computers. Users must:

> ...attend to the information provided by the computer, and the feedback it provides in response to their actions in determining their own next actions.

That is, an interaction occurs between the user and the survey. The user's actions affect the survey, and the survey's reactions affect the user. For web-based surveys, interacting with the computer can also affect how respondents cognitively process survey questions.

So how should issues related to navigating and interacting with surveys be treated when evaluating potential errors? Groves et al. (2004) considered navigation concerns to be part of the comprehension process under the response formation model. Hansen and Couper (2004) address some of the additional processes users go through in their model for the self-administered CAI (Fig. 2.2).

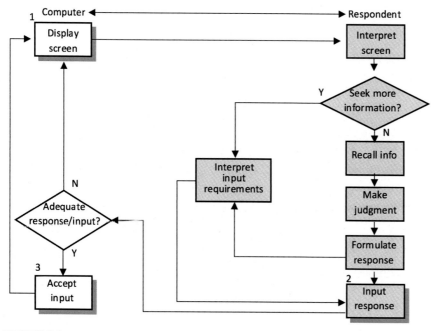

FIGURE 2.2

Model of self-administered computer-assisted interviewing interview. *Reproduced with permission from Hansen, S. E., & Couper, M. P. (2004). Usability testing as a means of evaluating computer assisted survey instruments. In S. Presser, et al. (Eds.), Methods for testing and evaluating survey questionnaire. New York, NY: Wiley.*

1. The model starts with the computer screen, displayed to the respondent.
   a. The respondent must then interpret the screen, which includes interpreting the intent of the question and interpreting the actions that need to be taken on the screen.
   b. The respondent then has a choice of seeking more information on the screen or going through the cognitive process of answering the question (e.g., recall, judgment, response), both of which require action on the part of the respondent.
2. Once the respondent has generated an internal response to the question, he or she inputs the response.
3. The survey then determines whether the input is acceptable.
   a. If the response is acceptable, the survey proceeds to the next question or action.
   b. If the response is not acceptable, the survey provides feedback to the respondent, such as an error message that indicates that the response is not adequate.

Note that a respondent must also navigate between survey pages or within a given survey screen.

Therefore when thinking about how respondents answer self-administered surveys, just evaluating the cognitive processes of comprehension, retrieval, judgment, and response is not enough. We also need to evaluate the *respondent—survey interaction*, as this affects the final data we can obtain from web surveys. That is, we want to assess how efficiently and effectively respondents can use the web survey to accomplish their goals in a way that is pleasing to them. A breakdown in the usability of a survey can affect how respondents answer survey questions.

> Just as a breakdown in one of the cognitive processes identified in the response formation model can affect the quality of data we receive, so can a breakdown in the usability of a survey.

USABILITY MODEL FOR SURVEYS

Building on the work presented by Hansen and Couper (2004), we propose a conceptual process model for the respondent—survey interaction involved in completing a survey. This interaction includes three key components: (1) interpreting, (2) completing, and (3) processing feedback (Table 2.2). Whereas the response formation model focuses on how respondents *comprehend* survey questions, the *Usability Model for Surveys* focuses on how respondents *use* surveys.

Table 2.2 Usability Model for Surveys

1. *Interpreting the design*:
   a. What meaning do respondents assign to visual design and layout?
   b. How do respondents believe the survey works?

2. *Completing actions and navigating*:
   a. How well does the survey support respondents' ability to complete tasks and goals?
   b. How well do respondents follow navigational cues and instructions?

3. *Processing feedback*:
   a. How do respondents interpret and react to the survey feedback in response to their actions?
   b. How well does the survey help respondents identify, interpret, and resolve errors?

In the Usability Model for Surveys, we highlight the three key usability processes that contribute to how accurate, effective, and satisfying the experience is for respondents. These processes are not mutually exclusive and often work in sequence with each other. As with the cognitive processes in the response formation model, a respondent must process each usability aspect successfully to prevent measurement error. If a respondent does not understand how the survey works, selects the wrong response, accidentally skips a question, or is unable to resolve an error, it will affect the quality of data received from the survey.

Listing these aspects separately from the cognitive processes emphasizes the need to identify potential breakdowns in survey usability, not just other sources of measurement error. Review and evaluate questionnaires with the explicit goal of preventing potential usability problems.

Response Formation Model—How respondents *comprehend* survey questions

Usability Model for Surveys—How respondents *use* surveys

The fact that usability testing should be an explicit pretesting goal does not imply that usability issues do not overlap with other potential quality concerns in questionnaires. You can try to focus on usability issues alone, but if participants tell you that they do not understand the question, do not ignore that finding. In fact, it is quite common to conduct combined usability and cognitive testing.

We propose the usability model for both self-administered and interviewer-administered surveys. With interviewer-administered surveys, we are still concerned with how the user (the interviewer) interacts with the survey, which is different from how the respondent uses a self-administered survey. Because interviewers are not answering the questions, they go through different cognitive processes than respondents. Yet, interviewers still interact with the survey in a way that could introduce errors.

Certainly, interviewers interact with a survey quite differently than respondents do because interviewers must also interact with respondents. Another reason that interviewers interact with surveys differently from respondents is that interviewers typically receive training on how to use a survey, and they usually complete the survey numerous times compared to respondents who typically use a survey once. A breakdown in the usability process for either a respondent or an interviewer can lead to measurement error.

In the following sections, we detail the three aspects that comprise the Usability Model for Surveys.

Interpreting the Design

When completing a survey, respondents must understand the intent of the survey question (cognitive process) as well as the actions they must take (usability process). Because comprehending how something works or behaves is uniquely different from comprehending language (e.g., question wording), they should be evaluated separately.

What Meaning Do Respondents Assign to Visual Design and Layout?

When respondents complete self-administered surveys, they must comprehend more than just the words used in the survey question. Respondents also assign meaning to different visual designs (Christian, 2003; Christian, Parsons, & Dillman, 2009; Tourangeau, Couper, & Conrad, 2004). Christian, Dillman, and Smyth (2005) posit that this "visual language" is as important as question wording when creating survey questions.

Much of this visual-language processing is automatic and subconscious. Tourangeau, Rips, and Rasinski (2004) identified five heuristics respondents use when interpreting visual design:

- Middle means typical
- Left and top mean first
- Near means related
- Up means good
- Like means close

During usability testing, we want to assess how respondents' interpretation of the visual design and layout affects how they believe the survey works and how they actually interact with the survey.

For example, in completing Question Q1a in Fig. 2.3, respondents must decide which button goes with which label before they can check the box that corresponds to their response. Due to the spacing of the words and the radio buttons, the respondent could easily think the radio button to the right of the answer is the correct choice. In Question Q1b, we see how a different visual design can improve understanding, making it easier for respondents to select the box that matches their choice.

Q1a. Example of horizontal response options:

    ○ Answer1 ○ Answer2 ○ Answer3 ○ Answer4

Q1b. Example of vertical response options:

    ○ Answer1

    ○ Answer2

    ○ Answer3

    ○ Answer4

FIGURE 2.3
The cluttered visual design of Q1a compared with Q1b makes it difficult to determine which radio button goes with which response options.

During usability testing, we can assess how participants interpret the visual design and how this interpretation affects their interaction with the survey. For example, respondents can have difficulty when the visual design is cluttered by unnecessary images, redundant information, or artistic flourishes that interfere with the task (see Fig. 2.4).

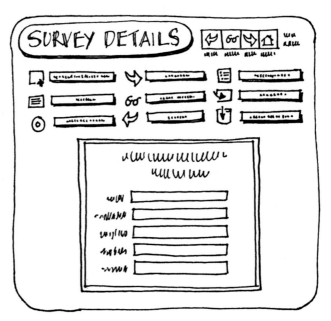

FIGURE 2.4
Unnecessary images, redundant information, and artistic decorations can negatively affect how a respondent interacts with the survey.

Interviewers, not just respondents, can be affected by the visual design and layout of survey questions on their computer screen. To help them administer a computer survey, the screen design can be tailored to include more or less information. For example, the screen may display both the question text to be read and the response box, or it can also display the preceding and subsequent question. Edwards, Schneider, and Brick (2008) found that telephone interviewers more easily administered the survey when multipart questions were presented on a single screen with all parts visible to the interviewer, rather than on separate screens with only one subpart visible at a time. Use of the single screen resulted in fewer errors (e.g., interviewer hesitation at participant confusion, wording changes, disfluent delivery) than multiple screens. In addition, interviewers preferred the single screen and reported less confusion.

Observe how a survey's visual design can affect the way that interviewers interact with and administer a survey to respondents. For some surveys, presenting too much information on one screen may be burdensome for interviewers. On another survey, it may be helpful to provide the necessary context needed when administering a string of related questions.

How Do Respondents Believe the Survey Works?

When respondents first interact with a survey, they have a *mental model* of how that survey should work, based on their experiences. This is particularly true when people interact with web-based surveys, as their mental model maps onto similar interactions in their environment, such as other web-based surveys, paper surveys, websites, mobile devices, and computers in general.

For many questions, the respondent's process of assessing how a survey works will be almost automatic. For example, Fig. 2.5 shows two identically worded survey questions. The question on the left has radio buttons, and the question on the right has check boxes. Most web-savvy survey respondents recognize that radio buttons allow for only one response, while check boxes allow for multiple responses.

4. What is your race?

   ○ White

   ○ Black

   ○ American Indian or Alaska Native

   ○ Asian or Pacific Islander

   ○ Some other race

5. What is your race?

   ☐ White

   ☐ Black

   ☐ American Indian or Alaska Native

   ☐ Asian or Pacific Islander

   ☐ Some other race

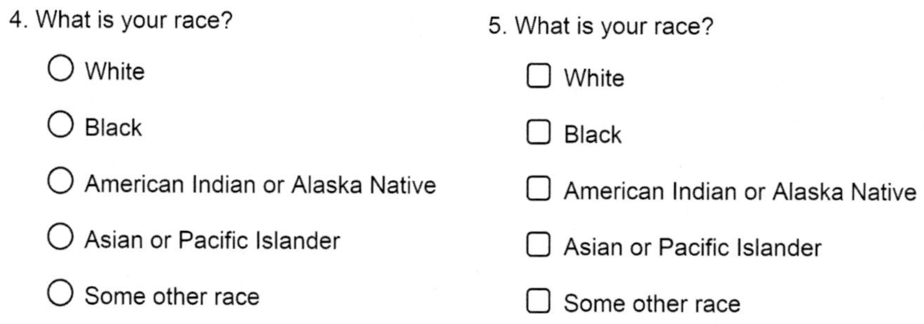

FIGURE 2.5

Survey respondents rely on design cues such as radio buttons (Question 4, left) or check boxes (Question 5, right) to determine how a survey functions.

However, if respondents do not know that check boxes allow for multiple selections, they may answer the question differently than someone who knows this convention. Instead of selecting all races that apply, respondents may select the category they identify with the most. Or they may select "Some other race," interpreting that to include people of multiple races.

One of Dillman, Tortora, and Bowker's (1999) principles for constructing web surveys is that a "respondent-friendly design must take into account both the logic of how computers operate and the logic of how people expect questionnaires to operate." One key purpose of usability testing is to evaluate whether the survey adequately supports a respondent's assessment and understanding of how the survey should function (i.e., the mental model). In the previous example, error can be introduced if the survey allows for multiple responses to be checked, but survey respondents do not understand that.

The more we can align survey design with respondents' behaviors, the easier the survey will be for respondents to use. A challenge arises as we incorporate more technological capabilities into surveys (e.g., buttons, links, images, videos, GPS). Respondents may not have specific mental models for these capabilities within a survey context, which makes user-centered design more challenging. In these instances, iterative usability testing is particularly advantageous as it allows for an initial design to be evaluated, tweaked, and retested to ensure that people understand how to use the survey.

Completing Actions and Navigating

How Well Does the Survey Support Respondents' Ability to Complete Tasks and Goals?

Web-based surveys have numerous features and capabilities that are not available on paper surveys. But with this increased flexibility often comes increased complexity. A basic web-based survey allows respondents to indicate their response by, e.g., selecting a radio button or typing into a text box. With more complex surveys, though, respondents may need to interact with the survey in additional ways to provide their answer to a question. For example, they may need to access a definition, see the previous question for context, play a video, enter multiple pieces of information, or indicate that they do not know an answer. Increased complexity can be particularly problematic in surveys where most respondents are one-time users. They do not have the benefit of repeated use or visits to improve their learning.

Despite the technological advances offered with web-based surveys, they must be simple and easy to use. For example, several experimental studies have shown that the greater the level of effort required to obtain a definition on a web-based survey, the less likely respondents are to read the definition. They are more likely to request definitions when only one mouse click is required, compared to two or more clicks (Conrad, Couper, Tourangeau, & Peytchev, 2006; Experiment 1). Respondents are even more likely to view definitions when they only need to rollover the term with the mouse cursor instead of click once (Conrad et al., 2006; Experiment 2). And, when definitions are always visible on screen, respondents are even more likely to read them, compared to when they have to rollover the definition (Galesic, Tourangeau, Couper, & Conrad, 2008; Peytchev, Conrad, Couper, & Tourangeau, 2010).

In the Peytchev et al. (2010) and Galesic et al. (2008) studies, responses to the survey questions differed for respondents who accessed the definitions compared to those who did not. Although the studies did not measure accuracy, per se, the differences in response distribution suggest that reading the definitions affected how respondents answered and interpreted the question.

These studies demonstrate that computer-centric, interactive features like rollover definitions can affect how respondents answer survey questions. Making surveys easier for respondents to use can reduce *satisficing* and improve data quality.

SATISFICING IN SURVEYS

Satisficing occurs when respondents are not willing or able to provide the effort (e.g., mouse clicks or movements, or mental calculations) to produce optimal answers to survey questions (Krosnick, 1991). The theory behind satisficing is that, because of the burdens associated with everyday life, people tend to use the smallest amount of effort necessary to satisfy a requirement (Simon, 1957). An example of weak satisficing is when a respondent selects the first reasonable response without reading through all responses to ensure it is the best response. Strong satisficing would be straightlining, when a respondent provides the same answer to all survey questions without actually considering the survey questions.

Krosnick (1991) notes that satisficing is related to three key factors: (1) task difficulty, (2) respondent ability, and (3) respondent motivation.

In usability testing, we assess aspects of the survey that may be unnecessarily difficult, which increase the respondent's cognitive burden and reduces accuracy. For example, if we notice that survey participants made errors because they were not reading instructions, we should reduce the amount of text by replacing some of it with visual cues. On web-based surveys, we can use autofills instead of making respondents remember their answer to a previous question.

By reducing complexity, we can increase motivation and improve the quality of responses obtained in surveys.

How Well Do Respondents Follow Navigational Cues and Instructions?

A number of design features affect how participants navigate surveys. These include determining what questions to answer, placement of instructions and introductions, placement of Next and Previous buttons, and navigation menus.

To answer survey questions, respondents have to get to the questions and correctly navigate from one question to the next. Geisen et al. (2013) found that usability participants testing a paper survey were immediately drawn to the first question and skipped over instructions or introductions. Participants "just want to get started," and question numbers essentially served as signposts to navigate through the instrument.

And whether the survey is on paper or web, this finding seems to hold. We have demonstrated in countless usability studies that survey respondents do not read instructions—unless they have to. Romano and Chen (2011) found that participants did not read instructions on a survey log-in screen but immediately looked for the actionable parts (where they needed to enter their user

Usability studies have shown that survey respondents often do not read instructions before attempting to complete the survey.

name and password) to begin the survey. This was problematic because during the sessions, participants asked why the survey was being conducted and why personal information was being requested—both of which were explained on the log-in screen (Fig. 2.6).

FIGURE 2.6

Fixation gaze plots showing that most participants did not read the instructions on the right side of the screen. *Reproduced with permission from Romano, J. C., & Chen, J. M. (2011).* A usability and eye-tracking evaluation of four versions of the online National Survey for College Graduates (NSCG): Iteration 2. *Statistical Research Division (Study Series SSM2011-01). U.S. Census Bureau. Retrieved from https://www.census.gov/srd/papers/pdf/ssm2011-01.pdf.*

In another example (Fig. 2.7), respondents looked back and forth between the two input options, trying to figure out how the sections worked together. They did not read the instructions above the questions, which explained how to use the sections.

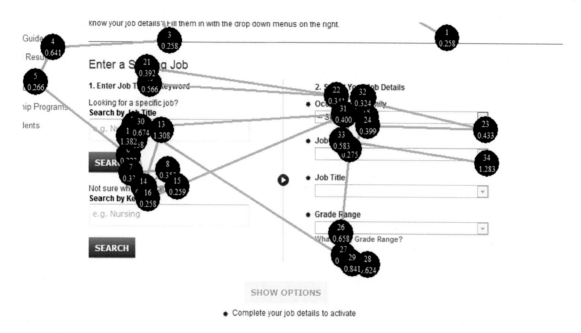

FIGURE 2.7
Fixation gaze plot shows that the participant looked back and forth between the two input options and did not read instructions.

Respondents are often completely reliant on the visual layout and design when deciding how to navigate through a survey. Therefore even more attention must be paid to the design of the survey and how it affects the way that respondents will navigate through it.

To illustrate this, imagine a series of survey questions presented on a screen in a two-column format (Fig. 2.8A). It is not immediately clear in what order a respondent should answer the questions. A respondent might take any of several pathways:

- Answer all questions on the first row and then go down to the second row (Fig. 2.8B).

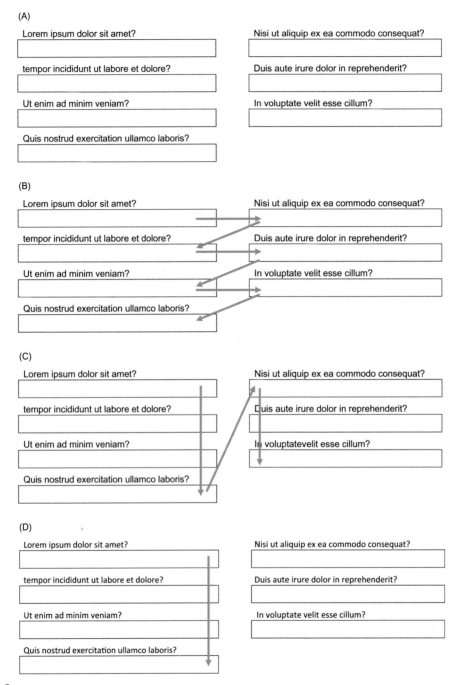

FIGURE 2.8

Respondents rely on visual cues to determine how to navigate survey instruments. (A) With a two-column format, the navigation pathway is unclear. A respondent might take any of several pathways. (B) Some respondents may answer all questions on the first row, then go down to the second row, and so on. (C) Other respondents may answer the first column and then answer the second column. (D) Respondents may miss the second column altogether.

- Answer all questions in the first column and then answer the second column (Fig. 2.8C).

- Miss the second column altogether and only answer the first column (Fig. 2.8D).

Questions in a single column are often easier for respondents to navigate correctly (Fig. 2.9). However, items that typically go together such as state and zip code can still appear side by side.

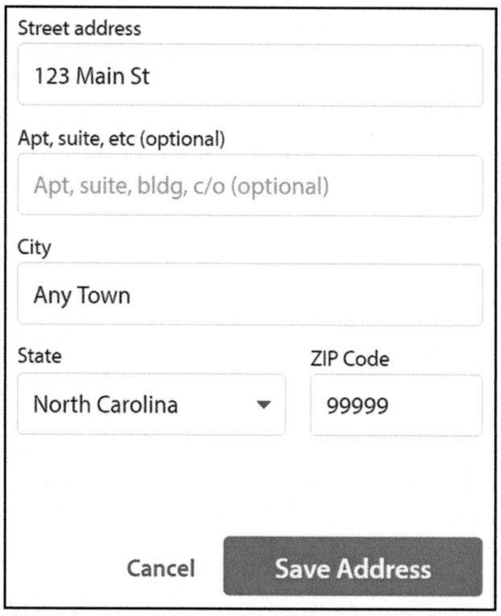

FIGURE 2.9
Use of a single-column format to facilitate navigation.

With paper surveys, usability issues are often related to navigational cues and instructions for skip logic. Many design considerations have been shown to improve usability of navigating skip logic on paper surveys—including using prominent question-numbering and using multiple visual design elements to emphasize skip patterns (Dillman, Smyth, & Christian, 2009).

On web-based surveys, navigational cues and instructions can be problematic too. For example, in a usability study for a web-based diary (Gareau, Ashenfelter, & Malakoff, 2013), participants were confused about the functionality of the Save and Submit button, shown in Fig. 2.10. "Some participants clicked this button after every row of data entry, others clicked it after completing each section, and others clicked it intermittently as it occurred to

Please report expenses for these people in your household:
Dan Smith, Amanda Smith, Ben Smith, Catherine Smith

Examples:

- breakfast buffet
- carry-out lunch
- dinner at restaurant
- pizza delivery
- Chinese takeout
- child's school lunch
- beer at happy hour
- pretzels at a ballgame
- wine at tavern
- croissant from cafe
- ice cream from truck
- wedding reception caterer
- soda from vending machine
- hot dog from convenience store
- popcorn and soda at movies

| Food and Drink Away from Home | Food and Drink for Home Consumption | Clothing, Shoes, Jewelry, and Acc. | All Other Products/Services |

Meal Type	Description	Where Purchased	Total Cost with tax and tip	Alcohol Included? (Check all that apply) Wine Beer Other	Total Alcohol Cost	Date Purchased	Clear
Breakfast	fast food breakfast sandwi	Fast Food, Take-out, C	$2.99	☐ ☐ ☐		03-11-2011	⊖
Dinner	dinner at restaurant	Full Service Places	$42.00	☑ ☐ ☐	$20.00	03-07-2011	⊖
Lunch	lunch at deli	Fast Food, Take-out, C	$9.54	☐ ☐ ☐		03-08-2011	⊖
Snack/Other	candy from vending machi	Vending Machines or M	$.75	☐ ☐ ☐		03-08-2011	⊖
Snack/Other	pizza from mall	Fast Food, Take-out, C	$2.50	☐ ☐ ☐		03-08-2011	⊖
Snack/Other	ice cream from truck	Vending Machines or M	$3.00	☐ ☐ ☐		03-09-2011	⊖
Snack/Other	coffee from coffee shop	Fast Food, Take-out, C	$4.57	☐ ☐ ☐		03-11-2011	⊖
Select One		Select One		☐ ☐ ☐		Select One	⊖
Select One		Select One		☐ ☐ ☐		Select One	⊖
Select One		Select One		☐ ☐ ☐		Select One	⊖

| Add Rows | Save and Submit |

FIGURE 2.10

The Save and Submit button was not clear to participants in a usability study. *Reproduced with permission from Gareau, M., Ashenfelter, K., & Malakoff, L. (2013). Full report for round 1 of usability testing for the consumer expenditure web diary survey. Center for Survey Measurement, Research and Methodology Directorate (Study Series 2013-24). U.S. Census Bureau. Retrieved from https://www.census.gov/srd/papers/pdf/ssm2013-24.pdf.*

them." Some participants expected to move to the next tab in the diary when they clicked it, and most participants were not sure how to submit their data when they were finished.

With web-based surveys, most skip logic is automatic. The survey program will only show respondents questions that they are required to answer. But, respondents can still face other navigational challenges. For example, a lot of research has been conducted on a basic navigational feature—the placement of the Next and Previous buttons. Some researchers argue that because the Next button is used more frequently, it should be on the left of the Previous button so that it is seen first and will be easier for users to reach (Couper, Baker, & Mechling, 2011; Dillman et al., 2009).

However, in a recent usability and eye-tracking study, Romano Bergstrom, Lakhe, and Erdman (2016) found that participants preferred the Next button to the right of the Previous button, and participants rated their survey experience more satisfactorily when Next was on the right. Eye-tracking data in this study showed that when the Previous button instead was on the right, it resulted in more fixations. This suggests that respondents were not expecting the Previous button to be in that location, and it took them longer to process the navigation. This is consistent with Couper et al. (2011) who found that the Previous button was clicked more when it was on the right. Since most respondents rarely use the Previous button to backup, more clicks are associated with worse usability.

These studies reveal that the way respondents expect to navigate through a web-based survey is driven by the way they navigate websites and other items in their environment. Respondents generally expect that right means "Next," and left means "backup," because this is consistent with general web navigation features as well as everyday items, as shown in Fig. 2.11.

> To the extent possible, we should design navigation features to match respondent's expectations of how these features should work.

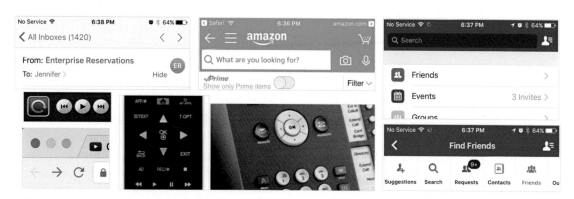

FIGURE 2.11

Respondents expect to navigate through web surveys the same way they navigate through other web products (email, web pages, browsers) and everyday items, like remote controls and phones.

In another usability and eye-tracking study, Bristol, Romano Bergstrom, and Link (2014) found that respondents easily understood the navigation on mobile versions of a survey, but they had difficulty following the navigation on the desktop version (see Fig. 2.12). On the mobile versions,

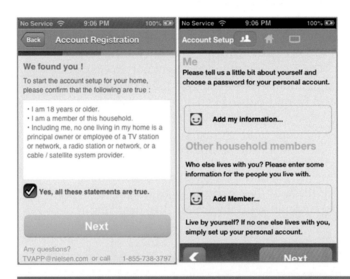

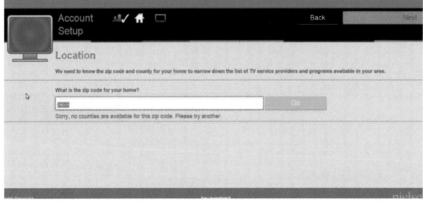

FIGURE 2.12

Respondents understood the navigation on the mobile versions (above two), but they had difficulty finding "Next" on the desktop version (bottom). *Reproduced with permission from Bristol, K., Romano Bergstrom, J., & Link, M. (2014). Eye tracking the user experience of a smartphone and web data collection tool. In Paper presentation at the AAPOR conference, Anaheim, CA, May 2014.*

the Next button was on the bottom of the screen. This matched users' mental models of moving down the screen as they answered questions, and then continuing down the screen to click on Next. On the desktop version, the Next button was located in the upper right of the screen. Respondents needed to move down the screen to answer questions and then go back up to the top of the screen to click on Next to advance. In the study, people looked around the screen and pressed Go numerous times, verbalizing that the survey was not working properly, before realizing the Next button was at the top of the screen. The Go button was toward the bottom of the screen, after the response, and this placement matched their mental model of where the "forward" navigation button should have been.

To the extent possible, we should design navigation features to match respondent's expectations of how these features should work.

Even when navigational features do match respondent's expectations, we must evaluate the potential effect navigation can have on other aspects of the survey. For example, Cook, Sembajwe, and Geisen (2011) tested a mobile survey that mimicked the finger-swiping motion commonly used to navigate through web pages on a mobile phone. Participants could use their finger in a swiping motion on the phone screen to navigate between survey questions.

Participants were familiar with the swiping function and enjoyed swiping between questions. Yet when participants swiped to navigate, occasionally they inadvertently changed their response to a survey question, particularly on check boxes. The initial placement of their finger to initiate the swiping motion registered as a selection, changing the participant's response. Some participants did not even realize that they had changed their response to the survey question, leading to inaccurate responses (Fig. 2.13).

Processing Feedback

How Do Respondents Interpret and React to the Survey Feedback in Response to Their Actions?

With interviewer-administered surveys, the interviewer provides feedback to the respondent. If an invalid response is provided, the interviewer will likely repeat the question or response options in order to get an accurate response. With self-administered web-based surveys, the computer or mobile device provides feedback to the respondent. This is one of the main distinctions between assessing usability of a paper survey and a web-based survey.

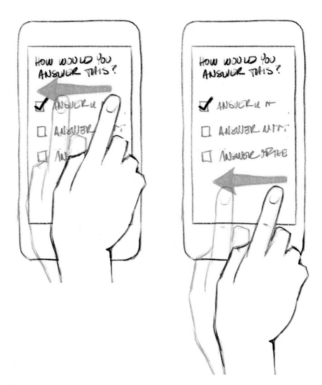

FIGURE 2.13
Swiping over a question response (left) instead of swiping on white space (right) resulted in participants inadvertently changing their response.

When respondents complete a web-based survey, they expect the survey to react to any action they take. For example, if they enter an answer and hit Next, they expect to be taken to a new page. If respondents click on a button or link, they expect something to happen in response. Respondents must then interpret that reaction to decide on their next action. If they are taken to a new question, they will answer that question. Instead, if the respondent remains on the same page after clicking Next, they must decide what needs to be done in order to move to the next screen.

In a well-designed survey, the feedback provided by the survey can help prevent errors. For example, it is common for respondents to accidentally miss a row in a grid question where several questions are grouped together in a table format. Several studies have found that providing dynamic feedback to survey respondents by graying out completed grid rows reduces item missing rates compared with traditional grids (Couper, Tourangeau,

Conrad, & Zhang, 2013; Galesic, Tourangeau, Couper, & Conrad, 2007; Kaczmirek, 2011).

However, respondents may misinterpret the feedback provided by the survey. Fig. 2.14 displays a survey in which respondents had to answer a question multiple times for different departments and programs. Due to the repetitive nature of the items and the limited screen space, rollover definitions were used instead of including definitions in the survey question. During usability testing, participants rolled their mouse over a definition or clicked on it. When the survey did not provide immediate feedback to the action, several participants moved the mouse away assuming that a definition was not available. It turned out that the programmer had built a 1-second delay into the rollover to prevent the definitions from coming up when they were not wanted.

As a result, several participants in the study did not realize that the survey included rollover definitions. Their mental models were correct in that moving the mouse over the term would produce a definition. However the delayed feedback provided by the survey changed their

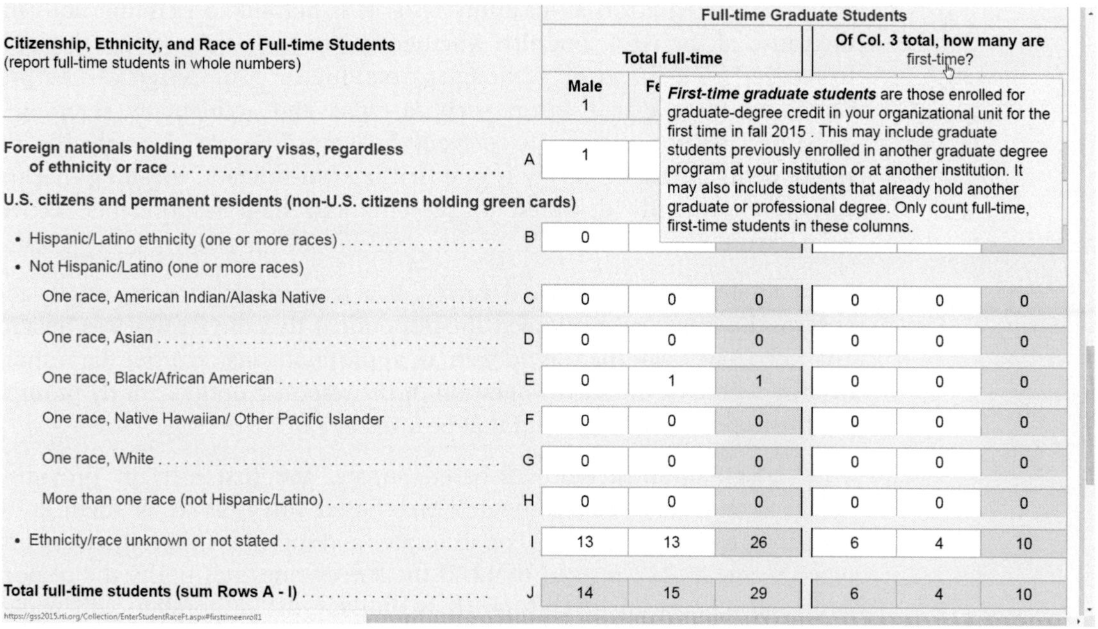

Full-time Graduate Students

Citizenship, Ethnicity, and Race of Full-time Students (report full-time students in whole numbers)		Total full-time: Male 1	Fe		Of Col. 3 total, how many are first-time?		
Foreign nationals holding temporary visas, regardless of ethnicity or race	A	1					
U.S. citizens and permanent residents (non-U.S. citizens holding green cards)							
• Hispanic/Latino ethnicity (one or more races)	B	0					
• Not Hispanic/Latino (one or more races)							
One race, American Indian/Alaska Native	C	0	0	0	0	0	0
One race, Asian	D	0	0	0	0	0	0
One race, Black/African American	E	0	1	1	0	0	0
One race, Native Hawaiian/ Other Pacific Islander	F	0	0	0	0	0	0
One race, White	G	0	0	0	0	0	0
More than one race (not Hispanic/Latino)	H	0	0	0	0	0	0
• Ethnicity/race unknown or not stated	I	13	13	26	6	4	10
Total full-time students (sum Rows A - I)	J	14	15	29	6	4	10

First-time graduate students are those enrolled for graduate-degree credit in your organizational unit for the first time in fall 2015 . This may include graduate students previously enrolled in another graduate degree program at your institution or at another institution. It may also include students that already hold another graduate or professional degree. Only count full-time, first-time students in these columns.

https://gss2015.rti.org/Collection/EnterStudentRaceFt.aspx#firsttimeenroll1

FIGURE 2.14

The rollover definitions were programmed with a 1-second delay. Respondents did not immediately realize that certain terms had associated definitions.

interpretation. By the next round of testing, the delay for the rollover definitions had been removed; participants successfully noticed, used, and
relied on the definitions.

How Well Does the Survey Help Respondents Identify, Interpret, and Resolve Errors?

Ideally, surveys have been designed in ways that prevent errors. We can do
this by designing effective web-survey questions (see Couper, 2008), providing informative feedback to respondents, and preventing common web
errors by adhering to usability guidelines, such as those proposed by
Quesenbery (2001):

- Make it hard for respondents to perform actions that are
  - incorrect,
  - invalid, or
  - irreversible.
- Plan for respondents to do the unexpected.

Despite our best designs, however, respondents may still encounter errors.
When observing errors in usability tests, it is helpful to examine not only
the cause of the error, but also whether and how the respondent was able
to recover from the error. Although errors due to poor design can be prevented to some extent, errors such as typos and accidentally skipping a
question are not as easy to prevent but must be easily resolvable for
respondents. A usable survey is one that is error-tolerant, meaning that the
survey is primarily designed to prevent, and help respondents recover
from, errors.

In an interviewer-administered survey, if a respondent provides an invalid
answer, the interviewer can alert the respondent that the answer was invalid.
The interviewer will then try to gain an appropriate answer from the respondent by repeating the survey question or the response options, or by prompting the respondent, "So would that be a yes or no?"

With a self-administered web-based survey, the first step in providing
feedback to respondents through a web-based survey is to let them know
that an error has occurred. For example, a respondent may inadvertently
type the age as 422 instead of 42. If the survey does not notify the respondent that 422 as an invalid age, it is unlikely the respondent will realize
the error.

Once an error is identified, the survey should adequately describe the error so
the respondent can identify it. To help respondents interpret error messages,
the messages should be positive, helpful, and near the problematic item.

Fig. 2.15 shows a typical error message from a mobile phone survey. The popup box notifies the respondent of an error, but it does not help the respondent to determine what caused it. The error message is general and located far from the problem, and the respondent may not know what fields are required. In this usability study, participants saw the error message and had to search the entire screen to find the missing field and correct it, as shown in the eye-tracking gaze plot in Fig. 2.15 (right).

 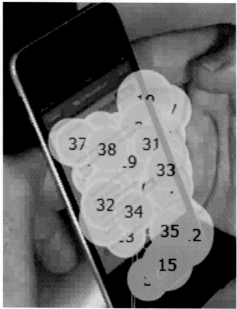

FIGURE 2.15

The error message does not indicate which field is missing and is not located next to the missed item (left). The gaze plot shows that the participant had to look all over the screen to find the missing field (right). *Reproduced with permission from He, J., Siu, C., Strohl, J., & Chaparro, B. (2014). Mobile. In R. Bergstrom, & A. Schall (Eds.),* Eye tracking in user experience design. *San Francisco, CA: Morgan Kaufmann.*

References

Biemer, P. (2010). Total survey error: Design, implementation, and evaluation. *Public Opinion Quarterly, 74*(5), 817–848.

Bristol, K., Romano Bergstrom, J., & Link, M. (2014). Eye tracking the user experience of a smartphone and web data collection tool. In *Paper presentation at the AAPOR conference, Anaheim, CA, May 2014.*

Chepp, V., & Gray, C. (2014). Foundations and new directions. In K. Miller, S. Willson, V. Chepp, & J. L. Padilla (Eds.), *Cognitive interviewing methodology* (pp. 7–14). New York, NY: Wiley.

Christian, L. M. (2003). *The influence of visual layout on scalar questions in web surveys* (unpublished master's thesis). Retrieved from <http://survey.sesrc.wsu.edu/dillman/papers.htm>.

Christian, L. M., Dillman, D. A., & Smyth, J. D. (2005). *Instructing web and telephone respondents to report date answers in a format desired by the surveyor*. Technical report #05-067. Social & Economic Sciences Research Center Pullman, Washing State University. Retrieved on <https://www.sesrc.wsu.edu/dillman/papers/2005/instructingwebandtelephone.pdf>.

Christian, L. M., Parsons, N. L., & Dillman, D. A. (2009). Designing scalar questions for web surveys. *Sociological Methods and Research, 37*, 393—425.

Conrad, F. G., Couper, M. P., Tourangeau, R., & Peytchev, A. (2006). Use and nonuse of clarification features in web surveys. *Journal of Official Statistics, 22*, 245—269.

Cook, S., Sembajwe, R., & Geisen, E. (2011). Can you see it now? Good: Usability testing of a mobile health application. In *Paper presented at the 66th American Association for Public Opinion Research, Phoenix, AZ*.

Couper, M. P. (2008). *Designing effective web surveys*. New York, NY: Cambridge University Press.

Couper, M. P., Baker, R., & Mechling, J. (2011). Placement and design of navigation buttons in web surveys. *Survey Practice*. <http://surveypractice.org.>

Couper, M. P., Tourangeau, R., Conrad, F. G., & Zhang, C. (2013). The design of grids in web surveys. *Social Science Computer Review, 31*(3), 322—345.

Davis, P., & Scott, A. (1995). The effect of interviewer variance on domain comparisons. *Survey Methodology, 21*, 99—106.

Dillman, D., Smyth, J., & Christian, L. (2009). *Internet, mail, and mixed-mode surveys: The tailored design method*. New York, NY: Wiley.

Dillman, D., Tortora, R., & Bowker, D. (1999). *Principles for constructing web surveys*. SESRC Technical Report 98-50, Pullman, Washington. Retrieved December 2, 2002 from <http://survey.sesrc.wsu.edu/dillman/papers/websurveyppr.pd>.

Edwards, B., Schneider, S., & Brick, P. (2008). Visual elements of questionnaire design: Experiments with a CATI establishment survey. In J. E. Lepkowski, et al. (Eds.),*Advances in telephone survey methodology*. Hoboken, NJ: Wiley.

Fowler, F. (2014). *Survey research methods*. Thousand Oaks, CA: SAGE Publications, Inc.

Galesic, M., Tourangeau, R., Couper, M. P., & Conrad, F. G. (2007). Using change to improve navigation in grid questions. In *Paper presented at the General Online Research conference (GOR'07), Leipzig, March*.

Galesic, M., Tourangeau, R., Couper, M. P., & Conrad, F. G. (2008). Eye-tracking data: New insights on response order effects and other signs of cognitive shortcuts in survey responding. *Public Opinion Quarterly, 72*(5), 892—913.

Gareau, M., Ashenfelter, K., & Malakoff, L. (2013). *Full report for round 1 of usability testing for the consumer expenditure web diary survey*. Center for Survey Measurement, Research and Methodology Directorate (Study Series 2013-24). U.S. Census Bureau. Retrieved from <https://www.census.gov/srd/papers/pdf/ssm2013-24.pdf>.

Geisen, E., Sha, M., Olmsted, M., Geber, E., Kenward, K., & Schoua-Glusberg, A. (2013). *Cognitive testing of roster, coverage, household count, and address questions for the 2020 census*. Unpublished technical report.

Groves, R. (1989). *Survey errors and survey costs*. New York, NY: Wiley.

Groves, R., Fowler, F., Couper, M. P., Lepkowski, J., Singer, E., & Tourangeau, R. (2004). *Survey methodology*. New York, NY: Wiley.

Hansen, S. E., & Couper, M. P. (2004). Usability testing as a means of evaluating computer assisted survey instruments. In S. Presser, et al. (Eds.), *Methods for testing and evaluating survey questionnaire*. New York, NY: Wiley.

Harzing, A. (2006). Response styles in cross-national survey research: A 26-country study. *International Journal of Cross Cultural Management, 6*(2), 243−266.

He, J., Siu, C., Strohl, J., & Chaparro, B. (2014). Mobile. In R. Bergstrom, & A. Schall (Eds.), *Eye tracking in user experience design*. San Francisco, CA: Morgan Kaufmann.

Kaczmirek, L. (2011). Attention and usability in internet surveys: Effects of visual feedback in grid questions. In M. Das, P. Ester, & L. Kaczmirek (Eds.), *Social research and the internet* (pp. 191−214). New York, NY: Taylor and Francis.

Krosnick, J. A. (1991). Response strategies for coping with the cognitive demands of attitude measures in surveys. *Applied Cognitive Psychology, 5*(3), 213−236.

Peytchev, A., Conrad, F., Couper, M., & Tourangeau, R. (2010). Increasing respondents' use of definitions in web surveys. *Journal of Official Statistics, 26*(4), 633−650.

Quesenbery, W. (2001). What does usability mean: Looking beyond 'Ease of Use'. In *Proceedings of the 48th annual conference, Society for Technical Communication, 2001, Chicago, IL*.

Romano, J. C., & Chen, J. M. (2011). *A usability and eye-tracking evaluation of four versions of the online National Survey for College Graduates (NSCG): Iteration 2*. Statistical Research Division (Study Series SSM2011-01). U.S. Census Bureau. Retrieved from <https://www.census.gov/srd/papers/pdf/ssm2011-01.pdf>.

Romano Bergstrom, J. C., Lakhe, S., & Erdman, C. (2016). *Next* belongs to the right of *Previous* in web-based surveys: An experimental usability study. *Survey Practice, 9*(1).

Romano Bergstrom, J. C., & Strohl, J. (2013). Improving government websites and surveys with usability testing: A comparison of methodologies. In *Proceedings from the Federal Committee on Statistical Methodology (FCSM) conference, November 2013, Washington, DC*.

Simon, H. A. (1957). *Models of man: Social and rational*. New York, NY: Wiley.

Stapleton, C. (2013). The Smartphone Way to Collect Survey Data. *Survey Practice, 6*(2).

Toepoel, V., Das, M., & van Soest, A. (2009). Design of web questionnaires: The effect of layout in rating scales. *Journal of Official Statistics, 25*(4), 509−528.

Tourangeau, R. (1984). Cognitive science and survey methods. In T. Jabine, M. Straf, J. Tanur, & R. Tourangeau (Eds.), *Cognitive aspects of survey design: Building a bridge between disciplines* (pp. 73−1000). Washington, DC: National Academy Press.

Tourangeau, R., Couper, M. P., & Conrad, F. (2004). Spacing, position, and order. Interpretive heuristics for visual features of survey questions. *Public Opinion Quarterly, 68*, 368−393.

Tourangeau, R., Rips, L. J., & Rasinski, K. (2000). *The psychology of survey response*. Cambridge: Cambridge University Press.

Willis, G. B. (2005). *Cognitive interviewing. A tool for improving questionnaire design*. Thousand Oaks, CA: Sage Publications, Inc.

CHAPTER 3

Adding Usability Testing to the Survey Process

Chapter 1, Usability and Usability Testing, provided an overview of usability testing, and Chapter 2, Respondent–Survey Interaction, discussed the principles of survey development and identifying survey error. This chapter brings the two concepts together and discusses how to apply usability principles to survey research to improve data quality as well as the user experience.

ITERATIVE DESIGN AND TESTING

When survey pretesting is done, it is often applied in a linear manner with the survey being revised before the next pretesting method is applied, as shown in Fig. 3.1.

FIGURE 3.1
The pretesting process conducted in a linear fashion.

However the main limitation of this linear approach is that the survey has been almost fully designed and programmed before usability testing begins. Consequently, the results of usability testing will not guide or shape the design of the survey instrument. When usability testing identifies problems at this late stage, deadlines and budget often prevent any substantial revisions.

Any usability testing is better than none, but to have the most impact, we recommend conducting it earlier in the survey development process using an iterative approach. You should usability-test early, work in stages as the survey is being developed, use fewer participants in more rounds, identify issues, revise, and test again. Integrate usability testing into the programming schedule as the survey is being developed so it can be conducted in

51

Usability Testing for Survey Research. DOI: http://dx.doi.org/10.1016/B978-0-12-803656-3.00003-8

stages, as specific aspects of the survey are being developed. Other pretesting methods can be conducted concurrently rather than sequentially. The benefit of this approach is that you can repeatedly design, test, and revise the survey, as shown in Fig. 3.2.

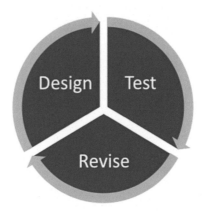

FIGURE 3.2
Iterative testing cycles through repeated states of designing, testing, and revising.

If an iterative approach of usability testing early and often is more effective, why is the linear pretesting approach used? Some reasons may include the following:

- *Usability testing was an afterthought.* Because usability testing was not included in the study design, it was not integrated into the budget or schedule, making it difficult to apply in an iterative fashion. Instead, it was just tacked to the end of the survey development process.
- *Iterative testing is (perceived as being) too expensive.* Conducting multiple rounds of testing may seem expensive, but it is not. It costs less to conduct iterative usability testing than to wait until the end when you might discover something big and costly. We typically pay usability test participants the standard $30–100 per hour—this is quite a bit less than the cost of programming or reprogramming when a new approach or design is needed.
- *Belief that large samples are needed.* Many survey researchers mistakenly believe that tests need large numbers of people to show problems. However, usability testing is largely qualitative. If even one respondent identifies a major problem, a correction is warranted.

- *Same way of doing things.* The linear approach is often used for other pretesting methods—it is common to first conduct an expert review, then cognitive testing, and then pilot testing. So researchers often apply usability testing in the same linear, stepwise manner. Yet usability testing should be more flexible and applied at multiple stages of question-naire development.

> Start early, work in stages as the survey is being developed, use fewer partici-pants in more rounds, identify issues, revise, and test again.

Reasons for More Rounds, Fewer Participants

Conducting more rounds of testing with fewer participants per round typically identifies more issues and does so more efficiently (e.g., picture 2 rounds with 5 participants each vs 1 round of 10 participants). You get diminishing returns from each additional participant in a round. At a certain point, additional participants often identify only problems you have already discovered. Ideally, you would continue testing with participants until you stop learning anything new. However, most projects do not have that kind of flexibility in schedule or budget.

The benefit of doing multiple rounds of testing with fewer participants compared to one big round of testing is that it allows researchers to test the solutions to problems. Identifying problems is often easier than fixing them, so you need to verify that the revisions (1) actually improve the survey and (2) do not cause additional problems elsewhere in it.

In addition, sometimes participants find it hard to see past glaring problems to the subtler ones. Testing a revised product may identify some less serious but still problematic issues that might have escaped notice in the first round, despite additional participants in it. Imagine a left-hand navigation menu that was so distracting that all participants used it to navigate instead of the Next and Previous buttons at the bottom of the screen. So the first round did not show how well participants could use those buttons to navigate through the survey. After the large usability issue (the distracting left-hand navigation menu) is fixed, you could use the next round of testing to assess the usability of those buttons and the screens they access.

Smaller rounds of testing also make it easier to summarize results. Easier sum-maries allow for expediency, both in disseminating findings to stakeholders and in revising the survey. This approach allows for a good balance between testing resources and revision resources. For example, a web-based survey might use the same response format for all survey questions.

Smaller Rounds Support Collaboration

Developing a survey requires input from a variety of stakeholders: the client who requests the survey, a project manager, subject-matter experts, questionnaire-design experts, and programmers, to name a few.

Usability testing conducted in a linear approach (with a large number of interviews conducted at the end of the survey development), does not usually foster collaboration among stakeholders. Each group of stakeholders is working independently, but there is a lot of room for a communication breakdown in this approach. For example, a noncollaborative usability test might go something like this:

1. Programmers program the survey.
2. Questionnaire-design experts administer the usability test sessions over a couple of weeks and write up the findings in a report that is delivered a few weeks after testing concludes.
3. The project manager, client, and possibly the substantive experts review the report.
4. The clients decide the changes that should be made, which get communicated to the questionnaire designers.
5. Questionnaire designers mark up a copy of the survey and present the changes to the programmers.
6. Programmers make the revisions.
7. Questionnaire designers test the survey again.

A more efficient approach is to encourage all stakeholders (clients, project managers, programmers) to observe usability testing live or remotely. Seeing is believing, and you want them to see the struggles that participants have. Reading about them in a report does not have the same impact as when stakeholders, clients in particular, observe them. Without that firsthand knowledge, they may not believe the magnitude of an issue. And observing usability tests is certainly more exciting than reading a report!

The reason programmers should observe is this: Sometimes questionnaire designers tell them to program questions in a certain way, but the reason for the changes may be unclear to the programmers. When programmers see how respondents interact with a survey they programmed, they can better understand the respondents' challenges, which can facilitate programming.

Iterative Usability Study Example

The following usability study (Geisen, Olmsted, Goerman, & Lakhe, 2014) highlights issues in one or more of the usability processes and shows how errors can be introduced. Following usability testing, the survey design was revised to improve the comprehension and action processes, which led to improved data quality.

The study was conducted on a version of the 2020 Census Household survey designed for Android smartphones. A study goal was to capture full names for all household members. Getting detailed name information, including middle and last names, assists the Census Bureau in identifying duplication of individuals who were counted at more than one address. Iterative usability testing was conducted to determine the most effective survey design for capturing accurate names for all household members.

The first design (Fig. 3.3A) used a one-box format with a prompt inside the text box that asked for the first, middle, and last names. The one-box format was chosen to accommodate multicultural names that do not conform to the typical American first, middle, and last name format. The prompt inside the box was chosen because it required less space on the small smartphone screen.

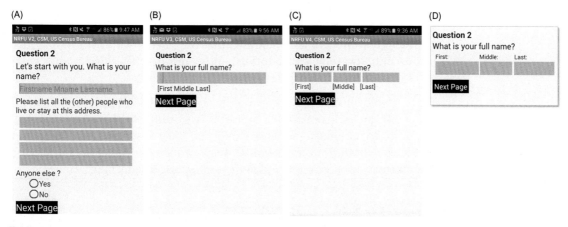

FIGURE 3.3
(A) Initial design: One box, prompt inside box. (B) Second design: One box, prompt below box: resulted in more complete names. (C) Third design: Separate boxes, prompt below: even more complete names but keyboard covered prompts. (D) Final design: Separate boxes, prompt above: resulted in the most complete set of names. *Reproduced with permission from Geisen, E., Olmsted, M., Goerman, P., & Lakhe, S. (2014). Planning for the future: Usability testing for the 2020 Census. Paper presented at the 2014 federal computer assisted survey information collection, Washington, DC.*

The first round of usability testing found that few participants entered their middle name, and some participants entered only their first name. This is what happened: Because the "name" question is easy for participants to answer, they immediately began typing without reviewing the prompt. Once they entered their first name, the prompt (to add the rest of their name) disappeared, leaving people to decide for themselves what to do next.

The second design (Fig. 3.3B) still used one text box, but this time, the prompt for the name appeared below the text box instead of in it. In addition, the question was revised to ask for "full name" instead of just "name." This version resulted in more complete names than the first design but still not many complete names overall.

The third design (Fig. 3.3C) used three separate "name" boxes to emphasize the importance of the middle name. The design worked better: People understood that three separate pieces of information were required. However, when the keyboard was activated, it covered the prompts that were below the text boxes; some participants were uncertain what information was required for each box (e.g., should they include middle name or maiden name in the middle box?).

The fourth design (Fig. 3.3D) also used three separate boxes, but the prompt was placed above the boxes. Consequently, participants had this information as they began entering their names, and the prompt was no longer covered by the keyboard. This resulted in almost all participants providing complete names.

There is still concern that some names might not match the first, middle, and last format. Of the few individuals in the study with names that did not fit this format though, they indicated that they were used to converting their names into the three-name format. More research, specifically with these types of respondents, is needed.

This example illustrates the benefit of iterative testing to evolve toward a better survey design. Efforts to prevent problems (e.g., using one box instead of three boxes to accommodate some respondents) may backfire and create more problems than they prevent. Because many of these outcomes are not predictable, there is no substitute for usability testing before launching a survey.

WHAT TO TEST AND WHEN

To apply an iterative usability testing approach to a survey, it helps to understand the types of testing that can be conducted at each stage in the survey development cycle.

The three primary types of testing are: *exploratory* or *formative testing, assessment* or *summative testing,* and *verification* or *validation testing* (Rubin & Chisnell, 2008).

- *Exploratory/formative testing.* Conduct exploratory usability testing at the beginning of the development process to guide the actual design of the survey—even if you do not have a single survey question finalized.

  At the early stages of survey development, much of the work is still conceptual. Exploratory testing can be used to evaluate the effectiveness or appropriateness of the high-level design before working out the more complicated details and nuances of your survey. Identifying problems in high-level design early can save countless hours in designing and programming.

Marquis, Nichols, and Tedesco (1998) suggest that at early stages of testing, the primary emphasis should be on evaluating the "interface design, arranging appropriate work sequences, and clarifying the meaning of words, icons, widgets, and other major features."

Exploratory testing also focuses on the users: Who are they and what tasks will they perform with the product? What do they think of the general concept or approach, and how does it match their mental models?

There is less emphasis on evaluating or observing user behavior during early testing because there may not be a product for the person to interact with.

Exploratory testing may not be needed if, e.g., survey designs are simple or based on a well-established design.

- *Assessment/summative testing.* Although this testing can happen at any point in the survey development cycle, it is usually done in development's early or middle stages, when prototypes exist for at least parts of the survey. It evaluates users' actual behaviors—how well people can actually use the product to complete a goal. It typically includes quantitative metrics as well as qualitative comments to evaluate effectiveness, efficiency, and satisfaction. It evaluates specific components of the survey and can provide insight on the high-level design or approach as well as a design's implementation.

Assessment testing is usually conducted over several rounds with improvements made between rounds. Subsequent rounds evaluate the improvements or new aspects of the survey as they are being developed. The quantitative metrics are tracked and compared across rounds, with the expectation that they will improve.

Sometimes a change as a result from usability testing leads to an unexpected issue in a later round. For example, Romano Bergstrom, Olmsted-Hawala, Chen, and Murphy (2011) conducted four rounds of testing in an iterative usability study. With each round, the fidelity increased: Round 1 used a low-fidelity paper prototype; Round 2 used medium-fidelity nonclickable HTML images; Rounds 3 and 4 used partially clickable web pages. Through the first three rounds of testing, usability increased, as measured by accuracy, efficiency, and satisfaction. But in the fourth round, usability declined because of a change made after Round 3. The iterative approach enabled the team to identify this issue and correct it.

■ *Verification/validation testing.* This usually occurs at the end of the survey development process just before the pilot test or survey launch. At this stage, it is helpful to test the whole survey, from logging in (if required) to completing/submitting the survey. The goal is to ensure the survey is free of any major usability concerns that would cause respondents to break off, or that would provide incorrect data. Another goal is testing how well the entire process works. Prior testing likely focused on testing certain aspects or sections of the survey in isolation.

Making any major modifications to the design or approach of your survey at this point is unlikely. The results of testing will be used to fine-tune and improve an existing design.

Fig. 3.4 shows common uses for testing surveys at each of these three stages in the development process. Testing conducted at each stage will vary by purpose and aspect of the survey to be tested.

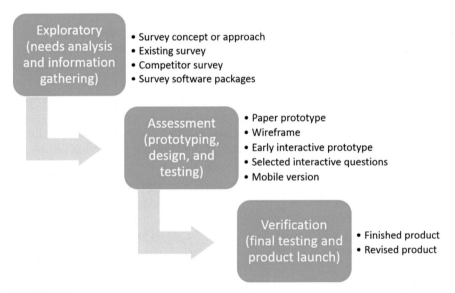

FIGURE 3.4
Usability testing throughout the survey development cycle.

Not every project needs usability testing at every stage, while some projects will require multiple rounds of testing throughout. The complexity of the project, budget, and your schedule all factor into the amount of testing the survey needs. To help you decide what type of testing is best for your survey, the following sections include examples of various survey products that can be tested at each stage and the benefits of usability testing these products.

We also discuss how you might integrate usability testing with other pretesting methods in some of these stages. During each of these stages, additional pretesting strategies such as an expert review or cognitive interviewing might be conducted in parallel or in combination with usability testing. For example, you can evaluate the usability of an early interactive prototype as you cognitively test draft survey items. During verification testing, you could conduct both cognitive interviewing and usability testing in a combined effort.

Survey Concept or Approach

Test the survey concept to evaluate the preliminary design or approach, particularly for complex surveys. For example, you may wish to answer the following:

- How well does the interface support the way respondents think about and answer the survey questions?
- Are the questions asked chronologically from past to present, and do respondents prefer to answer from present to past?
- Does the organizational structure of the survey support how respondents think about the task?
- Should you ask participants to recall a series of specific events and then ask questions about each event, or should you ask the follow-up questions immediately after asking about each event?

Strictly speaking, this type of testing is not usability testing. It may be conducted using focus groups, card sorting, or in-depth interviews. We discuss this here because you rarely can address the nuances of the specific survey design usability until you evaluate the high-level design with potential respondents.

For example, imagine that your team is tasked with designing a mobile application for a diary survey that will be used in a travel study. The goal of the diary survey is to collect geocoded locations of all of the places a person visits in 24 hours. The survey also needs additional details for each location, such as the mode of transportation (e.g., car, bus, walking), how long it took the respondent to travel between locations, how many people accompanied the respondent, and whether and how much the respondent paid for parking. The data will be used to create predictive travel models used for city planning.

Although there are several ways to design a diary survey for this purpose, it should be easy for respondents to use—and to remember to use—while they travel.

Exploratory usability testing can evaluate different preliminary survey designs with potential respondents. Reactions to these high-level designs can guide the development of the rest of the survey.

For example, to reduce the burden on respondents, you may want to minimize the amount of information that is collected in real time. Therefore you may design a survey that asks for some information in real time and collects the rest later. You can interview different types of participants, such as those who use public transportation only and families with children, and those without, to determine how to divide up the information reported "now" versus later. At this point, you may or may not have simple drawings, illustrations, or prototypes of the survey to show respondents. You would ask questions that would affect the potential design such as the following:

> How easy or difficult would it be for you to provide your total travel time
> every time you changed locations?

If you have early mobile designs to test, you can have participants interact with paper prototypes on a mobile phone, as shown in Fig. 3.5 (Craig, 2016). In this example the participant interacts with a 3D-printed model of a mobile phone with paper prototype "interfaces."

FIGURE 3.5

A participant works on an early paper prototype. *Reproduced with permission from Ecotonos. https://ecotonos.com/products/ux-phone and Craig, E. (2016). http://radicalresearchsummit.com/emma-craig/.*

Existing Survey

Conducting usability testing on an existing survey can be helpful if the plan is to continue fielding the survey each year, and the team is open to making changes and improvements. You can get feedback on ease of use and identify potential ways to improve the design.

In particular, testing an existing survey can be beneficial before implementing a large redesign of a survey. Observing how potential respondents interact with and use the survey can help you develop new survey questions.

For example, in 2007, the Survey of Graduate Students and Postdoctorates in Science and Engineering (GSS) was redesigned.

DESCRIPTION OF GSS

The GSS—sponsored by the National Science Foundation (NSF) and the National Institutes of Health (NIH)—provides data on the number and characteristics of graduate students in research-based master's or doctoral programs in science, engineering, or selected health (SEH) fields and on postdoctoral (postdoc) appointees, and doctorate-holding nonfaculty researchers in SEH fields. NSF uses the results of this survey to assess shifts in graduate enrollment and postdoc appointments and trends in financial support. For more information, visit: http://www.nsf.gov/statistics/srvygradpostdoc/.

Before redesigning the GSS, a usability test was conducted with the existing paper form (Fig. 3.6). The original landscape-oriented form asked for race/ethnicity by sex and student status (full time vs part time) for each graduate department in science and engineering.

Usability testing showed that participants were overwhelmed by the requested amount of information on the page. In addition, participants often missed or misunderstood the race headings (one race only: non-Hispanic/Latino; one race only; more than one race; unknown). So the format was simplified (Fig. 3.7). The new survey used portrait orientation instead of landscape, asked only about one group of students (e.g., part time) at a time, and revised the race and ethnicity categories.

If a survey is transitioning to a new data-collection mode, conducting usability testing on the current survey can guide the development of the new design. For example, in transitioning a survey from paper to web, you might

Question 2 (continued)

Please report on a headcount basis (the number of people in whole numbers).

Consistency check: Row 5, Column K, should match Question 3, Row 7, Column M (full-time women).
Row 6, Column K, should match Question 3, Row 6, Column M (full-time men and women).

Part-time and full-time status by sex (Use your institution's definition of part-time/full-time status.)	Race/Ethnicity and Citizenship of Part-Time and Full-Time Graduate Students Enrolled, Fall 2007 (Enter numbers of students; do not use fractions or decimals.)									Foreign	Total[1]
	U.S. Citizens and Permanent Residents										
	One race only non-Hispanic/Latino					One race only	More than one race		Unknown		
	Black/ African American A	American Indian/ Alaska Native B	Asian C	Native Hawaiian/ Pacific Islander D	White E	Hispanic/ Latino F	Hispanic/ Latino G	Non- Hispanic/ Latino H	Unknown (race not stated) I	Temporary visa holders J	Sum of A thru J[1] K
1. Men enrolled part-time											
2. Women enrolled part-time											
3. Total part-time[1]											
4. Men enrolled full-time											
5. Women enrolled full-time											
6. Total full-time[1]											

Rows 7 and 8: A *first-time* graduate student is one who has enrolled for graduate credit at the institution at which he or she is pursuing a degree for the first-time in the fall 2007 term.

7. Of full-time total (Row 6), how many are *first-time*?											
8. Of first-time total (Row 7), how many are *women*?											

[1] The shaded rows and column for the totals will be automatically calculated on the Web survey.

Please explain significant differences from last year's survey responses or provide other comments.

FIGURE 3.6

Existing paper survey form for GSS that was tested before redesign.

Citizenship, ethnicity, and race of part-time students (report students in whole numbers)	Part-time graduate students		
	Male 1	Female 2	Total[1] 3
Foreign nationals holding temporary visas, regardless of ethnicity or race......... A			
U.S. citizens and permanent residents (non-U.S. citizens holding green cards)			
• Hispanic/Latino ethnicity (one or more races)......... B			
• Non-Hispanic/Latino (one or more races)			
One race, American Indian/Alaska Native......... C			
One race, Asian......... D			
One race, Black/African American......... E			
One race, Native Hawaiian/Other Pacific Islander......... F			
One race, White......... G			
More than one race (non-Hispanic/Latino)......... H			
• Ethnicity/race unknown or not stated......... I			
Total part-time students (sum Rows A–I)[1]......... J			

Please explain significant differences from the 2007 survey or provide other comments here

[1] Row and column totals are calculated automatically if you report via the Web survey

FIGURE 3.7

The revised form broke the survey question into multiple components to make it easier for respondents to understand and answer. The form also revised racial and ethnic categories to match how schools and universities recorded this data for their students.

aim to answer questions such as these when you conduct usability testing on the paper survey:

- How do people navigate through the instrument?
- Do they complete it chronologically or flip back and forth between pages?
- Do they notice and use the provided definitions?
- What do they like and not like about the survey?

Answering questions such as those and observing what works well and what does not work will inform design of the web-based survey.

Similar Survey or Competitor Survey

This technique is used extensively in usability testing of websites. For example, if you were developing a new website for an airline, you might conduct usability testing of the websites of the three main competitors. You would use the insights gained to avoid features that people find annoying and frustrating.

As with websites and other products, a survey may share many similarities with other surveys, although, also like websites, all surveys have unique aspects. Similarly, surveys can benefit from usability testing competitors' surveys. The more similar the survey is to the current survey you are designing in the type of questions used (e.g., matrix style questions, sliders), content, length, and look, the more useful the insights will be.

If you cannot access competitors' surveys, another option is to test a similar survey developed for another project. In this case, you probably do not care about the actual survey questions but want to understand how people interact with the survey. You might aim to assess the following:

- Are people able to use navigation features easily?
- When filling out grids, do people have difficulty clicking the correct radio button?
- Are the Next and Previous buttons where people expect them to be?

Or perhaps you created the mobile travel-diary survey mentioned earlier. Now a different client asks you to create one for a different metropolitan area. Although this client has slightly different needs and interests, testing the earlier survey can provide useful insights for the new survey design. In this example, you want to conduct cognitive interviewing to evaluate the content of the survey questions too.

You can also learn a lot about how potential respondents interact with survey instruments, in general, by testing any survey.

Survey Software Packages

Many of the examples described so far assume that custom survey programming is being used for web-based surveys. However, depending on the needs of your survey, off-the-shelf *survey software* packages may be more than sufficient. These software programs allow nonprogrammers the ability to build web-based surveys. Usability testing can be used to decide which package is best for your survey and survey respondents. Most of these programs allow for free trials or month-to-month charges, so you can use this time to evaluate a variety of survey questions using each of the platforms. The results of usability testing can be weighed against ease of designing questions, types of question formats available, costs, and other factors.

Paper Prototype

Paper prototyping is a methodology that consists of creating simple illustrations of the product to facilitate design, development, and testing. Paper prototypes are often used to flesh out a particular design as well as to share ideas among survey designers, programmers, and stakeholders during the user-centered design process.

You can show paper prototypes to real users to get feedback on the design. Consequently, paper prototypes are often used on custom survey-design applications where programming a mock-up could be time consuming and costly.

Although paper prototypes can be used in exploratory testing, they are more frequently used in assessment testing, once the fundamental survey design or approach has been established and can be demonstrated visually.

Paper prototypes can range substantially in complexity. For example, a paper prototype could be a simple sketch of what certain questions or aspects of the survey look like. Fig. 3.8 shows a sketch of a survey question to be programmed using a slider. When you use a low-fidelity prototype like this, you can get information about what people would do and if they understand the general concept. On the other hand, for off-the-shelf survey software that already had a slider, a paper prototype would not be necessary.

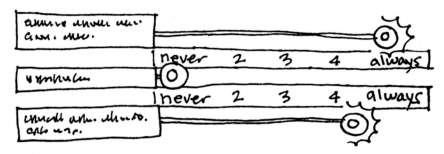

FIGURE 3.8
Hand-drawn prototype of a slider-style question.

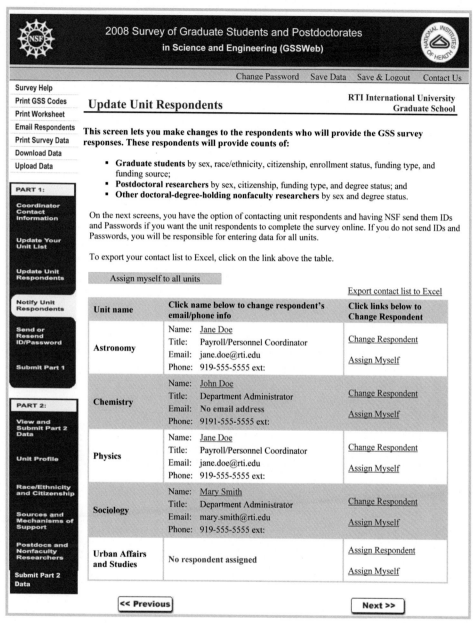

FIGURE 3.9
Microsoft Word paper prototype.

Fig. 3.9 shows a more sophisticated paper prototype that was developed in Microsoft Word, printed out, and shown to participants as part of the GSS redesign. Fig. 3.10 is a screenshot of the fully programmed survey. The prototype was developed to show the survey design to the web programmer,

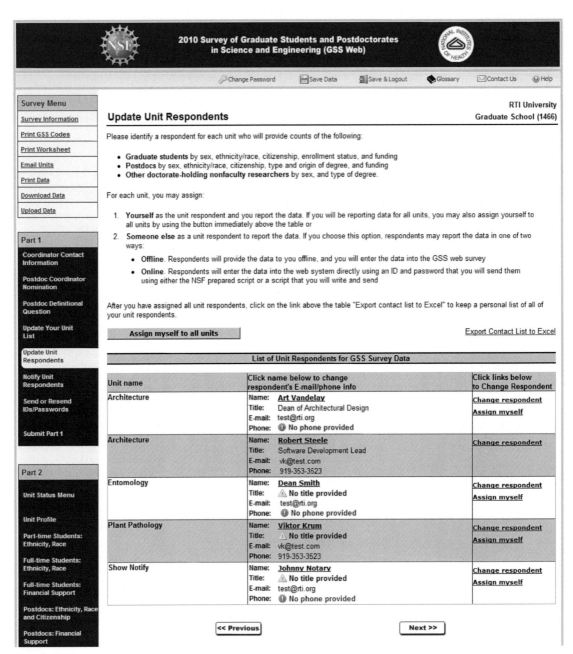

FIGURE 3.10

Programmed survey, based on paper prototype.

but it also could have been tested with participants to evaluate the general approach and layout before programming.

Conducting usability testing with paper prototypes has a number of advantages:

- *Early start.* Involving users in your initial designs and concepts provides feedback that can guide the rest of the survey development.
- *Cost effective.* Sketching out a concept on paper or mocking it up using a program, such as Microsoft Word, is cheaper than programming a fully functioning instrument. This is particularly true with a design that is complex and likely to change based on user feedback.
- *Improved collaboration.* Allows individuals from different disciplines to share ideas and concepts more easily.
- *Easy.* Programming or coding skills are not required. Similarly, basic paper prototypes do not require the use of graphic designers. They can be created by anyone.
- *Rapid evaluation and testing.* Survey development schedules are often rigid. Paper prototyping allows for quick evaluation and testing of certain aspects of the survey design.

> Get feedback on your design from real users by showing them prototypes before investing time and resources in programming.

Wireframe

Wireframes are like the skeleton of a web page. Similar to paper prototypes, they are used to lay out the basic structure and design of a website page. Although the wireframe might have headings or labels, it typically does not have actual content or has only limited content. It might have a link, but clicking on the link does not take the user to another location. Wireframes can be shown to participants as a printout or on a computer screen.

The advantages of the wireframe are similar to those of the paper prototype, but wireframes have the additional benefit of allowing you to work within the survey's actual confines. For example, how does a grid or matrix style question actually look when designed with your survey software program? How many columns can be used before the question text is too small or spans too many lines?

Fig. 3.11 shows a low-fidelity wireframe that was used in the first round of an iterative usability study (Romano Bergstrom et al., 2011). It shows the website's structure, major headers, and navigation features, but the text is all filler. Participants in the study were given tasks, and they told the moderator where they would click, if it were a live, working website. For example, participants were asked: "What percent of the population in California and Texas were white and college educated in 2006? Is there a way to visualize this information?" When participants said they would enter "California" and "Texas" into the box on the lower left and then click on the Map tab, the moderator then placed the paper wireframe shown in Fig. 3.12 over that section. The moderator played the role of the computer by showing what would occur next.

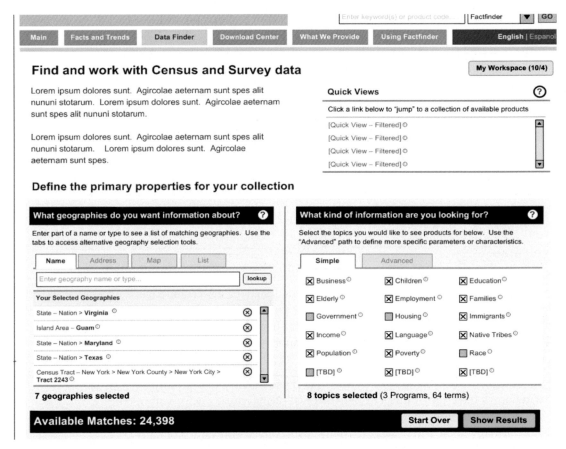

FIGURE 3.11

Low-fidelity wireframe used in the first round of an iterative usability study. *Reproduced with permission from Romano Bergstrom, J. C., Olmsted-Hawala, E. L., Chen, J. M., & Murphy, E. D. (2011). Conducting iterative usability testing on a Web site: Challenges and benefits.* Journal of Usability Studies, 7, 9–30.

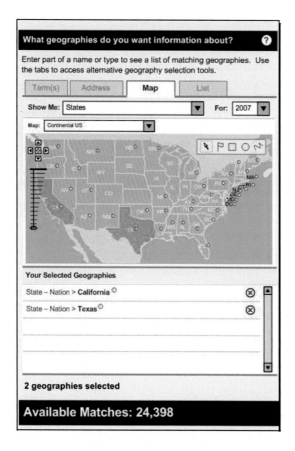

FIGURE 3.12

Low-fidelity wireframe paper used with the wireframe in Fig. 3.12. The moderator played the role of the computer by placing the paper over the wireframe when participants said where they would click. *Reproduced with permission from Romano Bergstrom, J. C., Olmsted-Hawala, E. L., Chen, J. M., & Murphy, E. D. (2011). Conducting iterative usability testing on a Web site: Challenges and benefits.* Journal of Usability Studies, 7, 9–30.

Fig. 3.13 shows a medium-fidelity, nonclickable HTML page that was used in the second round of testing. Participants were given tasks and were asked where they would click to complete the tasks. The moderator then displayed the next screen that would appear.

Before anything had been programmed, wireframes enabled us to learn whether people understood the general concept and how to use the website. As shown in the changes from Round 1 of testing (Fig. 3.11) to Round 2 (Fig. 3.13), many changes were made to the overall look and feel to make the site more intuitive. It was useful to start with paper and static screenshot wireframes to test the overall concept before time and energy had gone into coding the final site.

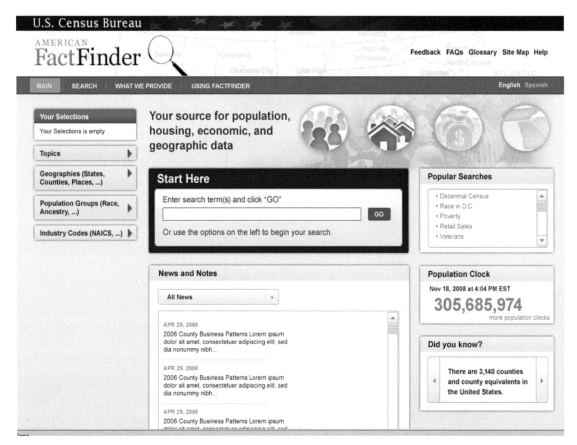

FIGURE 3.13
Medium-fidelity wireframe used in the second round of an iterative usability study. *Reproduced with permission from Romano Bergstrom, J. C., Olmsted-Hawala, E. L., Chen, J. M., & Murphy, E. D. (2011). Conducting iterative usability testing on a Web site: Challenges and benefits. Journal of Usability Studies, 7, 9–30.*

Early Interactive Prototype

The benefit of an early prototype is that you can test the survey with just a few questions to get feedback about the site overall. This feedback can be used to modify the design and apply the improved design for all survey questions. Participant feedback can focus on what people think of specific images. For example, you may aim to learn the following:

- Would people use the request PDF button?
- Do they know what it means?
- How do people react to having to scroll to see questions?
- Do people know how to save data?
- How/when do they use the navigation links?

Early prototype testing gives you feedback about certain aspects of the survey while other content is being developed or survey questions are being cognitively tested. This is a great way to incorporate user-centered design, maintain your schedule, and reduce costs by reducing the amount of reprogramming needed.

Fig. 3.14 is an example of an early interactive prototype. The left-hand navigation window in Fig. 3.14 shows about 10 sections to the survey. Although the content of each section is different, the types of question formats are similar across each section (e.g., radio buttons, text entry). Other aspects of the survey are the same across sections as well, including the navigation menu, the use of hover-over definitions, and other functionality.

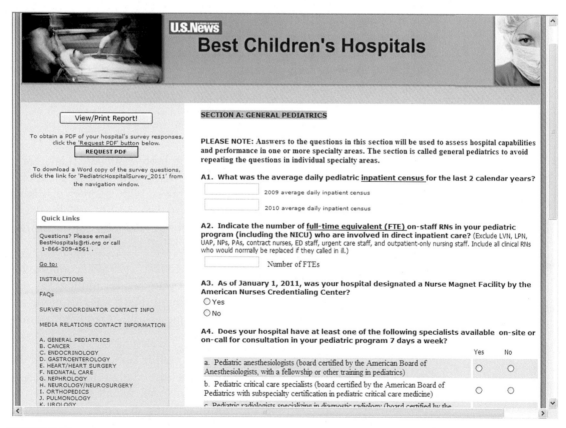

FIGURE 3.14

Example of an early interactive prototype used on the Pediatric Hospital Survey conducted as part of the Best Children's Hospital rankings, which are published annually by US News & World Report and have been conducted by RTI International since 2004. For more information, visit www.rti.org/besthospitals.

Selected Interactive Questions

Many surveys rely on the use of standard survey question types: check all that apply, radio buttons, drop-down menus, or write-in boxes. Most of the time, these question-type standards do not need usability testing. However, occasionally it is not clear how well a standard will work in a specific situation. For example, can participants find their answer in a drop-down menu with a long list of response options? Nielsen (2010) notes that "ordinal sequences" or "logical structuring" is often preferred over alphabetical sorting for long lists. However, it may not be clear what a participant considers logical structuring, or maybe alphabetical order is the most logical structure for some questions. In these cases, even a standard questionnaire format can benefit from usability testing.

Other good candidates for usability testing are surveys that require any custom programming. Interactive questions that can benefit from usability testing are questions that use mouse-over definitions and questions with embedded functions, such as a "calculate total" button. One question format that has been historically problematic—and could benefit from usability testing—is the grid style question.

Mobile Version of a Survey

"If you're doing a web survey, you're doing a mobile survey" (Link, Lai, & Bristol, 2013). Many respondents complete web-based surveys on mobile devices such as smartphones and tablets. Doing so with a survey that is not designed for mobile devices can lead to poor data quality and break-offs. This phenomenon, dubbed "unintentional mobile response," can be as high as 20% on some surveys (Buskirk, 2013).

Olmsted-Hawala, Nichols, Holland, and Gareau (2016) conducted a usability study of a survey that had not been optimized for mobile. Fig. 3.15 displays two of the screens on mobile. They found that it was frustrating and difficult for participants to respond to many questions that required zooming in to read the questions and response options.

Now many software programs have built-in mobile optimization tools that detect the device being used and optimize the design for that device. However, mobile optimization does not work well for all survey-question types, and some software programs optimize better than others. Therefore it is worth evaluating how usable a survey is even when optimized.

For some surveys, mobile optimization may not be sufficient. And even when surveys have been mobile optimized, unexpected usability issues can still occur. Sometimes it is most efficient to have a separate survey design for mobile devices and computers.

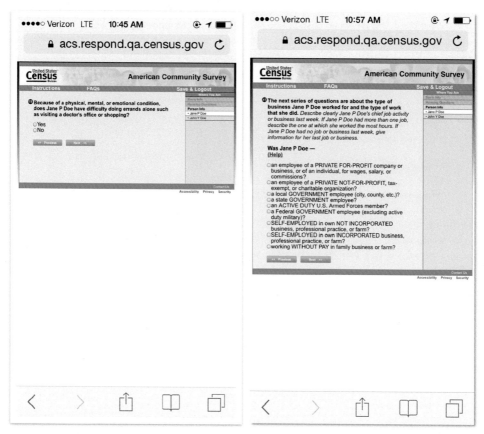

FIGURE 3.15

Two screens of a survey that was not optimized for mobile. *Reproduced with permission from Olmsted-Hawala, E. L., Nichols, E. M., Holland, T., & Gareau, M. (2016). Results of usability testing of the 2014 American Community Survey on smartphones and tablets Phase I: Before optimization for mobile devices. Research and Methodology Directorate, Center for Survey Measurement Research Report Series (Survey Methodology #2016-03). U.S. Census Bureau. Available online at http://www.census.gov/srd/papers/pdf/rsm2016-03.pdf.*

Romano Bergstrom (2016) conducted a usability study of a survey that had been optimized for mobile—Fig. 3.16 shows the desktop version and Fig. 3.17 shows the mobile version. Even though the overall survey had been optimized for mobile, there were usability issues with the grid questions. As shown in Fig. 3.17, the respondent needed to click on the dropdown for each item on the mobile version. However, some participants only made the first selection then clicked on Continue at the bottom of the screen without answering the remaining questions. Another problem with the mobile version design was that the response options were hidden until the respondent clicked on the dropdown, which made it difficult to understand what was being asked.

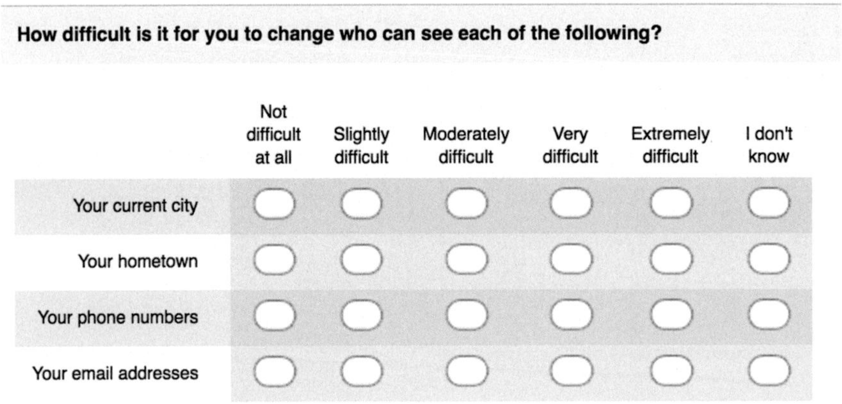

How difficult is it for you to change who can see each of the following?

	Not difficult at all	Slightly difficult	Moderately difficult	Very difficult	Extremely difficult	I don't know
Your current city	◯	◯	◯	◯	◯	◯
Your hometown	◯	◯	◯	◯	◯	◯
Your phone numbers	◯	◯	◯	◯	◯	◯
Your email addresses	◯	◯	◯	◯	◯	◯

FIGURE 3.16

Grid question on a desktop version of a survey. *Reproduced with permission from Romano Bergstrom, J. C. (2016). Empirical evidence for the value of usability testing surveys.* Presented at the International Conference on Questionnaire Design, Development, Evaluation, and Testing (QDET2), Miami, FL.

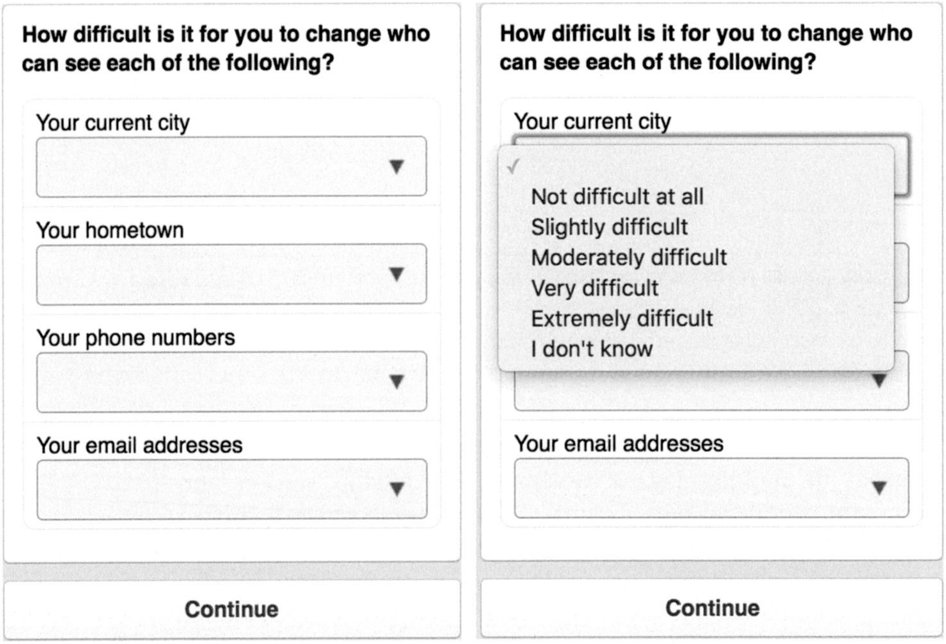

FIGURE 3.17

Mobile optimized version of the Fig. 3.16 survey. *Reproduced with permission from Romano Bergstrom, J. C. (2016). Empirical evidence for the value of usability testing surveys.* Presented at the International Conference on Questionnaire Design, Development, Evaluation, and Testing (QDET2), Miami, FL.

The mobile version was redesigned so that each item in the grid appeared on a separate page as shown in Fig. 3.18.

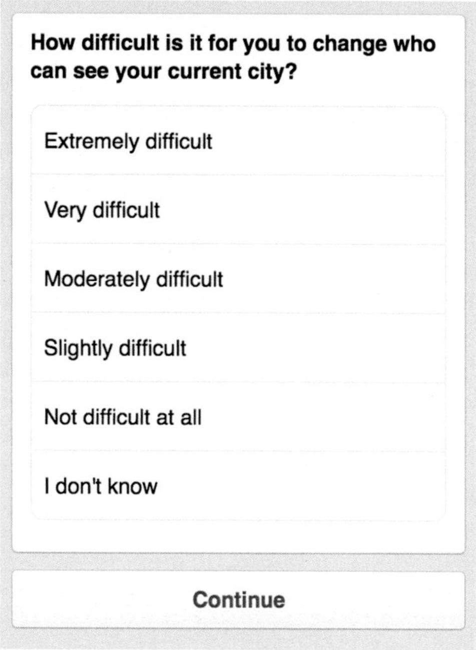

How difficult is it for you to change who can see your current city?

Extremely difficult

Very difficult

Moderately difficult

Slightly difficult

Not difficult at all

I don't know

Continue

FIGURE 3.18
Revised mobile version of the survey in Fig. 3.16. Each item that appeared in a grid on the desktop version appeared on a separate page on the revised mobile survey. *Reproduced with permission from Romano Bergstrom, J. C. (2016). Empirical evidence for the value of usability testing surveys.* Presented at the International Conference on Questionnaire Design, Development, Evaluation, and Testing (QDET2), Miami, FL.

Avoid survey-question designs that are known to be problematic on mobile devices, such as grids (Mavletova & Couper, 2014; Sterrett et al., 2015; Wang, McCutcheon, & Allen, 2015). Rather than conducting usability testing on such questions, incorporate alternate strategies into the design, such as the use of stacked grids (Richards, Powell, Murphy, Yu, & Nguyen, 2015) or asking questions one at a time (Romano Bergstrom, 2016). Usability testing can evaluate any concern with these designs.

> When designing and scheduling usability testing, think about smartphone respondents, and be aware of challenges.

Other conventions that work well on desktop and laptop computers, such as radio buttons, need adjusting for smartphones too. Usually more space is required between options to ensure that respondents can accurately select their answers with their fingers. As a result, many designers choose to make the entire response option into a button.

Be sure to factor usability testing on a mobile device into the overall planning and scheduling for your usability study. Surveys that use a mobile-specific design can benefit from all of the types of testing described in this chapter. Exploratory testing can provide insights on the specific design and approach. Paper proto-types and wireframes can explore a specific design before developing it.

A caveat about usability testing on a mobile device is that it will not necessarily provide insights on potential mode effects. Mode effects occur when the use of one survey mode creates differences in the data collected compared with another mode. Detecting mode effects often requires assigning respondents to experimental conditions using quantitative methods because certain respondents will prefer to answer in one mode compared with another. Therefore teasing out mode effects from respondent error may be difficult if respondents who choose mobile are different from respondents who complete the survey on a computer.

Fully Programmed or Revised Survey

Even when early testing is done, we recommend conducting usability testing on the final survey as well. If earlier rounds of usability testing were conducted, testing at this stage will focus on verifying or confirming that earlier problems have been fixed and no new problems have been introduced. If no earlier testing was done, testing at this stage is intended to verify that the survey instrument has no major problems or concerns. In both cases, the purpose is to verify that people can complete the survey effectively, efficiently, and with satisfaction (or at least without frustration).

The survey may have already been cognitively tested, but it is also common to conduct a test where you are focused on both the cognitive processes of answering the survey questions and the usability of the instrument—a combined cognitive/usability test. This can be conducted within the same sessions, where participants complete tasks that evaluate usability and answer questions about interpretation, or the usability and cognitive tests can occur separately, but simultaneously. For example, Romano Bergstrom, Hunter Childs, Olmsted-Hawala, and Jurgenson (2013) conducted simultaneous cognitive and usability tests on an interviewer-administered survey: the cognitive tests focused on comprehension, accuracy, and the abil-ity to answer survey questions by respondents, and the usability test focused on the ability for interviewers to complete the survey. Concurrent testing enabled us to identify areas for improvement for interviewer training based on how respondents reacted to questions in cognitive interviews and how interviewers dealt with the issues during the usability test.

Usability testing at this stage is often done before conducting a pilot test, but it can also be done after the pilot to explore any unusual findings in the questionnaire such as high item nonresponse or unexpected responses.

USABILITY TESTING CONTINUUM

Testing early and often may not be necessary or even possible for some surveys. When deciding which type of testing to conduct on your survey and when, it may help to see where your survey fits on the usability testing continuum, as shown in Fig. 3.19.

Usability testing continuum

Less Testing	More Testing
Existing surveys	New surveys
Short surveys	Long surveys
Simple surveys	Complex surveys
No special web features	Web-centric features
Off-the-shelf	Custom software
Single mode	Multiple modes
One-time surveys	Surveys repeated yearly
Limited time/budget	Moderate time/budget

FIGURE 3.19
Usability testing continuum.

For example, for existing surveys, you may not need extensive testing if you want to test only survey aspects that do not perform well or if you do not want to make large changes that might affect trends.

For short surveys that can be programmed quickly and easily, conducting testing at multiple stages in the development may not be necessary. Similarly, simpler or more standard surveys may not need to be tested at all stages. In these cases, usability testing can often be combined with cognitive interviewing.

References

Buskirk, T. D. (2013). Smarter smartphone surveys 201: Data collection methods and survey design considerations. In: *Presented at the American Association of Public Opinion Research*. Available at <http://www.aapor.org/source/education/webinar_recordings.cfm#.UsmPYNrnYfg>.

Criag, E. (2016). <http://radicalresearchsummit.com/emma-craig/>.

Ecotonos. <https://ecotonos.com/products/ux-phone>.

Geisen, E., Olmsted, M., Goerman, P., & Lakhe, S. (2014). Planning for the future: Usability testing for the 2020 Census. In *Paper presented at the 2014 federal computer assisted survey information collection, Washington, DC*.

Link, M., Lai, J., & Bristol, K. (2013). Accessibility or simplicity? How respondents engage with a multiportal (mobile, tablet, online) methodology for data collection. In: *Presented at the annual conference of the American Association for Public Opinion Research, Boston, MA*.

Marquis, K., Nichols, E., & Tedesco, H. (1998). Human—computer interface usability in a survey organization: Getting started at the census bureau. In: *Proceedings from the survey research methods section of the American Statistical Association*.

Mavletova, A., & Couper, M. P. (2014). Mobile web survey design: Scrolling versus paging, SMS versus E-mail invitations. *Journal of Survey Statistics and Methodology, 2*(4), 498–518.

Nielsen, J. (October 4, 2010). *Alphabetical sorting must (mostly) die* [Web log post]. Retrieved from <https://www.nngroup.com/articles/alphabetical-sorting-must-mostly-die/>.

Olmsted-Hawala, E. L., Nichols, E. M., Holland, T., & Gareau, M. (2016). *Results of usability testing of the 2014 American Community Survey on smartphones and tablets Phase I: Before optimization for mobile devices*. Research and Methodology Directorate, Center for Survey Measurement Research Report Series (Survey Methodology #2016-03). U.S. Census Bureau. Available online at <http://www.census.gov/srd/papers/pdf/rsm2016-03.pdf>.

Richards, A., Powell, R., Murphy, J., Yu, S., & Nguyen, M. (2015). Gridlocked: The impact of adapting surveys grids for smartphones. In *Presented at the annual conference of the American Association for Public Opinion Research, Hollywood, FL*.

Romano Bergstrom, J. C. (2016). Empirical evidence for the value of usability testing surveys. In *Presented at the International Conference on Questionnaire Design, Development, Evaluation, and Testing (QDET2), Miami, FL*.

Romano Bergstrom, J. C., Childs, J. H., Olmsted-Hawala, E., & Jurgenson, N. (2013). The efficiency of conducting concurrent cognitive interviewing and usability testing on an interviewer-administered survey. *Survey Practice, 6*(4), ISSN: 2168-0094.

Romano Bergstrom, J. C., Olmsted-Hawala, E. L., Chen, J. M., & Murphy, E. D. (2011). Conducting iterative usability testing on a Web site: Challenges and benefits. *Journal of Usability Studies, 7*, 9–30.

Rubin, J., & Chisnell, D. (2008). *Handbook of usability testing: How to plan, design, and conduct effective tests*. Indianapolis, IN: Wiley.

Sterrett, D., Stern, M., Rugg, G., Raker, E., Baek, J., & Bilgen, I. (2015). The effects of grids on web surveys completed on a mobile device. In *Presented at the annual conference of the American Association for Public Opinion Research, Hollywood, FL*.

Wang, M., McCutcheon, A., & Allen, L. (2015). Grids and online panels: A comparison of device type from a survey quality perspective. In *Presented at the annual conference of the American Association for Public Opinion Research, Hollywood, FL*.

CHAPTER 4

Planning for Usability Testing

Now that you have learned about the importance of usability as a survey pre-testing methodology, you are ready to begin planning your own usability study. The first things to consider are whom you are going to invite to participate in the study, where the study will be conducted (e.g., in the lab vs the field), what participants will do, and then, what equipment you will need.

PARTICIPANT SELECTION

In reality, how many people you recruit often comes down to budget—how much time, money, and resources you have for the usability study. It is okay if you can afford to conduct only a quick study with a handful of users in a couple of rounds. You will still identify some large usability issues as long as that handful represents the actual users—this is the single most important element of recruiting.

Once you conduct usability testing, you and your team (including stakeholders) will know the full value of this process, so trying to get more resources will likely be easier. But if this is your first usability test, it might be harder to get resources devoted to this step.

Regardless of the total number of participants you will recruit, you must recruit study participants who represent potential respondents—the people who would actually complete the survey in the real world. To do this, you must determine what the target population is for your survey: Who should be included ("in scope"), and who should be excluded ("out of scope"). For example, if the target population for a survey is recent college graduates, it would not make sense to test the survey with undergraduates or with people who graduated more than 20 years ago. Including participants who are out of scope may result in both false negatives (missing findings that members of the target population would have identified) and false positives (erroneously identifying problems that the target population would not have).

79

Usability Testing for Survey Research. DOI: http://dx.doi.org/10.1016/B978-0-12-803656-3.00004-X

Determining Participant-Selection Criteria

To ensure your usability test sample is representative of the target population, recruit participants from the major groups reflected in that population. For a survey of recent college graduates, you might include people who attended 2- and 4-year colleges, large and small schools, private and public schools, etc. Including the major groups will allow you to identify the most common types of usability problems respondents in the survey would experience.

In addition to the major groups representative of your population, determine whether there are any other characteristics that are related to the objective of the survey and might affect how people respond. For example, participants who transferred between colleges will likely have different experiences from students who completed all of their studies at one school. If *these differences are likely to impact how respondents will use and answer the survey*, recruit people from both groups. An example is a survey that includes a number of questions about students' classes and experiences each year. In that case, excluding transfer students would not identify usability issues that were problematic for that group only.

Continuing with the college example, you may decide that you will recruit five participant groups, which include recent graduates:

1. who transferred from one college to another
2. from 2-year colleges
3. from 4-year small public colleges or universities
4. from 4-year large public colleges or universities
5. from 4-year liberal arts colleges

The next consideration is demographic characteristics—sex, race/ethnicity, age, education (although this will not apply in the college example), and income. With a small sample, do your best to obtain a balance. For example, if the sample size is 10 participants (two in each participant group), those 10 people should represent a mix of demographics. If you are conducting multiple rounds of testing, continue striving for demographic balance across all rounds. The mix will rarely be perfect—e.g., one participant group might end up with only two females in one round instead of five. That's okay because our goal is representing people who are like our end users; it is not to achieve statistical significance. So do your best to recruit diverse participants and to balance across rounds of testing.

If the survey is web-based, make sure that participants' computer and web experience reflects that of the actual survey users. If you are to assume that *anyone* may complete your survey via the web, regardless of their experience, recruit both types of users—"expert" and "novice." During recruitment, you will need to identify participants' relative level of experience. Ask questions that get at the amount of computer and web usage per day and week. For example, self-reported questions that you can use include (Romano Bergstrom, Olmsted-Hawala, Rogers, & Krosnick, 2011):

1. How much experience have you had with computers *to use the Internet*? Please check one option. (Response options: A great deal; a lot; a moderate amount; a little; none)

2. How much experience have you had with computers *to do things other than use the Internet*? Please check one option. (Response options: A great deal; a lot; a moderate amount; a little; none)

However, these typical questions are vague, and people may compare themselves to their peers or use other shortcuts when responding to these questions. Their reflection may not be an accurate measure of their skill, so ask more specific, objective questions to assess computer and web experience, such as perceived difficulty doing specific things on the web (Romano Bergstrom, Olmsted-Hawala, Rogers, et al., 2011). For example:

3. How difficult is it for you to learn to use websites that you have not visited before? (Response options: Extremely difficult; very difficult; moderately difficult; slightly difficult; not difficult at all)

4. Computer windows can be minimized, resized, and scrolled through. How difficult is it for you to manipulate a computer window? (Response options: Extremely difficult; very difficult; moderately difficult; slightly difficult; not difficult at all)

5. How difficult is it for you to use the Internet? (Response options: Extremely difficult; very difficult; moderately difficult; slightly difficult; not difficult at all)

A more objective way to ask about computer and web experience is to have participants report how often they do certain things using the computer or web. Research has shown no differences among older and younger adults when asked to subjectively report computer and Internet experience (items 1 and 2 above). However, when asked to report frequency of particular activities (items 6 and 7 below), those demographics differ. Older adults report fewer specific activities compared with younger adults (Romano Bergstrom, Olmsted-Hawala, Rogers, et al., 2011). Some objective questions you can use include:

6. During the last week, how many times did you use the Internet *to find information about*:
   Finances (e.g., accounting, stocks, mutual funds) _____
   Health or medicine _____
   Housing _____

Local community activities (e.g., public events) _____
News _____
Organizations (e.g., political groups, American Medical Association)
_____
Other people (e.g., home addresses, phone numbers, email addresses)
_____
Personal social activities (e.g., friends' parties) _____
Places (e.g., museums, hotels) _____
Public transportation _____
Recipes _____
Sports _____
Television shows _____
Travel _____
Weather _____

7. During the last week, how many times did you *use the Internet to*:
Access social networking sites (e.g., Facebook) _____
Buy things _____
Conduct personal banking _____
Contact people via email _____
Contact people via video chat _____
Download music _____
Download, look at, order, and/or edit photos _____
Gather information for work _____
Make travel reservations _____
Pay bills _____
Play games _____
Read news _____
Search library holdings or databases _____
Sell things _____
Visit discussion groups _____
Watch shows or videos _____

Although these questions may not be necessary for all your studies—they are long and burdensome—they may help to ensure responses that indicate actual, not perceived, experience.

> An objective way to ask participants about computer and web experience is to ask people to report *how often* they do certain things.

If you are testing on a mobile device (and you are providing the device), you should recruit participants who are familiar with the device being used. For example, if you are testing a survey on an Android smartphone, recruit participants who use Android smartphones and not iPhones. This will reduce the amount of usability issues that are associated with the device instead of the survey.

DETERMINING SAMPLE SIZES

To identify potential problems with the survey, a small nonprobability sample works well in most cases; it does not take many people to start seeing trends in usability issues. A large, probability sample is unnecessary because you do not need to generalize the usability test findings to the population (i.e., estimate what percentage of all respondents would have a usability issue).

> A large probability sample is not necessary for usability studies because you do not need to generalize the usability test findings to the population.

When you are conducting iterative usability testing, the sample needed for a single round is usually small (5−10 participants). Changes are made based on findings, and we test again, and this iterative process continues until (ideally) optimal usability is achieved, we stop learning anything new or a product deadline approaches (Romano Bergstrom, Olmsted-Hawala, Chen, & Murphy, 2011). In survey design, optimal usability is when the survey can accurately capture respondents' responses. You may set out to conduct two rounds of testing, and then realize you need more because major issues were still identified with the second round. On the contrary, you may set out to conduct four rounds of usability testing, but then you realize you only need two rounds because the survey performs well. Over a number of these iterative tests, you will end up talking with 10−80 people, depending on how many rounds you conduct.

Nielsen and Landauer (1993) found that the number of unique usability problems found in a usability test conducted with n users can be predicted using Eq. (4.1):

$$X = \{N(1 - (1 - L)^n)\} \tag{4.1}$$

where X is the total unique usability problems, N is the number of problems known, L is the proportion of unique usability problems discovered by a single participant, and n is the number of participants.

Analyzing the number of usability issues found across a large number of projects, Nielsen and Landauer found that, on average, the value of L was 0.31.

That is, the average participant identified 31% of all usability issues identified in a given round of testing. The plot of the formula above with a value of $L = 0.31$ is shown in Fig. 4.1.

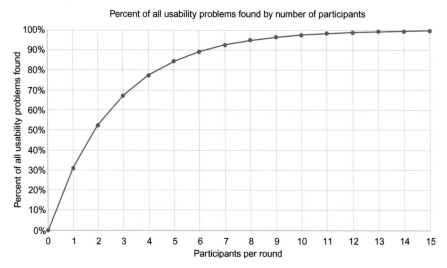

FIGURE 4.1

Percent of all usability problems found by number of participants. *Adapted from Nielsen, J., & Landauer, T. K. (April 24–29, 1993). A mathematical model of the finding of usability problems. In* Proceedings of ACM INTERCHI'93 Conference *(pp. 206–213). Amsterdam, The Netherlands.*

This shows that one participant identifies 31% of all usability problems, two participants identify 52%, and three participants identify 67%. Each additional participant identifies fewer and fewer new problems, with a total of 15 participants needed to identify all the usability issues. Eight participants identified about 95% of all problems, and seven additional participants identify the last 5% of problems.

Consequently, Nielsen and Landauer (1993) and other web-usability leaders, including Krug (2005), recommend testing a product with five participants per round of testing, and for multiple rounds of testing. This approach identifies about 85% of the issues at each round, on average, at a third of the cost of identifying 100% of the issues.

Naturally, the actual proportion of unique usability problems discovered by a single participant varies from project to project. And it is unclear whether participants who test surveys identify the same proportion of problems as participants who test websites. Therefore, we should note that five participants will not always find 85% of the problems, but it will likely find the biggest problems. And unlike websites, surveys rarely change after they are launched. Therefore, it may be necessary to test with more than five participants in each round to ensure identifying a greater percentage of total errors before the launch.

More participants per round are also needed when different subgroups answer survey questions differently (e.g., 2-year vs 4-year college graduates on a survey of recent college graduates). These respondents may receive different questions, or, due to differences in background and history, they may interact differently with the same questions. You will need more participants in each round to ensure that all survey questions are tested in general and for all subgroups in particular. You will want to include 1−5 participants per subgroup in each round depending on the total number of subgroups identified as well as your budget and schedule.

Another consideration when determining sample size is how your web-based survey will be accessed. You will want to test across as many environments and devices as possible because different platforms will detect different usability issues.

Continuing the example about recent college graduates, you may decide that you need 15 participants in each round. This allows you test five participants with for each major device or operating system: laptop/desktop, Android (smartphone and tablet), and Apple iOS (smartphone and tablet). This also permits three participants in each of the five subgroups (transfers, 2-year colleges, 4-year small public colleges, 4-year large public colleges, and 4-year liberal arts colleges). And in each round, remember to include participants with different demographics, computer and web skills, and any other variable that may affect how people respond.

Although small samples work well for most studies, there are occasions where large sample sizes are necessary to determine significant differences between designs. An example would be testing an existing survey prior to a redesign. You may want to determine baseline usability before embarking on iterative testing to improve the design. Or you may want to determine the best design among a few possibilities. In these cases, you will want a large enough sample to determine statistical significance to make a decision about which design offers an improvement. For large samples, we recommend conducting remote unmoderated testing because you are less interested in qualitative data and more interested in quantitative data. The sample size is no longer "a handful of participants," and now you must calculate effect size and the number of participants needed to obtain significance (Sauro & Lewis, 2016).

PARTICIPANT RECRUITMENT

Once you have decided which types and how many people to recruit, you will need to figure out how to get them to talk to you. In general, people are open to providing feedback. You just have to find them and incentivize them to talk to you! The following recruitment strategies may be helpful. Each strategy has its pros and cons.

Existing Participant Lists (Existing Frame)

You may recruit from lists of your survey's end users, your target respondents. This may be useful if, e.g., you are planning a satisfaction survey for a government agency or surveying users of an interface. In these cases, you are targeting people who recently interacted with the agency or interface.

While these existing lists may yield participants that match your criteria, they often yield only a small percentage—maybe 10%—of successful recruits. This low success rate may be because people did not expect the contact, so they are less likely to respond to the invitation than people who have opted into lists and want to participate in research studies. So be ready to recruit off the list as well.

No Participant Lists (Constructed Frame)

Here, we outline recruitment methods for when you do not have a list. Consider using more than one method, as different methods of recruiting will yield different recruits (Antoun, Zhang, Conrad, & Schober, 2016). Although some methods are more cost-effective, others lead to more demographically diverse recruits.

- *Use a research firm who has a participant database.* The quick, large pool of potential participants is rather reliable—people have opted in to participate in studies, so they are open to being contacted. However, these people tend to be "professional participants," and they likely have opted into many such databases. The cost per participant may be higher than other methods too. Using a research firm is helpful when you want to recruit general population as well as specific criteria.

- *Hang fliers in nearby coffee shops, schools, libraries, etc.* This technique is perfect for targeting people in the local community, and it is inexpensive. It is a bit of work—you have to print the fliers and go out into the community to hang them, and you may have limited reach. However, this technique is valuable when targeting specific populations (e.g., students at a nearby school) and people who do not use the Internet. It is also great for getting people who can come in to participate during their lunch breaks or before/after work.

- *Place ads online on social media.* Social media allows you to target very specific interests and demographics, and it can be done quickly. It can be costly because often you are charged by the click. Many more people will click on the ad than will participate in the study. It is valuable when targeting general and specific populations. Keep in mind that you are recruiting people who use social media.

- *Place ads in the newspaper classifieds.* This can be conducted online or in print. You will get lots of responses quickly. Beware though—people who are recruited via classifieds are often unemployed, and they may lie about criteria just so they can participate in the study and get the incentive. In general, classifieds work when recruiting people from the general population, and when you use the print classifieds, you can recruit people who do not use the Internet.

- *Snowball (word-of-mouth).* The snowball method works really well when you need specific populations—people who you have already recruited will tell their network about the study. The downside is that people may know each other, and the sample might not be so varied or representative.

Some populations can be hard to recruit, including the following:

- Doctors and clinicians
- Lawyers and judges
- People with low heath-literacy levels who have special medical conditions
- High-income people, such as people who own two yachts
- VPs of tech companies
- Technical enterprise app developers
- Highly skilled people with specific skill sets
- People who have never used common products or services (such as a debit card)
- People with disabilities.

Some of these populations are hard to recruit because we cannot offer sufficient compensation for their time or they are simply too busy. For others, it may be hard to get them to come to you. And for others, it may just be hard to find them.

But hard does not mean impossible or not worth trying. To reach special populations, you might consider offering a referral incentive to people in your network who will help you recruit. Or you might ask for help from another organization. For example, if you want to recruit blind users, you could contact an organization that assists blind people.

TESTING EQUIPMENT, ENVIRONMENT, AND MATERIALS

Develop a checklist as part of your plan and use it before and after you get to the test site. The checklist below may help you get started:

USABILITY TESTING CHECKLIST

Equipment and Environment
- ☐ Separate or divided rooms for laboratory usability testing: observation, testing, and control rooms
- ☐ Chairs and tables for equipment
- ☐ Recording equipment: audio and video, screen capture
- ☐ Computers, laptops, power cords, mouse, and keyboard
- ☐ Telephone (landline or cell phone)
- ☐ Streaming: screen-sharing or video conferencing, video chat
- ☐ Eye-tracking equipment
- ☐ Mobile "sled"
- ☐ Clock to monitor timing

Materials
- ☐ Printed materials for paper survey or prototypes
- ☐ Printed scripts or moderator's guide
- ☐ Printed worksheets for observers
- ☐ Clipboard, pens, and highlighters to easily take notes
- ☐ Incentives for participants (gift cards, payment)

Staff
- ☐ Personnel to moderate or take notes
- ☐ Translator for non-English-speaking participants

Usability Testing Equipment

In this section, we'll talk about what equipment you will need to collect and record data during a usability session.

Recording Equipment

Audio, video, or screen recordings are paramount for capturing much of the observational and self-reported data that occur in a usability session. At a minimum, record the audio and use a note-taker to document on-screen observations. A better approach, though, is to record both the participant's screen and the audio. Even with a note-taker, it can be virtually impossible to capture both the verbal exchange between moderator and participant as well as document the participant's behavior (e.g., trying to click on parts of the screen that are not clickable, pages visited, and features used). When you look at your paper or computer to record notes, you no longer look at the participant's screen and may miss something that occurs.

A common additional feature to tie into the recordings is a camera that can be used to capture the participant's face so that you can see their expressions and capture nonverbal cues. Recording the participant's face is valuable when you conduct eye tracking too. Without facial recording, you have no way of knowing if any missing eye-tracking data is because of an issue with hardware or software or because the person looked away or blinked.

Audio Recordings

To improve the quality of audio-recordings, you will want to use an external microphone rather than relying on your device's internal microphone. External microphones can be positioned near the participant to capture audio, and they are better at capturing voices and minimizing other noises such as shuffling papers or keyboard typing. For remote testing using web conferencing, you often have an option to use the web to call into a conference line, and the conference line is recorded.

Screen Recordings for Desktop/Laptops

The choices of screen recorders for laptop and desktop computers range from free to one-time price to subscription-based. Most of the fee-based companies offer free trials, so you can see which product works best for your needs. Here are the key features that you should look for.

- *Application- versus Web-based Recording.* Recorders that are application-based (installed on the computer) typically have better output quality than web-based (which stream video over the web such as web conferencing systems). Web-based recordings may be over-pixelated and delayed. However, for most purposes, web-based recording quality is more than adequate. For remote usability testing or when participants are using their own devices, web-based recording may be your only option.
- *Image Capture.* This feature is valuable for adding high-quality still examples to presentations and reports. A product that combines video and image capture can be convenient.
- *Screen Sharing.* Software that allows for simultaneous screen recording and screen sharing is more convenient than using separate products.
- *Logging Software.* Some screen recorders have features that help with logging observations, such as marking when a task begins and ends or documenting the success or failure of a task. This software can then compile the data from all sessions and produce quantitative metrics, such as task completion times or success rates.
- *Mouse Movements.* Some screen recorders can capture the mouse cursor and mouse clicks, which can help in identifying times when the

participant tried to click something that was not clickable. For example, in Fig. 4.2, the red triangle denotes that the user made a left mouse click just to the right of the radio button, so no selection was made. The mouse-click feature showed that the participant skipped the item accidentally rather than intentionally.

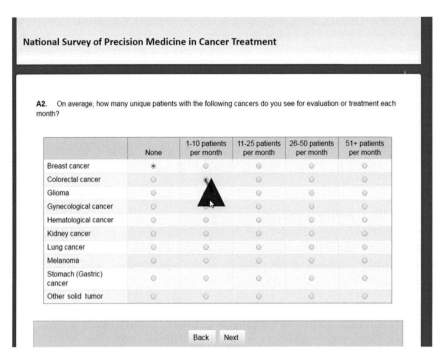

FIGURE 4.2
Example of a screen recorder that captures mouse movements and clicks.

- *Keystrokes and Screen Text.* Capturing participants' keystrokes or screen text can be useful, e.g., to identify whether shortcut keys were used or incorrectly typed. For example, interviewer-administered surveys often have shortcut keys (e.g., Alt + F8 to exit).

- *Face Recording.* Some recorders have the ability to incorporate a web camera along with the screen recording. You can use your computer's built-in web camera or an external one that plugs into the computer. This feature is often included as a picture-in-picture recording, allowing you to see the participant's face along with what the participant is doing on the screen.

- *No Installation Required.* If participants will use their own computer, use web-based software that does not require downloading or installing. With web-based recording, usually the moderator sends the participant a link to join an online meeting. The researcher can then hand over control of the survey to the participant and use the software to record the session over the web.

- *Editing Software.* Screen recorders with built-in editing software make it convenient to create highlight reels to demonstrate the key usability issues that occurred during testing.

Keep reevaluating options such as software types, capabilities, and quality advance. Like so many other components of usability testing, no one size fits all. Tailor the product to your study needs based on the number of interviews being conducted, the level of analysis, the presence or absence of observers, remote vs in-person, etc. The software with the most capabilities often has a higher learning curve or higher cost, so choose the product that has only the features you need.

> There are many different software available to help you record usability sessions and log what participants say and do. Be sure to check them all and choose a product that meets your needs. Keep reevaluating your options—software types, capabilities and quality continue to advance. And your needs may be different for different studies.

Screen Recordings for Mobile Devices

Choices of screen recorders for mobile devices are somewhat limited. Some mobile devices do not allow for recording outside of the application itself. To record on these devices, screen-recorder applications must include a built-in browser that participants have to use. This can be problematic if participants also need to access other applications or browsers on their device to complete a survey. Another limitation is that many screen-recorder apps are not available or consistent across platforms (e.g., Apple vs Android vs Windows). Still another limitation is difficulty for you or observers to see the participant's screen and actions. As a result, we recommend two alternate approaches for recording usability sessions on mobile devices.

1. *Use a mobile "sled" or platform* (and your laptop's screen-recording software). A "sled" is a platform that holds a mobile phone or tablet. Usually it is light and portable, allowing participants to pick up the device and use it as they normally would. A digital camera is affixed to the top of the sled to record both the device screen and the participant's hands. You can purchase a sled or make your own using a selfie stick and webcam, as shown in Fig. 4.3.

   If you do not have a sled, you can set up an external camera that records a platform or space on the desk. Use a white sheet of paper to indicate to

FIGURE 4.3
The mobile device is placed on a mobile sled, made from a selfie stick and webcam. The webcam connects to a nearby laptop so the moderator and observers can view the participant's screen and hand movements.

participants the general area that they should stay in during the session, see Fig. 4.4.

The camera is then connected to the computer to let you and observers see the participant's screen and hand movements without having to look over the participant's shoulder, as shown in Fig. 4.4. If needed, you can use a second camera to record the participant's face. To record the session and stream the view to observers, use the screen-recording software on your laptop.

The benefits of this method are many: It is portable, quickly set up, does not require the participant to download software, works with any mobile device, and does not rely on Internet access.

2. *Remote, mobile screen sharing.* Another option is to use mobile screen sharing software to view the mobile device on a computer. You then use screen-recording software on the computer (or via the web) to record the session. It also supports remote, mobile usability testing because the participant and moderator do not need to be in the same place. A limitation is that participants must download the screen sharing app and enter a PIN provided by the moderator to allow the moderator access to view the participant's screen. Participants may not want to download software to their device, and they may have privacy concerns with allowing a moderator to view their screen. Another limitation is that there can be a lag and the screen image can sometimes appear pixelated depending on Internet speed.

Eye-Tracking Equipment

Recent advancements in eye-tracking technology have made eye tracking more affordable and easy to use. In fact, many eye-tracking companies

FIGURE 4.4
The participant uses their device within the white area on the desk, and a webcam records the space. Another webcam is used to record the participant's face. Both are streamed to a nearby laptop that the moderator uses to see the participant's screen. This view is recorded and streamed to observers.

rent equipment, so you do not have to invest in the entire system. Modern eye-tracking equipment is unobtrusive and uses technology that has been built into both computer monitors and stand-alone devices. Fig. 4.5 displays a participant in a survey usability study. The paper survey and the eye tracker rest on a platform, and an overhead camera records the physical space. Fig. 4.6 displays eye tracking for a mobile survey.

With eye-tracking *glasses*, people can move freely in a given space. The glasses connect to a battery pack that the participant wears, and the battery pack streams to a nearby computer, as shown in Fig. 4.7. But the recorded view is where the participant looks, so if the participant looks away, you will not see what is happening on the screen. If you are simultaneously assessing load time for certain survey items, you may need a second camera—such as one on a mobile sled—for recording the physical space.

Using eye-tracking equipment may require you to ask participants to adjust the direction of their gaze or the angle of the device. For example, if they hold the device too low, the eye tracker may not capture their gaze. The glasses need to be seated just right on the face or they will not record the eyes.

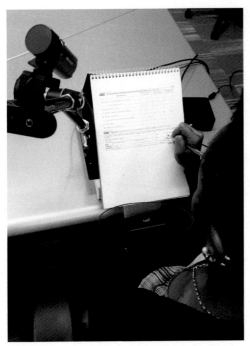

FIGURE 4.5
A participant completes a paper survey while her eyes are tracked. The eye tracker is at the bottom of the platform. *Reproduced with permission from Jarrett and Romano Bergstrom (2014).*

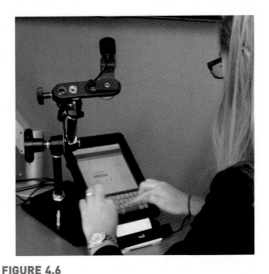

FIGURE 4.6
A participant completes a survey on a tablet while her eyes are tracked. The eye tracker is at the bottom of the platform below the mobile device. *Reproduced with permission from He, J., Siu, C., Strohl, J., & Chaparro, B. (2014). Mobile. In J. C. Romano Bergstrom, & A. Schall (Eds). Eye tracking in user experience design. San Fransico, CA: Morgan Kaufmann.*

Where to Conduct Sessions

Next, you will plan where the sessions will take place and how you are going to conduct them. The most common location types of usability tests are:

1. Laboratory
2. In-the-Field
3. Remote: Moderated and unmoderated

There are many considerations when choosing the best method for your study. For example, some key differences are as follows:

- *Laboratory*:
  - It is a controlled environment, with no external distractions.
  - You can record and communicate from a control room and allow the participants to emmerse themselves in the product.

FIGURE 4.7
A participant wears eye-tracking glasses while completing a survey.

- Observers can watch from another room and provide additional probes (via moderator) in real time.
- You can incorporate physiological measures (e.g., eye tracking, EDA, EEG).
- There are no travel costs.
- *In-the-Field*:
  - Participants tend to be more comfortable in their natural environments.
  - You can recruit hard-to-reach populations (e.g., children, doctors).
  - The moderator travels to various locations.
  - You will bring equipment (e.g., video/audio recorder, eye tracker).
  - These are natural observations.
- *Remote*:
  - Participants are in their natural environments (e.g., home, work).
  - You can use web conferencing or video chat (moderated sessions) or online programs (unmoderated).
  - You can conduct many sessions quickly.
  - You can recruit participants in many locations (e.g., states, countries).

We describe each of these in detail, and then we discuss how to determine which method is right for you.

Laboratory Usability Testing

When conducting laboratory usability testing, you will need to figure out the room(s) and equipment setup. For example, when conducting web-based survey testing on mobile devices, you will likely want some sort of platform for the device to sit on (e.g., a "sled") to record the screen and to allow observers to view the screen. You will also need to figure out where the participant will sit, where the moderator will sit, and where observers will sit.

A traditional usability lab (Fig. 4.8) contains three rooms:

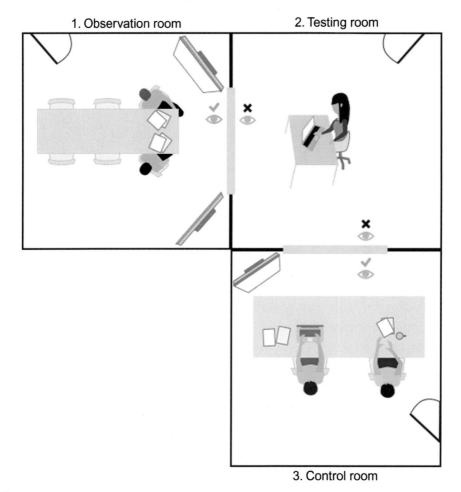

FIGURE 4.8

Traditional Usability Lab: Observers view the livestreaming of the participant and the participant's screen from another room. The moderator and note-taker work from a separate room.

1. Observation: Observers view through one-way glass or by livestreaming of the participants and their screens on monitors. This separate room allows for discussion about the observation. It also helps participants to feel more at ease without observers in the same room.

2. Testing (i.e., the Participant Room): As participants work alone, they can immerse themselves in the product.

3. Control: The moderator (and maybe a note-taker) control cameras and talk to the participants through microphones and speakers.

But many other usability practitioners prefer to sit next to or across from the participant. Although this may be good for building rapport, it can affect task performance because it distracts the participant. Let's say the moderator asks the participant to complete the survey and think aloud. When participants get confused, they may look at or talk to the moderator—e.g., asking if they got something "right." This is an even larger problem with eye-tracking studies; of course, you need the participant to look at the survey and not at the moderator!

Even if you do not have a lab with the three separate rooms, you can emulate this environment with inexpensive trifold dividers, shown in Fig. 4.9. And if you do not have dividers, you can sit behind the participant in the same room, shown in Fig. 4.10. The likelihood of people turning around to talk to the moderator during the session or trying to peer around the divider is lower than if you are sitting right next to them (although some participants really try, as shown in Fig. 4.11).

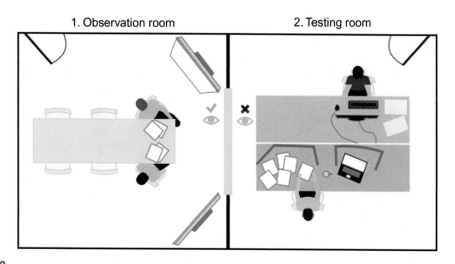

FIGURE 4.9
Usability "Lab" with trifold dividers—"Testing Room" on the right. Observers view from behind one-way glass and a monitor to see participant's screen.

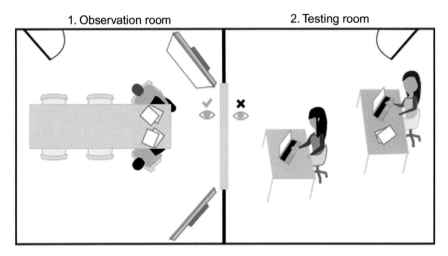

FIGURE 4.10
Testing room where the moderator sits behind the participant. Observers view from behind one-way glass and a monitor to see participant's screen.

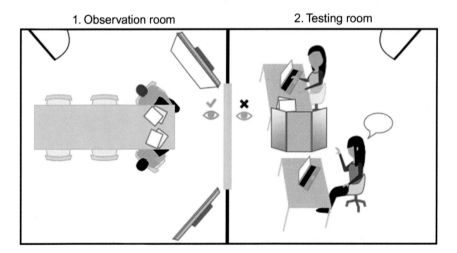

FIGURE 4.11
Testing room where the moderator sits behind a barrier and the participant tries to peer around the barrier to talk to the moderator during the session. Observers view from behind one-way glass and a monitor to see the participant's screen.

Even if you do not have a formal usability lab, you can emulate one by setting up trifold dividers between you and the participant or by sitting behind the participant. Try not not sit next to the participant—they likely will turn to talk to you throughout the session, and this interaction can interfere with the usability test.

It is important to note that you do not have to have a formal observation room with a one-way mirror in order for stakeholders to observe. With the use of screen-sharing and web conferencing, you can set up an observation room in any conference room. The point of a large observation room is that it allows for both observation and discussion.

Even if you do not have a formal observation room, you can stream usability sessions to a conference room, so people can observe together and discuss what they are learning.

Some benefits of laboratory usability testing include the following:

- You have the opportunity to follow up with participants if they say or do something unique.
- You can interrupt what they are doing, if necessary, to move them along to another task.
- You can also learn some unique things by allowing participants to follow routes that are untraditional or otherwise unanticipated, and you can follow up with them about their experience.
- It is a controlled environment, with no external distractions.
- You can record the sessions using your equipment (audio, video, screen recording)
- You can incorporate biometrics (e.g., eye tracking, electrodermal activity, facial coding, EEG)
- You can use paper prototypes.

In-the-Field Usability Testing

There are different considerations for conducting usability testing in the field, especially when outside of your geographical area. You likely will need to find a local research partner who knows the area and can recruit people who, e.g., are on the same side of town so you will not waste time sitting in traffic when traveling from one session to the next, in a given day. You have even more to consider when people speak a different language than you. In that case, you likely will need to find a research partner who can conduct the recruitment and the interviews. So you can understand what is going on when you observe the sessions, this research partner can also supply some-one to translate in real time. Whether the partner or you conduct the ses-sions, make sure you bring along the proper equipment to display the survey and record the session.

As you might imagine, figuring out the room(s) and equipment setup is more difficult with in-the-field testing than it is in the lab: You don't know what the participant's home or office setup will be like. You can recruit peo-ple who have their own computer or mobile device, but have a back up ready as well.

Allowing people to use their own devices provides for a real-world setting, but every participant may have a different experience. Just think about all the avail-able models of smartphones! If participants use their own phones, you may detect usability issues with only some of them, due to the phone model and the way it displays the survey. But if you detect an issue that you see with only the one participant who has a particular phone model, it may be an important issue. You may need to conduct another round of testing that includes more people with that particular model phone.

As with lab testing, you will need to record what is happening on the screen. For web-based surveys completed on laptops or desktops, the need to record is a good reason to use your own computer: You can install inexpensive screen-capture recording software on your computer but probably not on your participants'. You might consider using a nearby video camera on a tri-pod, but we do not recommend this—these recordings from afar do not tend to be good quality.

For web surveys on smartphones, you can record the screen as you would in the lab: Place the phone into a "sled" that plugs into a nearby computer (shown in Fig. 4.12), and then record the screen in the same way you would record a laptop screen. This also allows observers to see the screen without needing to huddle awkwardly and distractingly around the participant.

Things often occur in-the-field that you must prepare for. For example, as shown in Fig. 4.12, family members may want to observe. Sometimes, the presence of a family member can interfere with participants' behaviors. For example, if the survey questions are about alcohol use, young adults may not answer honestly when their parents are nearby. Instead they may quickly look for an appropriate response and make that selection. And while we are not necessarily testing the accuracy of the response, we do want participants to make realistic selections so we can assess usability of the survey. If they are making answers up, we might miss critical issues. For example, if all the young adult participants select the first option and

FIGURE 4.12
In-the-field testing. The participant holds the sled that holds the mobile device. The session is taking place outside, where the Internet connection is better than in the home. The participant's mother stands nearby, watching the session.

do not look for the most accurate option, we might miss a usability issue with long scrolling response options.

Remote Usability Testing

For *moderated sessions*, you work from your office or home, and the participant works from their office or home. The telephone may be sufficient to conduct the interviews. You can mail materials ahead of the session, and during the call, participants can walk through the survey. But it is best to see what participants are doing. So for a web-based survey, the best remote-testing solution is video conferencing, which allows you to see the participant, and either of you to share your screen (St. Onge, Alvarado, & Stettler, 2014). It also allows you to record nonverbal aspects of communication, which are indicators of the experience (Sundaram & Webster, 2000). You begin the interview by seeing each other and chatting about what you will be doing, building rapport, making sure they understand what you are asking them to do. Then you can send them a link to a survey and ask them to share their screen while they complete it, or you can share your screen and give them control of the mouse, see Fig. 4.13.

The participant will stream the screen, and you can stream the session to stakeholders, so they can view in real time. You may use a second computer to log into the streaming, record the session, take notes, and

FIGURE 4.13
Remote moderated testing, where the moderator can see the participant's face, and a note-taker sits nearby, unseen by the participant.

communicate with your observers. If you use live chat to communicate with them, use a separate platform so the participant does not see the exchange (e.g., use Facebook Messenger to communicate with the observers so they do not use the chat function in GoToMeeting, which may be used to stream). In fact, if participants and observers are on the same line, it is good practice to disable the chat function on the tool that participants are using.

Unmoderated sessions, as the name suggests, do not include any interaction with the participants at all. They receive an invitation to participate, and you will receive the data when they are finished. Before that can happen, you need to choose a testing platform for hosting the sessions. Common platforms include UserZoom, UserTesting.com, TryMyUI, and Loop11. Each varies by cost and payment structure—e.g., you may need to buy an annual license or you can pay per response. Each also varies by features, such as recording the participants' screen while they work and providing you with the recording. In addition, some companies provide analysis, whereas others provide the raw data. The importance of the different components may differ by study, and these will guide your decision on which platform to use.

If you select a platform that has a participant panel, you will need to set up the platform to recruit the participants you need. Alternatively, you can conduct your own recruitment and send participants a link to your test. Either way, you merely need to set up your sessions in the platform you are using and hit Go. With the panel, invites automatically go to people who have opted into the panel. If you are conducting your own recruitment, you email them the link. Then you can sit back and relax while the data is collected quickly!

Edgar and Mockovak (2012) found remote, unmoderated testing provided useful first impressions regarding how participants completed survey tasks and that these findings corroborated the results from their laboratory testing. Although most participants provided useful think-aloud verbalizations, for those that did not, there was no way to get those participants "back on track." The main disadvantages were that each session was limited to only 20 minutes compared with an hour for in-lab participants. The tasks had to flow logically from one to the next since there was no moderator to set up a task. All probes had to be written in advance so they had to apply to all participants regardless of how they completed a task. They also did not have automated measures of time-on-task or task success and had to calculate those after the fact.

Choosing the Best Method

Both remote and in-person sessions can be useful, and there appears to be no difference in usability metrics: task completion, time on task, severity of issues discovered (Brush, Ames, & Davis, 2004; Tullis, Flieschman, McNulty, Cianchette, & Bergel, 2002). Although remote sessions may take a little longer to set up because you have to figure out the technical equipment, you can reach more diverse participants from many geographical areas, and there is no restriction on time and place (Bartek & Cheatham, 2003). People use their own devices, so you may detect usability issues that you would not detect when using a device you provide.

Remote unmoderated sessions allow you to collect lots of data quickly, but there is no moderator follow-up. With moderated interviews, you build rapport and can ask questions about participants' comments and actions. Also with in-person sessions, there are no distractions, and you can control the environment. On the contrary, in remote sessions, although participants are often distracted by family or colleagues (Bartek & Cheatham, 2003), this represents the real world, where they may be distracted while completing surveys.

In-the-field testing is ideal when it is important to see people in their environment. For example, web connectivity may be poor in emerging markets, and you may seek to understand the issues those markets have with the survey. The only way to really know the impact of poor connectivity on performance is to go there and see it live. In-the-field testing also is ideal for surveys that involve people using other things in their environment to complete the survey. For example, a survey for small businesses may require respondents to refer to items in their offices. In this case, it would be valuable to see how people complete the survey at the place of business, including if merely findings things is a barrier to completing any part of the survey.

We often use a combined approach—remote unmoderated sessions for quantitative data, and moderated sessions for qualitative data. Sometimes, one precedes the other, and sometimes they happen concurrently. In a recent study, after a week of laboratory iterative testing (Monday: five usability sessions; Tuesday: revised design; Wednesday: five sessions; Thursday: revised design; Friday: five sessions), results were inconclusive. We were too close to launch date for more in-person testing, so we conducted remote unmoderated testing over the weekend.

We programmed two new versions of the survey and conducted a first-click test, comparing the new versions to the original tested version. We asked people where they would click; once they clicked, they were asked, "Why did you click there?" More than 800 people participated in each condition. On Monday, the click data and open-ended responses showed a clear "winner"—one design that people understood better than the other two. We were able to proceed as scheduled, with the data to ensure confidence in the survey design.

TIPS FOR AGILE TESTING

Don't have much budget? Don't have much time? Don't worry. You can still conduct some quick usability-test sessions. For a web-based survey, you can bring your laptop and sit beside the participants and watch them complete the survey. You can use inexpensive screen-recording software, or at least audio-record with something as simple as your smartphone. And if you don't have an audio-recorder, you can take notes in real time. For usability testing on mobile devices, you can sit beside the participant. If you don't have time or budget to recruit, you can ask someone you know to complete the survey. Just ask someone who is most like an end user and who does not know much about the project. Although these conditions are not perfect, it is still best to conduct some usability sessions with someone(s) than not to conduct any at all.

PRACTICAL CONSIDERATIONS

So now you are ready to conduct your usability interviews. You know whom you are going to recruit and the equipment and setup you will need. There are a couple other things to consider during planning.

How Long Should the Sessions Be?

For remote unmoderated sessions, sessions should be as short as possible because the likelihood of participant dropout is higher than for moderated sessions. For moderated sessions, a general rule for one-on-one sessions is about an hour. Some are as short as 30 minutes, and some are as long as 90 minutes. Avoid sessions that are longer than 90 minutes to avoid fatigue getting in the way of quality data.

How Do I Incentivize People to Participate?

We generally pay participants, and we often pay in cash for in-person sessions. But you can also use gift cards or some other token of appreciation. Depending on the time and effort required to participate, the incentive should be sufficient to ensure people actually show up for their sessions. For example, pay more for an in-person 60-minutes session, where people have to come to a lab, than for a 60-minutes remote session, where they can work from home. Hard-to-reach and specialized populations (e.g., doctors, lawyers, people with special skills) are often paid more as well.

Appropriately high incentives can actually save money on staff labor by making it easier to recruit and reducing the number of no-shows and cancelations. On the other hand, incentives that are too high may be considered unethical because participants may not feel that they can afford not to participate.

For remote unmoderated sessions, you pay much less than for moderated sessions (or even nothing, as in the first-click study mentioned above). For example, Edgar, Murphy, and Keating (2016) reported paying 75¢ per 5-minute task (equivalent to $9 an hour) to participants recruited through Mechanical Turk and the equivalent of $30 an hour to participants recruited through Facebook and TryMyUI. By contrast, participants in an in-person, moderated interview received the equivalent of $53 per hour.

How Do I Get Stakeholders Involved?

The best way to get stakeholders both involved and excited about the research is to include them early and often. When you begin planning the research, tell relevant stakeholders what you are planning and ask for anything additional they would like to learn. Tell them that you will *try* to get it all in—don't commit to every single thing that people want to learn. Imagine if 10 people all add 10 questions to your debriefing interview! You probably wouldn't have the time. But you can try to cleverly fit in the relevant questions. For example, you can give every other participant an alternate set of follow-up debriefing questions.

Another way to get stakeholders involved—and get buy-in—in usability testing is to invite them to observe as many testing sessions as possible. Across numerous projects, we have discovered that having stakeholders present during the interviews leads to more changes made to the product and faster. For example, consider our example of a usability test of a survey being redesigned for the web. No client observed the first round of testing. Although the report recommended major changes, clients wanted to make only minor ones. So we decided to conduct the second testing round at the clients' location so they could observe. In the observed interview, a participant made the same error that was made in the first round of testing. Although the clients had already seen a report and presentation that described that error, it did not make an impression until the clients observed the error in real time. In fact, they were astounded at how problematic it was, so they immediately suggested a revision to address the error.

This is all too common. On a different survey, Emily tried to explain to the programmer how the survey needed to be revised to correct a participant's usability issue. The programmer insisted that he had programmed in line with web convention, and that the recommended revision would not work. "We were at a standstill. I knew that the current design did not work, but the programmer was sure the new design would not work either. So I asked him to observe the next usability session. When he watched a participant interact with the survey, he immediately realized the problem, and we were able to find a design that both resolved the error and was feasible from a programming perspective." Seeing is believing. Observation greatly increased the ability to communicate improvements and the speed of implementation.

Encourage programmers, clients, decision-makers and any stakeholders to observe usability testing live. Watching usability test sessions live is more exciting than reading a report anyway! Send observers calendar invitations to remind them. Furthermore, observation supports a collaborative process incorporating the viewpoint of the team. Even if all stakeholders cannot observe every usability session, encourage as much observation as possible. You might even *require* at least one observer per session.

If people cannot attend in person, provide short, specific, and immediate updates.

Provide livestreaming so they can observe remotely if needed. And you can provide recordings with specific time marks or make shorter clips of relevant findings. However you choose to share, do it quickly. Waiting a few weeks to share findings with the team will ensure that they are NOT engaged.

Live chat sessions (e.g., with Facebook Messenger or the streaming tool) let observers ask questions in the moment, instead of waiting until the end of the session. But take care that the conversation does not interfere with your main role—to interview the participant and successfully run the session. Whether you chat on your phone or a laptop, place it off to the side and on silent. Do not respond to the chat session, just glance over at it during the session so you are aware if observers have questions. (This is also a good way for them to let you know of any technical issues.)

You can also give observers worksheets to complete during or after each session. Items on the worksheet can include participant quotes, time stamps, main takeaways, and novel findings. Encourage them to complete the worksheet at the end of each session because after a few sessions, it is impossible to remember who said or did what. Figs. 4.14 and 4.15 are two examples of basic observation forms that provide boxes for participant comments and usability issues/problems.

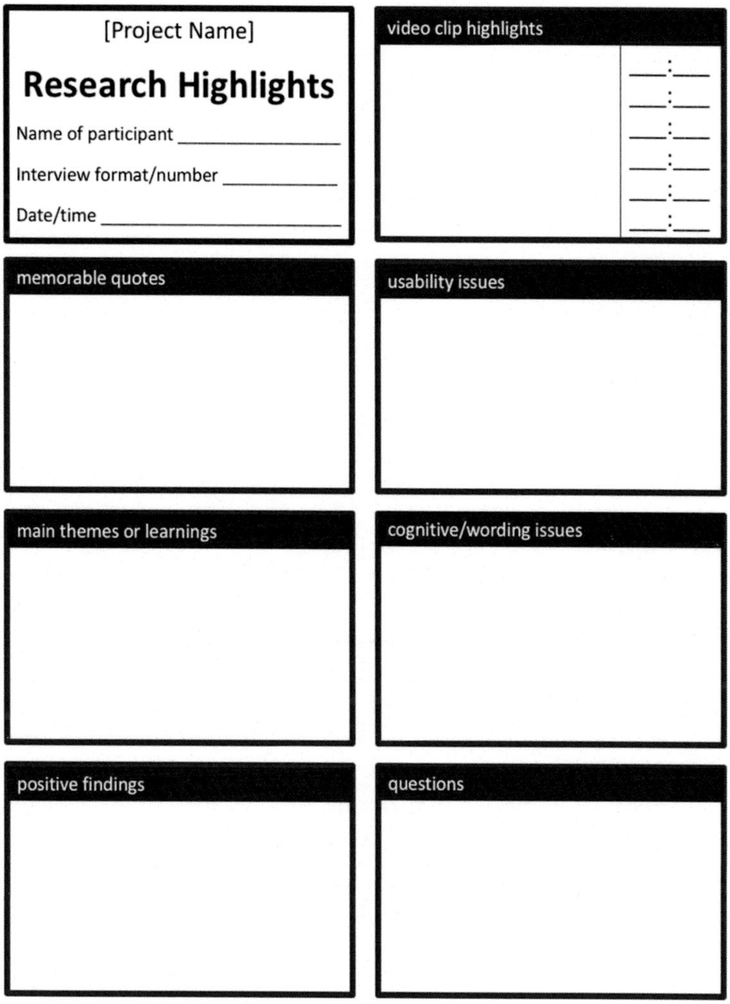

FIGURE 4.14
Example of a form that observers can use to document their observations.

Task 1: Your supervisor would like to review a printed copy of your survey responses before you submit the survey. How would you do that?	
Participant Comments:	
Usability issue/problem:	
Task 2: After reviewing the responses, your supervisor indicated that the number of employees at your company is actually 525. Please revise your company's response to that question accordingly.	
Participant Comments:	
Usability issue/problem:	

FIGURE 4.15
Another example of a form that observers can use to document their observations.

Between sessions, debrief with the observers to highlight the main takeaways. Ask observers what was interesting to them and if they would like anything else covered in upcoming sessions. At the completion of all sessions of the day, debrief with observers about the main learnings from the day and next steps. You may decide during this discussion to change something in the moderator's guide before the next sessions.

Send a short email to the team summarizing what you learned that day and any changes that you are making. You can also send links to videos in this email and ask for any questions.

How Many Sessions Can I Conduct in a Day?

As you would expect, the number of daily session varies by moderator and session length. You can conduct as few as one a day to as many as 10, with breaks between or not. For more than five sessions in a day, consider using two moderators to share the load.

References

Antoun, C., Zhang, C., Conrad, F. G., & Schober, M. F. (2016). Comparisons of online recruitment strategies for convenience samples: Craigslist, google AdWords, facebook, and amazon mechanical turk. *Field Methods, 28*(3), 231–246.

Bartek, V., & Cheatham, D. (2003). *Experience remote usability testing, Part 1: Examine study results on the benefits and downside of remote usability testing.* <http://www.ibm.com/developerworks/library/wa-rmusts1/wa-rmusts1-pdf.pdf> Accessed 07.08.15.

Brush, A., Ames, M., & Davis, J. (2004). A comparison of synchronous remote and local usability studies for an expert interface. In *Extended Abstracts of the 2004 Conference on Human Factors and Computing Systems-CHI '04.*

Edgar, J., & Mockovak, B. (2012). Unmoderated pretesting. In *Paper presented at the 2012 federal computer assisted survey information collection, Washington, DC.*

Edgar, J., Murphy, J., & Keating, M. (2016). Comparing traditional and crowdsourcing methods for pretesting survey questions. *Sage Open.* Available from http://dx.doi.org/10.1177/2158244016671770, Published 23 October 2016.

He, J., Siu, C., Strohl, J., & Chaparro, B. (2014). Mobile. In J. C. Romano Bergstrom, & A. Schall (Eds.), *Eye tracking in user experience design.* San Francisco, CA: Morgan Kaufmann.

Krug, S. *Don't Make Me Think,* 2005, New Riders; Berkeley, CA.

Nielsen, J., & Landauer, T. K. (April 24–29, 1993) A mathematical model of the finding of usability problems. In *Proceedings of ACM INTERCHI'93 Conference* (pp. 206–213). Amsterdam, The Netherlands.

Romano Bergstrom, J. C., Olmsted-Hawala, E. L., Chen, J. M., & Murphy, E. D. (2011). Conducting iterative usability testing on a Web site: Challenges and benefits. *Journal of Usability Studies, 7,* 9–30.

Romano Bergstrom, J. C., Olmsted-Hawala, E. L., Rogers, W. A., & Krosnick, J. A. (2011). Age-related differences in reported computer and internet usage based on question type: 'A Great Deal' of variability. In *Poster presentation at the AAPOR Conference, Phoenix, AZ, May 2011.*

Sauro, J., & Lewis, J. R. (2016). *Quantifying the user experience: Practical statistics for user experience* (2nd ed.). San Francisco, CA: Elsevier, Morgan Kaufmann.

St. Onge, H., Alvarado, H., & Stettler, K. (2014). Using WebEx for usability testing: Considerations for establishment surveys. In *Paper presented at the 2014 federal computer-assisted survey information collection, Washington, DC.*

Sundaram, D., & Webster, C. (2000). The role of nonverbal communication in service encounters. *Journal of Services Marketing,* 378–391.

Tullis, T., Flieschman, S., McNulty, M., Cianchette, C., & Bergel, M. (2002). An empirical comparison of lab and remote usability testing of web sites. In *Proceedings of the usability professionals' association conference, Orlando, FL.*

CHAPTER 5

Developing the Usability Testing Protocol

As you develop your test materials, consider your objectives so that you test and measure only relevant usability aspects. Including every aspect that can possibly be tested may be overwhelming, and it is just not necessary.

This process starts with determining your testing focus, which will guide everything in the sessions. Make sure your team and stakeholders are all on the same page.

IDENTIFYING TESTING FOCUS/CONCERNS

In a usability test, we want to know if participants can complete the survey without any major problems. But the testing focus has to be more specific. For example, you may wish to learn the following:

- How well do people understand the instructions?
- Do people read the entire question and response options before responding? If not, what do they read?
- Can people use the Next and Previous navigation buttons correctly?
- Do people know what to do on each screen?
- How easily do people find the information they need to answer the questions?
- When people do not understand something or have a question, do they use the FAQs?
- Are the FAQs helpful/sufficient? What is missing?
- How helpful/unhelpful are the definitions when people use the hover-overs?
- Are people able to correctly select their job from a long list of potential jobs?
- When do people use the left navigation, if at all?
- Can people use sliders correctly to select the desired response?

111

Usability Testing for Survey Research. DOI: http://dx.doi.org/10.1016/B978-0-12-803656-3.00005-1

Note how specific these questions are. They are also actionable, allowing you to use the results to improve the survey.

IDENTIFYING MEASURES TO COLLECT

To avoid collecting too much or too little data during the test, decide ahead of time what types of data you will collect.

Qualitative Versus Quantitative

Both qualitative and quantitative data are useful, so we usually collect a bit of both. Quantitative data collected in usability tests is not intended to be generalizable to the large population of interest; they are used solely to identify and understand potential usability problems. For stand-alone quantitative metrics to be valuable, you need a large sample size, which can be cost-prohibitive and often not that informative. For example, knowing that the task success rate across all participants was 20% in Design A versus 80% in Design B is not meaningful on its own. What is meaningful is the qualitative data—knowing why participants were not able to complete a task. Are all participants having the same problem or are different participants having different ones? Furthermore, knowing why participants had a problem gives insight into how to fix it. As a result, we often cross reference any quantitative measures, such as the percent of respondents who successfully complete a task, with the qualitative data: our observations and any comments made by participants during and after the session.

> Both qualitative and quantitative data are useful, so collect a bit of both.

The balance of qualitative to quantitative information desired may change depending on the stage of testing. Testing conducted very early in the development cycle tends to rely more on qualitative information while late-stage testing may rely more on quantitative data. However, with the rise of remote unmoderated testing, conducting quantitative usability studies at any stage has become more feasible.

Performance Measures

Table 5.1 summarizes the most common *performance measures* you can collect from qualitative and quantitative data. You should relate usability metrics to a specific focus or concern, such as navigating the FAQs, rather than to the entire survey.

Table 5.1 Quantitative and Qualitative Usability Metrics

Metric	Quantitative Usability Measure	Qualitative Usability Measure
Accuracy	Percent of steps/tasks completed successfully	Description of errors people make while completing tasks
Efficiency	Time to complete tasks	First click
	Number of clicks required to complete tasks	Click pattern
Satisfaction	Satisfaction ratings on a survey	Comments about the experience via think aloud
		Responses to predetermined debriefing questions
		Responses to follow-up questions from the moderator
Ease of use and learnability	Difficulty ratings on a survey	Comments about the experience via think aloud
		Problems people have while trying to complete tasks
Attention and/or confusion	Time to first fixation to a particular area of interest	Comments about the experience via think aloud
	Total number of fixations to a particular area of interest	Responses to follow-up questions from the moderator
	Mean fixation duration to a particular area of interest	Eye-tracking gaze plots
		Eye-tracking heat maps

Accuracy

The most typical *accuracy* measure is quantitative: the percentage of participants who successfully complete a task. The data is usually recorded simply as a 1 for tasks completed successfully and a 0 for tasks not completed successfully. Sometimes a task may receive a half point if participants completed half of the task. For example, you may ask participants what they would do if they had a question about a survey item, and they may respond that they would click on the FAQs link. But then they select the wrong FAQ. So they got to the right page but not the right answer.

We often capture qualitative measures of accuracy as well: the description of the errors people made while completing tasks. In the FAQ example, qualitatively, we might describe what FAQ the participant clicked on and why their attention was drawn to that question (e.g., the location of the FAQ or the wording of the FAQ).

Efficiency

Efficiency is also usually quantitative. The most common efficiency measure is how long it takes participants to complete tasks. Start timing when the participants actually begin the task (e.g., not when they are reading instructions), and end timing when they say they have found what they are looking for. (Before the test starts, prompt participants to tell you when they have found it.)

The number of clicks required to complete a task is also a useful efficiency metric. Count all of the clicks, including the use of the back button. For example, finding the relevant FAQ might require a minimum of two clicks. However, you might observe that people first click around a lot (i.e., "hunting and pecking"), looking for the information, and on average it takes them eight clicks. You then need to infer why people cannot find the correct FAQ in two clicks. Is it due to design? Labeling? Perhaps something else?

When examining quantitative efficiency metrics you will want to look at three things:

1. Was the task less efficient than expected (e.g., took longer or required more clicks)?
2. Was the task less efficient than tasks of similar length and complexity?
3. Did efficiency vary greatly by participants?

Qualitative information can also apply to efficiency: It is often useful to record the first click people make. This can highlight navigation issues—whether people can get started down the right path to complete a task. In fact, research has shown a correlation between first click accuracy and overall task success: People who make the correct first click are more likely to complete the task successfully than those who make an incorrect first click (Tullis & Albert, 2008).

Efficiency data can help you identify usability issues that accuracy data might not reveal. If participants can complete all tasks successfully, you may conclude that there are no usability issues. However, by examining the efficiency data, you may learn that one task in particular took much longer to complete than expected: although the most efficient route to complete the task required only 3 clicks, participants made 18 clicks on average.

Satisfaction

To measure *satisfaction*, we ask how satisfied people are with the task or survey. We can collect quantitative satisfaction data at two different time points: when participants have completed all the tasks (to identify issues related to the whole survey), and/or after each task.

Some popular satisfaction questionnaires are:

- SMEQ: Subjective Mental Effort Questionnaire (post-task; 1 item; Sauro & Dumas, 2009)

- SUS: System Usability Scale (post-session; 10 items; Sauro & Lewis, 2012)
- QUIS: Questionnaire for User Interaction Satisfaction (24 items; Chin, Diehl, & Norman, 1987)

We can also qualitatively evaluate satisfaction. The participants' verbalizations and reactions throughout the usability session are a wonderful indicator of how satisfied they are. For example, grunting and cursing are sure signs that people are not satisfied! You can also follow up with people at the end of the study during the debriefing interview to ask about specific things they said or did during the session. For example, you can say, "I noticed when you got to this page, you cursed. Can you tell me a little bit about that?" You also can follow up in the debriefing interview with open-ended satisfaction questions. For example, you may want to ask all your participants what the best part and worst part of the survey were. Forcing people to decide on one of each may provide great insight into the things that really bothered people.

> Key performance measures include accuracy, efficiency, satisfaction, ease of use and learnability, and attention/confusion.

Ease of Use and Learnability

Ease of use is especially important for self-administered surveys since there is no interviewer present to explain how to use the survey. If the survey is too complicated, people will simply not respond.

Like satisfaction measures, *ease of use* can be quantitatively measured after participants have completed all the tasks, and/or after each task. The Single Ease Question (Sauro & Dumas, 2009), shown in Fig. 5.1, is an example of

FIGURE 5.1

Single Ease Question. *Reproduced with permission from Sauro, J., & Dumas, J. S. (2009). http://www.measuringu.com/papers/Sauro_Dumas_CHI2009.pdf.*

an ease-of-use question that can be asked following each task (*Note*—we can also number the response options or fully label each response options).

Like satisfaction, ease of use can also be measured qualitatively from the participants' verbalizations and reactions. Additional qualitative measures are our observations of the types of problems participants had as they completed a task.

Learnability, on the other hand, is important for interviewer-administered surveys. Interviewers can be trained on how to administer surveys and record responses, and we can measure the learnability of a survey. Ideally, the survey is so easy to use, that you will not need to worry about how quickly interviewers can learn to use it. In some circumstances, though, such as when there is no time to make design changes to the survey, you may be interested in knowing that the survey is at least learnable with training and practice.

Attention

Researchers often ask participants if they noticed particular elements during a usability study. However, this is not the best way to assess what captures people's attention for several reasons. First, even though we tell participants that we are testing the product, not *them*, they still want to "please the moderator" and "ace the test." So when you ask people what they are looking at, they want to "get it right" and may wait to answer until they are sure that they are looking at the "right" thing. Second, it is impossible for people to accurately tell us *when* they looked at something. Albert and Tedesco (2010) compared participants' explicit ratings and verbalizations to eye-tracking data and found great variability in what people reported noticing and what they had actually seen. Many participants in the study had "false alarms"—they said they saw elements, but in fact, they did not.

Attention is best measured implicitly, and eye-tracking equipment is the easiest way to do it. It allows us to noninvasively collect data about:

- what people look at
- how many times they look at various things
- the order in which they look at things
- how long they look at things.

> Noting what aspects of the survey participants pay attention to is best measured implicitly, and eye-tracking equipment is the easiest way to do it.

This type of data is much more reliable than asking people to report what they are looking at. We can get both qualitative and quantitative data for eye tracking, and we usually use them together. For example, we may identify a particular area of interest (AOI), such as the secondary left navigation menu, and we want to assess not only whether people use the left navigation menu, but also whether and when they even notice it. For example, we may collect *time to first* fixation to that AOI to assess how long into the survey it took for people to notice the navigation menu, and *how many times they look at it before actually using it*. Then we may examine the qualitative-gaze plots, which display the order of fixations, so we can understand what else they looked at before clicking on that navigation menu (Romano Bergstrom, Olmsted-Hawala, & Bergstrom, 2016).

Repeat fixations (looking back and forth at something) before making a click can be an indicator of confusion. Although you can explicitly ask participants if they found parts of the survey confusing, this may not be a valid indicator. Participants may be reluctant to admit they were confused.

Multiple Methods: Self-Report, Observational, Implicit

Usability data can be further bucketed into three bins: self-report, observational, and implicit (Fig. 5.2). The two most common types of data are self-report (participants' perceptions about their experience: why they think they do things) and observational (directly measurable based on participants' behavior: how they do things).

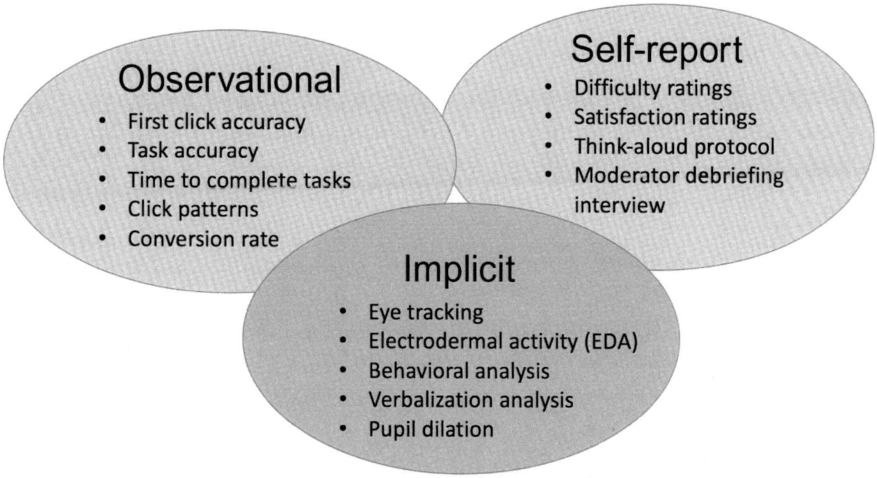

Observational
- First click accuracy
- Task accuracy
- Time to complete tasks
- Click patterns
- Conversion rate

Self-report
- Difficulty ratings
- Satisfaction ratings
- Think-aloud protocol
- Moderator debriefing interview

Implicit
- Eye tracking
- Electrodermal activity (EDA)
- Behavioral analysis
- Verbalization analysis
- Pupil dilation

FIGURE 5.2

Three types of usability metrics. *Adapted from Romano Bergstrom, J. C., & Strohl, J. (2013). Improving government websites and surveys with usability testing: A comparison of methodologies. In* Proceedings from the Federal Committee on Statistical Methodology (FCSM) conference, Nov 2013, Washington, DC.

People are explicitly aware of *self-report data*, which often come in the form of questionnaire and probe responses and verbalizations. These data generally add value above and beyond what we can observe in sessions (Tolvonen, Choi, & Nevala, 2011). However, participants often have a chance to think about their responses, which may introduce bias, so you also need *observational data*. You measure behaviors that may be more natural or not be expressed verbally or directly. These types of data typically include performance measures (e.g., reaction time, accuracy) and observed behaviors (e.g., click behavior).

In most usability studies, researchers collect self-report and observational data. While self-report and observational data are easy to obtain, people are often aware of their actions and verbalizations. Because people often want to "get it right," they may do something they would not ordinarily do, which may interfere with data. Therefore, we might also collect *implicit data*, the most unbiased form of user-experience data. These data measure behavior and physiology that are difficult or impossible for people to be aware of. They include eye tracking, pupil dilation, and electrodermal activity, which users cannot control. Pupil dilation and electrodermal activity can provide insight into interactions that are exciting. While they are relatively novel in the field and are outside the scope of this book, we anticipate that these metrics will be more pervasive in years to come. Similarly, behavioral and verbalization analysis often are not used with usability testing because of the amount of time they take. But they can be used when you want a purer analysis of verbalizations and behavior. For example, using linguistic analysis programs, we can assess how many positive and negative verbalizations people make without having to ask them how positive or negative they feel about a product (Olmsted-Hawala & Romano Bergstrom, 2012).

Whenever possible, include implicit measures—i.e., collect data that people cannot articulate, even if they try. This data enables us to understand the unbiased interactions with the interface.

Eye Tracking
Eye tracking is the most common type of implicit data used for usability-testing surveys. It is not typically conducted in isolation—we use it only with other methods to understand what people are looking at *while they are doing something*. If you wish to understand merely what attracts attention when people passively look at something, like a print advertisement, an "eye-tracking study" alone may be sufficient. You can ask people to look at an advertisement for 30 seconds, and you can assess where their attention is during those 30 seconds. But in survey usability testing, we want to understand attention while people are completing tasks, such as responding to questions, looking for information, or navigating to the next screen. We combine the eye-tracking data with the behavioral data, which can provide insight into issues that we may not detect without eye tracking.

Eye tracking has been used to study how people perceive question stems, response options, and images within self-administered surveys (Jarrett & Romano Bergstrom, 2014). The existing research mostly focuses on web-based surveys and is limited to a few key papers. In each of these studies, eye tracking provided information that was helpful above and beyond the self-report and observational data. For example, Redline and Lankford (2001) found that participants did not read linearly, and they skipped around the survey. Galesic, Tourangeau, Couper, and Conrad (2008) found that participants spent more time looking at options on the top of a list of responses. They also found that participants who take the time to read the entire response list also read the instructions and other parts of the questionnaire. Lenzner, Kaczmirek, and Galesic (2011) found that longer fixation time on question stems indicated comprehension issues. Libman and Smyth (2012) looked at smiley faces as symbolic language and found that participants with low literacy levels moved faster to look at the smiley faces in the web survey. In one paper-based survey study, Walton, Romano Bergstrom, Hawkins, and Pierce (2014) used eye tracking to understand a decline in response rate after design changes had been made and found that attention to brand and motivational language likely played a role—both of these were less attended to the new design (see Fig. 5.3).

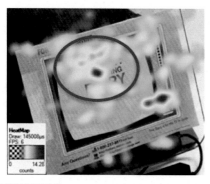 

FIGURE 5.3

"Old" Diary (left) and "New" Diary (right). The Nielsen brand received more attention on the old diary than the new diary. The motivational language (lower right blue circle) was not attended to on the new diary (right). *Reproduced with permission from Walton, L., Romano Bergstrom, J., Hawkins, D., & Pierce, C. (2014). User experience testing and eye tracking inform paper diary design. In Proceedings from the human computer interaction international conference, June 2014, Crete, Greece.*

Before the test, identify "AOIs" for each screen. On a survey, typical AOIs are the instructions, question stem, input field, response option text, navigation buttons, or navigation menu. You can then obtain location, duration, and movement data for each AOI.

The basic units of eye-tracking data that you will collect are *fixation count* (location), *fixation duration*, and *saccades* (movement) (Schall & Romano Bergstrom, 2014).

- *Fixation count.* A fixation is when the eye is relatively still. We use fixations to determine where participants look as they complete a survey. We use fixation *counts* to assess which areas of the page get more or less attention. We also assess the order in which people look at various elements—fixations are often numbered—to see how people process survey elements. Repeat fixations (e.g., fixating on a link numerous times before making a click) can indicate confusion.

- *Fixation duration.* We can also measure how long participants spend looking at a particular location. Each duration is usually extremely short—only milliseconds. Increased duration is associated with processing and suggests complexity, interest, or engagement.

- *Saccades.* These measure a participant's eye movements between fixations to create a visual hierarchy that can show the order that participants view certain elements on the screen.

While eye tracking is certainly meaningful in many ways, it is not always the best solution. Jarrett and Romano Bergstrom (2014) outline different types of survey questions and which types benefit the most from eye tracking. The elements to consider are (1) gaze: where the person is looking and (2) attention: what the person is attending to, which may or may not be the same as their gaze.

> Eye tracking works best when both gaze and attention are at the screen.

Fig. 5.4 plots attention and gaze for different types of questions (Jarrett & Romano Bergstrom, 2014). For example, when respondents answer questions that they know easily, such as name and date of birth, both their gaze and attention are at the screen. These "slot-in" questions produce the best eye-tracking data. For "third-party" questions, where respondents have to ask someone else for the information, neither the respondent's gaze nor attention is on the screen and eye-tracking data cannot be collected. For "gathered" questions, where the respondent has to get their answer from another source (e.g., look at a receipt, refer to hardcopy materials, perform an online search), gaze may be intermittently recorded. While eye-tracking data can be collected, it will not be useful.

Typically, the worst scenario for eye tracking is when gaze is on the screen, and attention is elsewhere, as in the case of responses that people must think up on the spot ("created" questions). For example, you may ask people a question that requires critical thinking (e.g., number of windows

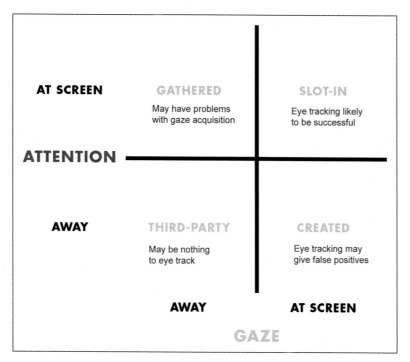

FIGURE 5.4

The best eye-tracking data will be when the person's gaze and attention are on the screen. *Reproduced with permission from Jarrett, C., & Romano Bergstrom, J. C. (2014). Forms and surveys. In J. Romano Bergstrom & A. Schall (Eds.), Eye tracking in user experience design. San Francisco, CA: Morgan Kaufmann.*

in their house), and while they are looking at the screen, they are counting windows in their head. In this case, the eye-tracking data does not indicate attention at all. (A parallel is when you are talking to someone on the telephone, and you are looking at something but not really "seeing" it because your attention is on the conversation.) So think about whether eye-tracking data will help to understanding users' attention for the questions on your survey.

CREATING TEST MATERIALS

Materials include your *script*—what you will say to each participant—as well as tasks/scenarios, the consent form, and satisfaction or ease of use scales (e.g., SUS). These materials combined, make up the usability testing protocol, also known as the *moderator's guide*.

The script ensures that each participant hears the same thing and that you do not forget any logistical procedures, like starting the video recording or telling the participant that observers are watching from another room.

The Script

Scripts generally contain these elements:

1. Introduction to you (your name, company, and role)
2. Information about the session (e.g., you will ask the participant to complete a survey, and you would like them to complete it as if they were at home)
3. What the person needs to do during the session (e.g., complete the survey, think aloud, tell you when something is not clear)
4. What you are going to do during the session (e.g., sit in the other room, record notes, and sometimes ask questions)
5. Other important information (e.g., observers are watching, you are making a video recording, the session will last 60 minutes)

Once you create a script, you can reuse it and tweak the parts that are relevant to the surveys you are testing. In fact, you can tweak the following script to make it relevant to your work.

Example Script

- Thank you for your time today. My name is [name]. I work here at [place], and I will be working with you today. In this lab, we evaluate how easy or difficult products are to use. We bring in people like you who are potential users of our products to try them out while there is still time to make changes to them.

- Today, we will be evaluating [name of survey] by having you work on the survey.

- There are two parts to our session. First, you will complete the survey. Then, at the end of the session, you will complete a questionnaire about your experience during the session. And then I will ask you some questions about the survey. The entire session should last about an hour.

- Before we start, there is a form I would like you to read and sign. It explains the purpose of today's session and your rights as a participant. It also informs you that we would like to record the session to get an accurate record of your feedback. Only those of us connected with the project will review the recording, and it will be used solely for research purposes. Your name will not be associated with the recording or any of the other data collected during the session.

- [Hand consent form; give time to read and sign; sign own name and date.]

- Thank you.

- Before we start, I want to tell you that you can't make a mistake or do anything wrong here. Difficulties you may run into reflect the design of the survey, not your skills or abilities.

- Where it works well, that's great. If you have a problem using parts of it, that is also great, because you will help us to identify these places.

- We are going to use your comments and data as well as comments and data from the other participants to give feedback to the designers of the survey. Your comments and thoughts will help them make changes to improve the survey.

- I did not create the survey, so please do not feel like you have to hold back on your thoughts to be polite. You are not going to hurt my feelings. I am a researcher, not a designer, and the main thing to keep in mind is that I am here to learn from you. Please share both your positive and negative reactions.

- While you are working, I would like you to think aloud. In other words, I'd like you to tell me what you are thinking, describe the steps you are taking, what you are expecting to see, why you are doing what you are doing, what you are going to do, and why. Tell me why you clicked on a link or where you expect the link to take you. Tell me if you are looking for something and what it is and whether you can find it or not.

- Do you have any questions about this "thinking-aloud" process?

- [Tell Participant about the letter that they would receive in the mail. When you instruct them to, they are to read it and proceed with the survey, as they would if they got the letter in the mail.]

- Ok, now we are ready to begin. I am going to go around to the other room and do a sound check. I will work from there and take notes, and I can see your screen. I will instruct you when to read this letter and when to begin. Also, here is the questionnaire you will complete at the very end. I will tell you when to complete this.

- [Set the task questions and questionnaire by participant.]

- I am going to leave, but we will still be able to communicate through a series of microphones and speakers. Do you have any questions?

- [Go to control room. Do sound check. Start video recording.]

- Can you hear me ok? Alright, now we are ready to begin. Please begin by reading the letter out loud. As you work, remember to talk to me about what you are thinking and feeling.

Scenarios, Tasks, and Probes

When setting up the protocol—what you are going to do during the usability sessions—you will need to determine what you are going to ask the participants to do. We use scenarios to get participants in the same frame of mind as if completing the survey in the real world, we then give them tasks to complete, and we use probes to help us gather additional information.

- *Scenario*—a real-life situation that you ask participants to put themselves in to test the instrument
- *Task*—something you want the participant to accomplish
- *Probe*—questions asked of the user to elicit additional information and feedback

We often use *scenarios* that help people get into a role that they would be in when completing the survey. These are grounded in the ways respondents might complete the survey in the real world. For example, Romano, Murphy, Olmsted-Hawala, and Childs (2008) asked participants to imagine they were standing in a respondent's doorway, administering the Census survey, to emulate the experience of the people who conduct follow-up interviews with households that do not complete the census. A main usability concern of the large trifold survey was that interviewers might struggle with the binder and forms when on a household's doorstep. In usability sessions, some participants dropped all of the items while conducting the interviews, and many said that it was awkward to manage all the items (see Fig. 5.5).

FIGURE 5.5

Scenarios are helpful when assessing situations, like interviewers standing and administering a large survey on respondents' doorsteps.
Reproduced with permission from Romano, J., Murphy, E., Olmsted-Hawala, E., & Childs, J. H. (2008). A usability evaluation of the NonResponse Followup Enumerator (NRFU) questionnaire form. Statistical Research Division (Study Series SSM2008-10). US Census Bureau.

During debriefing, some participants commented that "...the form was difficult to hold. I was juggling everything," and that "the size and shape (of the form) were difficult to handle and hard to maneuver." In addition, some participants folded the pages back to align the names on the left side, and this was a concern because it might interfere with data capture.

Vignettes can be used to test hypothetical scenarios with participants that you might not be able to test otherwise. In the study mentioned above (Romano Bergstrom et al., 2008), we assessed specific relationships that were thought to pose potential recording problems: nanny, foster daughter, and half-sister relationships. Respondents needed to reference the Information Sheet in Fig. 5.6 to determine the appropriate relationship. These would fall into the other nonrelative, other nonrelative, and sister categories, respectively. In usability testing, participants struggled with correctly recording all three relationships, and so we recommended adding a probe for interviewers to use with respondents when administering the survey.

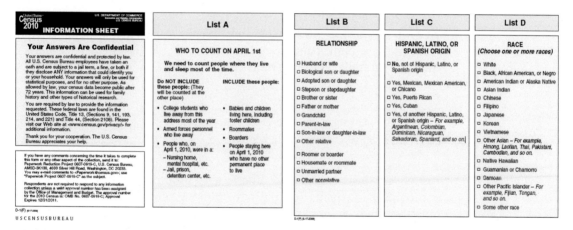

FIGURE 5.6

Vignettes are helpful when participants need to imagine unique situations like completing the census for a difficult-to-record household (Romano et al., 2008). In this study, participants were provided vignettes with household situations so we could evaluate the usability of the Information Sheet.

Scenarios and vignettes should be short and simple—you want people to understand them, act on them, and complete the survey, not get caught up trying to remember the scenario or vignette.

Scenarios are usually accompanied by *tasks*. For a simple survey, the task may just be completing the survey, "Please complete this survey as you normally would at home." More specific tasks may include having participants log out and resume an interview, find a definition, find a contact number if they had a question or use a navigation menu.

The following scenario and task was used on the Survey of Graduate Students and Postdoctorates (GSS) to evaluate how well participants could add new graduate departments and remove departments that were no longer active (Fig. 5.7).

Scenario: Your graduate school will include the following PhD programs this year:

- *Biology*
- *Chemistry*
- *Marine, Earth, and Atmospheric Sciences*
- *Physics*
- *Spanish*

Task: Please update the list of departments, programs, and research units that should be included in the survey for this year.

There is not always a one-to-one relationship between tasks and scenarios. You may have participants complete the same task for different scenarios or complete multiple tasks under the same scenario.

> Scenarios and vignettes should be short and simple—you want people to understand them, act on them, and complete the survey, not get caught up trying to remember the scenario or vignette.

Lastly, we use *probes*—or interjected prompts—when necessary, to encourage participants to continue thinking aloud. Probes must remain objective and as noninvasive as possible. For example, we often use "keep talking" or "mm hmmm" as probes to quietly encourage people to think aloud, as opposed to asking "what are you thinking?," which may interrupt their process (Olmsted-Hawala, Murphy, Hawala, & Ashenfelter, 2010).

You can also ask more specific probes when you will not be interrupting the participant's natural process. For example, at the end of a natural break in the survey (e.g., when the survey topics transition), you can stop the participant and ask about their experience with the previous section.

Developing and administering probes is discussed in Chapter 6, Think Aloud and Verbal-Probing Techniques.

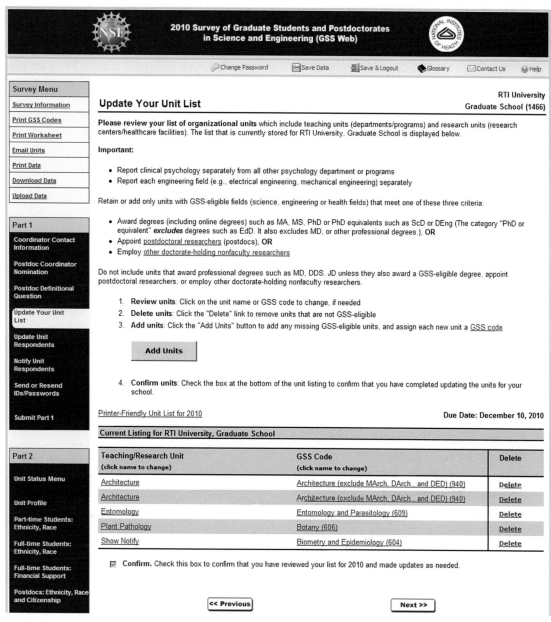

FIGURE 5.7

Scenarios and tasks were used to test how well survey participants could add new graduate departments and remove old departments.

EXAMPLE: SCENARIOS AND TASKS

Study: Again, let us imagine that you are tasked with designing a study to assess the usability of a web-based travel diary. Respondents are supposed to record all the places they have traveled in the past 24 hours. For each location, they need to report specific information, such as how long it took to get to there from the previous destination and who they traveled with.

Testing Focus/Concerns

- In what order do participants add trips (e.g., newest to latest, latest to newest, most salient to least salient, longest to shortest)?
- In what order do people process the elements of each trip (e.g., do they enter the place or time first?), and how does the survey match this mental model?
- What challenges do participants have when adding a new trip?
- How do people handle compound trips such as dropping a child off at school on the way to work?
- What trip information do participants have difficulty recalling?

Performance Measures

- Quantitative
    - Number and percent of tasks completed successfully
    - Time to complete a task
    - Errors of omission (e.g., locations visited in the past 24 hours that were omitted)
    - Errors of commission (e.g., locations not visited that were accidentally included)
    - Difficulty ratings

- Qualitative
    - Order in which people enter information
    - How much of the instructions are read
    - Observations regarding ease of use
    - Participant verbalizations
    - Debriefing interview

    Scenario 1: "You have been asked to complete a travel survey about all the places you visited in the last 24 hours."
    Task 1: "Please complete this diary as you normally would at home."

    Scenario 2: "You realized that you forgot to add a trip you took yesterday."
    Task 2: "How would you add a missed trip to the diary?"

    Scenario 3: "You remember that you did not travel to [location] in the past 24 hours."
    Task 3: "How would you remove this trip from your diary."

References

Albert, W., & Tedesco, D. (2010). Reliability of self-reported awareness measures based on eye tracking. *Journal of Usability Studies, 5,* 50—64.

Chin, J. P., Diehl, V. A, & Norman, K. (September 1987). Development of an instrument measuring user satisfaction of the human-computer interface. In *Proc. ACM CHI '88 (Washington, DC)* (pp. 213—218). CS-TR-1926, CAR-TR-328.

Galesic, M., Tourangeau, R., Couper, M. P., & Conrad, F. G. (2008). Eye-tracking data new insights on response order effects and other cognitive shortcuts in survey responding. *Public Opinion Quarterly, 72*(5), 892—913.

Jarrett, C., & Romano Bergstrom, J. C. (2014). Forms and surveys. In J. Romano Bergstrom, & A. Schall (Eds.), *Eye tracking in user experience design.* San Francisco, CA: Morgan Kaufmann.

Lenzner, T., Kaczmirek, L., & Galesic, M. (2011). Seeing through the eyes of the respondent: An eye-tracking study on survey question comprehension. *International Journal of Public Opinion Research, 23*(3), 361—373.

Libman, A., & Smyth, J. (2012). Turn that frown up-side down: The use of smiley faces as symbolic language in self-administered surveys. In *Paper presented at 2012 AAPOR annual conference, Orlando, Florida, May 2012.*

Olmsted-Hawala, E. L., Murphy, E. D., Hawala, S., & Ashenfelter, K. T. (2010). Think-aloud protocols: A comparison of three think-aloud protocols for use in testing data-dissemination web sites for usability. In *Proceedings from CHI, April 2010, Atlanta, GA.*

Olmsted-Hawala, E. L., & Romano Bergstrom, J. C. (2012). Think aloud protocols. Does age make a difference? In *Proceedings from the society for technical communications summit, May 2012, Chicago, IL.*

Redline, C. D., & Lankford, C. P. (2001). Eye-movement analysis: A new tool for evaluating the design of visually administered instruments (paper and web). In *Proceedings of the section on survey research methods, American Statistical Association. Paper presented at 2001 AAPOR annual conference, Montreal, Quebec, Canada.*

Romano, J., Murphy, E., Olmsted-Hawala, E., & Childs, J. H. (2008). *A usability evaluation of the NonResponse Followup Enumerator (NRFU) questionnaire form.* Statistical Research Division (Study Series SSM2008-10). US Census Bureau.

Romano Bergstrom, J. C., Olmsted-Hawala, E. L., & Bergstrom, H. C. (2016). Older adults fail to see the periphery during website navigation. *Universal Access in the Information Society, 15*(2), 261—270.

Romano Bergstrom, J. C., & Strohl, J. (2013). Improving government websites and surveys with usability testing: A comparison of methodologies. In *Proceedings from the Federal Committee on Statistical Methodology (FCSM) conference, Nov 2013, Washington, DC.*

Sauro, J., & Dumas, J. S. (2009). <http://www.measuringu.com/papers/Sauro_Dumas_CHI2009.pdf>.

Sauro, J., & Lewis, J. R. (2012). <https://www.amazon.com/Quantifying-User-Experience-Second-Statistics/dp/0128023082/ref = dp_ob_title_bk>.

Schall, A., & Romano Bergstrom, J. (2014). *Eye-tracking book, Morgan Kaufmann.*

Tolvonen, R., Choi, D.-S., & Nevala, N. (2011). Ergonomics product development of a mobile workstation for health care. *Journal of Usability Studies, 7,* 40—50.

Tullis, T. S., & Albert, B. (2008). *Measuring the user experience* (pp. 256—257). Boston, MA: Morgan Kaufmann Publishers.

Walton, L., Romano Bergstrom, J., Hawkins, D., & Pierce, C. (2014). User experience testing and eye tracking inform paper diary design. In *Proceedings from the human computer interaction international conference, June 2014, Crete, Greece.*

CHAPTER 6

Think Aloud and Verbal-Probing Techniques

Think aloud and *verbal probing* are two methods for obtaining participant verbalizations (self-report data) during a usability test. For think aloud, participants talk about what they are thinking and doing while completing tasks. With verbal probing, moderators ask participants targeted questions about their experience completing the survey. These verbalizations help you understand what participants think about the survey, whether they misinterpreted the design, and why they encountered difficulty completing tasks.

A usability study may incorporate one or both of these methods, but think aloud is the primary method used by usability professionals to test websites and other products (Barnum, 2010; Dumas & Redish, 1999; Nielsen, 1993).

THINK-ALOUD APPROACH

The traditional think-aloud interviewing method was developed by Ericsson and Simon (1984, 1980) to understand the processes used in working memory. Loftus (1984) was the first to suggest using the approach for survey-question evaluation, specifically how people answered autobiographical questions. This approach has since been adapted and popularized as a standard survey-pretesting method in the form of cognitive interviewing (Willis, 2005).

During cognitive interviewing, the moderator typically reads the survey question to the participant, who answers it, adding any thoughts or opinions that came up while forming the answer. Here is an example of a survey question with a think-aloud response:

MODERATOR:

In the past 30 days, what time did you usually go to bed on weeknights?

131

Usability Testing for Survey Research. DOI: http://dx.doi.org/10.1016/B978-0-12-803656-3.00006-3

PARTICIPANT:

11 p.m., I guess. I do usually go to bed around 11 p.m. during the week. However, I watch the news in bed most nights, so I don't actually go to sleep until after it's over, around 11:30.

In this example, the participant had a different answer for the time she usually went to bed versus the time she usually fell asleep. This lets the researcher know that the question, as written, is ambiguous and may yield inconsistent responses. Some survey respondents may answer for the time they went to bed, and others may answer for the time they fell asleep. The think-aloud approach shows that even when participants are able to answer a question quickly and without difficulty, the survey question might not be capturing the intended information.

When conducting usability testing for a survey, the process is similar. You will want participants to tell you what they are thinking as they work on the survey or complete specific tasks. You want to understand their cognitive processes—how they interpret and answer the survey questions—as well as how they interact with the survey. You will learn about issues with question wording, labels, and design. For example, participants may have difficulty finding contact information, and they verbalize that they usually find it in the upper right corner, but they cannot find it there.

To be valuable, the think-aloud approach should elicit more than a description of what participants are doing, for example, "I'm entering my answer into the box." We can usually determine what they are doing by observation alone. Ideally, the think-aloud approach will allow us to assess participants' higher-level thinking processes as they complete a task.

To illustrate this, let's say the participant's task is to answer the survey question about the time she usually goes to bed by entering the response on a mobile phone (see Fig. 6.1).

Okay, so I'm going to click on the button here to enter the time. Ah, the scrolling clock. Hmmm…why's it set for 4:05? Oh, that's what time it is now. I see. That's kind of annoying though because I have to change both the hours and the minutes. I would be easier it if it was just set at some standard time like 8 o'clock. I am just going to leave it at 11:05 rather than scroll down to 11:00 exactly because that's kind of tedious.

FIGURE 6.1
Example of a survey tool for a clock feature.

The time in Fig. 6.1 was set to the current time to prevent any biases associated with selecting some other default (e.g., 10 p.m.), which might suggest to participants an average or normal bedtime. Yet, the think-aloud method showed that the participant was not able to efficiently provide the actual time she went to sleep because adjusting the input fields required too much effort. A different input field for entering time may be needed to make it easier for a respondent to answer correctly.

Fig. 6.2 and the subsequent conversation show another example of the type of insights that participants' think-aloud comments can provide.

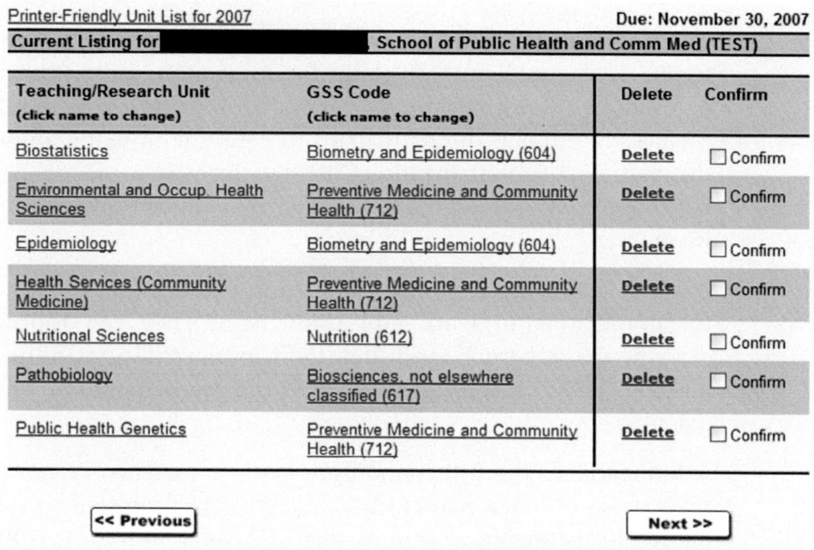

Printer-Friendly Unit List for 2007		Due: November 30, 2007	
Current Listing for █████████████	**School of Public Health and Comm Med (TEST)**		
Teaching/Research Unit (click name to change)	**GSS Code** (click name to change)	**Delete**	**Confirm**
Biostatistics	Biometry and Epidemiology (604)	Delete	☐ Confirm
Environmental and Occup. Health Sciences	Preventive Medicine and Community Health (712)	Delete	☐ Confirm
Epidemiology	Biometry and Epidemiology (604)	Delete	☐ Confirm
Health Services (Community Medicine)	Preventive Medicine and Community Health (712)	Delete	☐ Confirm
Nutritional Sciences	Nutrition (612)	Delete	☐ Confirm
Pathobiology	Biosciences, not elsewhere classified (617)	Delete	☐ Confirm
Public Health Genetics	Preventive Medicine and Community Health (712)	Delete	☐ Confirm

[<< Previous]   [Next >>]

FIGURE 6.2
A list of teaching and research units that the participant is asked to verify using a think-aloud process when completing a survey.

PARTICIPANT SCENARIO & TASK:

This is a list of teaching and research units that you provided on this survey last year. Please review the list to verify whether these units are still offered at your school.

THINK-ALOUD RESPONSE:

Ok. I like this table format. It is easy to scan quickly. Biostats . . . Yes, we still have that department. [Clicks Confirm] Ok. That was easy. Now, wait. What if I made a mistake? Can I unclick Confirm? [Unclicks Confirm]. Yes, I can. Good. [Clicks Confirm again.] That's important.

Now, I'm not sure what "Biometry and Epidemiology (604)" means so I'm going to click it just to see what happens . . . .

The participant talks about how she feels about the survey. We also learn about her expectations for how the survey should work. Given that "confirm" is a check box, she assumes she will be able to check and uncheck the box. We learn that she is satisfied when the survey matches her expectations. We also learn that she is not familiar with everything on the page, but this unfamiliarity does not seem problematic to complete the task.

With the think-aloud method, you will often identify what was easy or difficult about the task, whether the participant had any misconceptions about the survey content or functionality, and how the participant felt about completing the task.

A key advantage of the think-aloud approach is that it provides unbiased feedback. The moderator explains the think-aloud process and may provide an example. After that, the moderator's role is relatively minor and mainly involves reminding the participant to continue thinking aloud. As a result, the participant's verbalizations are relatively free of any bias that could be triggered by the moderator asking a direct question or interfering in any way.

Another advantage is that the think-aloud process is generally easy for moderators to learn and implement. They can follow a script to describe the approach, and then their primary responsibility is to provide periodic, unobtrusive feedback to the participant to show they are listening.

A limitation of the think-aloud approach is that it may not help on automatic tasks or when participants' thoughts are processed so quickly that the participant is unable to express them (Davis & Bistodeau, 1993; Ericsson & Simon, 1980; Sugirin, 1999). When participants are asked autobiographical questions, such as their name, age, and sex, they do not typically verbalize how they come up with their answer. Asking people to think aloud for these types of questions may not yield useful findings, and it may slow them down. Similarly, Rubin and Chisnell (2008) found that the think-aloud technique tended to be problematic when participants completed tasks that are usually performed on "autopilot." The act of thinking aloud introduced *reactivity* effects, in which participants' heightened awareness interfered with their ability to complete the task.

Another limitation is that thinking aloud is difficult for some participants. While the think-aloud approach is relatively easy for moderators to learn, it is not normal for most people and can make them feel uncomfortable.

Concurrent Versus Retrospective Think Aloud

There are two main think-aloud methods for usability testing:

- *Concurrent Think Aloud (CTA)*. Participants think aloud as they complete tasks.
- *Retrospective Think Aloud (RTA)*. Participants think aloud or explain what they were doing during the task as they look at screenshots of the survey or a video replay of the usability test.

There are a number of differences between these two approaches, and the best approach will depend on the goals of your study. Table 6.1 summarizes the key differences between the two approaches.

Table 6.1 Differences Between Concurrent and Retrospective Think Aloud

Concurrent Think Aloud (CTA)	Retrospective Think Aloud (RTA)
- Immediate thoughts (good recall) - Procedural comments - May affect task performance and usability metrics - Can interfere with eye-tracking data - Shorter session length - Less natural	- Relies on memory (recall failure) - Explanatory comments - No effect on task performance or usability metrics - Accurate eye-tracking data - Session length increases - More natural

RTA works best on surveys that have some or full functionality, such as selected interactive questions, early interactive prototypes, finished products, and mobile versions. You can observe how participants use and interact with the survey without the potential disruptions in task performance that can be caused by CTA or verbal probing. The observations can then be supplemented with qualitative feedback from respondents. Think aloud may not work well for early or exploratory testing, which usually requires more moderator involvement and verbal probing.

A more detailed discussion on the differences between CTA and RTA follows:

- *Recall.* CTA is based on the think-aloud approach originally developed by Ericsson and Simon (1980), in which verbalizations shed light on a participant's working memory. This allows researchers to identify participants' immediate, initial reactions to the survey. Participants' comments are provided in real time, which results in less editing or forgetting of their thoughts.

  By nature, RTA is no longer a means of exploring a participant's working memory and deviates considerably from the traditional CTA approach. Instead, RTA relies on participants' recall of what they were thinking when they initially completed the survey. As such, RTA is fallible because participants may not recall what they were thinking. In addition, certain information, such as whether they saw a specific button, may never have been encoded in the participant's memory in the first place.

- *Procedural versus explanatory comments.* There is some evidence that CTA tends to provide more descriptive or procedural feedback, whereas RTA tends to provide more insights and cognitive processing (Bowers & Snyder, 1990; Ohnemus & Biers, 1993; Olmsted-Hawala & Romano Bergstrom, 2012; Page & Rahimi, 1995). This is because a participant's working memory, employed with CTA, includes mainly what is necessary to complete the task. Use of RTA, on the other hand, gives participants more time to process and assign meaning to their tasks.

  Olmsted-Hawala & Romano Bergstrom (2012) found that participants who used CTA in a usability study spoke more positive words (e.g., smart, hopeful) than participants who used RTA, and that participants who used RTA spoke more insight words (e.g., complex, meaning, prove) and cognitive processing words (e.g., ambiguous, hesitate, solutions) than participants who used CTA. Participants who used CTA also spoke more present tense words than participants who used RTA.

- *Effect on task performance and usability metrics.* RTA has no effect on task performance or usability metrics—this makes sense as participants are completing tasks without the dual task of thinking aloud. The effect of CTA on task performance is inconsistent. Although many studies have found no difference between CTA and RTA, a few studies have found that CTA negatively affects performance and usability metrics compared with RTA.

  Ericsson and Simon (1984, 1980) have found that CTA slows down participants' cognitive processing. Although participants may take longer to formulate an answer, *how* they go about recalling their answers does not appear to change. This suggests that whether participants think aloud or not, they will answer the survey question in much the same way.

  A difference between cognitive interviewing and usability testing is that participants are not just answering questions, but they are performing actions in real time. Several usability testing studies show little to no difference on task performance (i.e., how participants complete tasks) and usability metrics such as accuracy, efficiency, and satisfaction (Capra, 2002; Olmsted-Hawala, Murphy, Hawala, & Ashenfelter, 2010; Van Den Haak, De Jong, & Schellens, 2004).

However, two studies have found that CTA can interfere with usability metrics. For example, Van Den Haak et al. (2004) found that accuracy and efficiency were lower with CTA compared to RTA, but the same types of usability issues were identified. Similarly, Krahmer and Ummelen (2004) found that CTA studies tend to have longer task performance times but no differences in accuracy.

In addition, the complexity of certain tasks may affect the quality of verbalizations provided during think-aloud. Ericsson and Simon (1980) observed that tasks that became more complex, creating a "high cognitive load" for participants, interfered with verbalizations. Individuals were simply not as good at thinking aloud during difficult tasks.

Olmsted-Hawala and Romano Bergstrom (2012) examined whether task complexity affected the impact of think-aloud on task performance. They found that middle-aged participants (ages 40−50), compared with younger and older adults, were more accurate and efficient on difficult tasks when using CTA compared with RTA. There were no differences between CTA and RTA in any age group for easy tasks.

- *Impact on eye-tracking data.* CTA may interfere with eye-tracking data. For example, Eger, Ball, Steens, and Dodd (2007), Guan, Lee, Cuddihy, and Ramey (2006), and Maughan, Dodd, and Watlers (2003) have found that CTA affects what people look at. Romano Bergstrom and Olmsted Hawala (2012) have found that CTA affects fixation data for older but not younger adults. CTA is particularly problematic for eye-tracking data when the moderator sits next to the participant, who often turns to look at the moderator, resulting in a loss of eye-tracking data (Bavelas, Coates, & Johnson, 2000, 2006).

- *Session length.* Although some studies have found that task completion times are longer with CTA, RTA takes longer to administer overall because it relies heavily on video replay of the session (Capra, 2002; Norman & Murphy, 2004; Van Den Haak, De Jong, & Schellens, 2003; Van Den Haak et al., 2004).

- *Participant comfort.* RTA permits working in silence, which is more natural for participants (Rosson & Carroll, 2002).

In sum, both approaches appear to work well in identifying potential usability concerns. If you value usability metrics, use RTA, and if you value real-time feedback about participants' thoughts, use CTA.

> If you value usability metrics, use retrospective think-aloud, and if you value real-time feedback about participants' thoughts, use concurrent think-aloud.

In our experience, CTA tends to identify more usability issues and takes less time to administer than RTA. Therefore, we often use CTA even though we know that the usability metrics might be less reliable. Or, we use a mixed approach, randomly assigning half of the participants to CTA and half to RTA. The approach may change for each usability study you conduct.

Implementing Think Aloud

Participants will need some help to understand what think aloud is, and why it is important. The following example of a CTA introduction explains the process. The example emphasizes that the usability test moderator wants to know what participants are thinking, not just what they are doing, and it demonstrates why thinking aloud is helpful to the moderator.

> *CTA Example:*
>
> *I would like you to fill out this survey just as you would if you accessed it online. While you are working, I would like you to think aloud. I can see what you are doing, but I don't know why you are doing it. So I need your help.*
>
> *So while you are working, I would like you to share what you are thinking, tell me what you are about to do, and why. Tell me if you are looking for something and what it is, and whether or not you can find it. If you get quiet, I may say, "what are you thinking?" And I would like you to continue telling me what you are looking for and what you are thinking.*
>
> *You can also help by pointing out anything that is confusing or unclear. We want your honest opinions about what you like or dislike about the survey, what worked well for you and what was difficult. If you find at any point that you are not sure what to do or are trying to figure something out, please tell me. I may not be able to answer your questions, but it is really helpful to hear this from you. This information will help us understand what we can do to improve the survey and make it work better.*
>
> *Do you have any questions before we begin?*

For RTA, the process is similar except you will wait until the participant has completed all tasks and then introduce cued think aloud. Instead of asking them to think aloud while completing tasks, ask them to think aloud as the watch the video play back: "As you watch the video, I would like you to think aloud. I can see what you did, but I don't know why you did it. So I need your help. I would like you to tell me what you were thinking while you were working."

In addition to the introduction, some moderators like to demonstrate think aloud or have participants practice the think-aloud process so they are comfortable before beginning the actual research session. You demonstrate or have participants practicing think aloud while doing a simple task, such as adding an event to a calendar. To prevent biasing the participant, the practice task should not be directly related to the survey or product being tested.

Encourage participants merely to keep a running stream of consciousness and avoid filtering their responses, making inferences, or explaining. These verbalizations are less reliable due to their subjective nature. To reduce this type of verbalization, Ericsson and Simon (1980) had the moderator physically separated from the participant. We recommend this approach for conducting usability testing as well (see Chapter 4: Planning for Usability Testing). On the other hand, in cognitive interviewing and combined cognitive/usability testing, the moderator tends to sit with the participant because there is more social interaction.

Since usability testing focuses on the user, we often find value in participants' subjective verbalizations as well. But, we do not want this to interfere with completing the tasks. Therefore, exploring participants' subjective experience in depth is usually conducted through verbal probing as part of the debriefing interview, which is administered after the participant has completed the tasks. For example, you can ask participants if they have had similar experiences with other surveys or you can ask them to tell you about another experience that was particularly difficult or easy. This allows participants to explain their actions. It does not interfere with their natural interaction while completing the survey when you wait until the end of the session to ask these types of thought-provoking questions.

Here are additional tips for facilitating think aloud during a usability test:

- *Prompt participants as needed.* Subtle prompts to continue thinking aloud helps both participants who have trouble grasping the think-aloud process initially and those who start out well and then stop thinking aloud as they get more involved in the survey or task. Rather than simply reminding participants to think aloud, these prompts indirectly encourage participants to continue expressing their thoughts verbally. Use of these prompts in the beginning of a usability session can help train participants to think aloud. Often, you will find that participants begin to anticipate these prompts and voluntarily start thinking aloud. Typical prompts include the following:
    - What are you thinking?
    - Tell me what you're doing.
    - Tell me what you are looking at.
    - Keep talking.
    - Tell me more about that.
  Ideally, these prompts are administered in a low voice, to keep from distracting or interrupting the participant completing a task. To minimize the interviewer's presence, some moderators prefer shorter

prompts, such as, "What are you doing?," but others prefer more conversational prompts such as "Can you tell me what you're doing?" These slight variations to the prompts above are fine. If you use other prompts than what we have shared here, be sure they do not interrupt the participants' thought process or affect their behavior. For example, asking people why they did something could derail them from their natural next moves.

- *Demonstrate that you are listening.* Participants are more likely to continue talking if they believe that you are listening. You can help to convey that attention by saying "mmm, hmm" or "uh huh" while they talk. You can provide supportive feedback such as "Thanks" or "That's helpful," as appropriate. Keep your feedback neutral, though. Overly positive feedback such as "Good" or "That's great!" can suggest to participants that certain comments are better than other comments and may affect future comments they provide.

- *Be patient.* Prompting too frequently may interfere with task completion, so do not prompt participants every time they fall silent. Give them the opportunity to volunteer their thoughts before prompting. If it is obvious that a participant is reading (and you have not asked him or her to read out loud), wait to prompt until he or she finishes.

- *Give reminders.* At the start of each new task, remind participants to think aloud, as needed. This may not be necessary for all participants. But for most, a reminder is helpful.

Despite these tips, there may be times when participants simply are not able to verbalize their thoughts well, and that is ok. The more complex a task is, the more difficult it is for participants to think aloud, due to cognitive burden. When complex tasks or participants with low cognitive ability prevent the use of CTA, you still have the benefit of observational data. In these cases, you can pay more attention to the behaviors (e.g., click patterns) and ask specific questions in the debriefing interview.

VERBAL-PROBING APPROACH

With this technique, the moderator asks the participant targeted questions (probes) about either survey content or functionality. The goal of verbal probing is to understand how participants interpret the design and to get insight regarding their experiences interacting with the survey. Probes can be general such as, "How easy or difficult was this task to complete?" or more specific: "How helpful or unhelpful was the Calculate Total button when answering these questions?"

With think aloud, participants verbalize what comes to their mind, but this may not address all the questions that researchers have. One of the main advantages of verbal probing is that it allows the moderator to explore a specific issue or usability problem more deeply. Direct observation may reveal that an aspect of the survey is problematic, but probing can be used to understand why something is problematic. Knowing why something is problematic is critical for addressing the issue. Moderators can ask targeted questions as needed.

> Knowing why something is problematic is critical for addressing the issue.

Another advantage of verbal probing is that it is easier for some participants. Responding to a direct question is easier for participants than having to provide a running commentary on their thought processes while completing tasks.

On the contrary, a disadvantage of verbal probing compared with think aloud is that verbal probing is more complex and nuanced and may be more difficult for some moderators to learn. The primary concern with concurrent verbal probing is that it may introduce bias in the qualitative information participants provide, particularly if probes are not well crafted. We can mitigate this by avoiding leading questions and only asking neutral, balanced probes. Learning how to draft and administer unbiased probes is critical.

Another limitation is that intense verbal probing can often increase the length of a session compared with think aloud, due to the time for the moderator to ask the questions, time for the participants to think about and provide their answers, and disruption in task performance. All of these factors result in sessions that are 1.5 to 2 times as long as sessions with CTA alone.

Concurrent Versus Retrospective Verbal Probing

As with the think-aloud approach, verbal probing can be used concurrently or retrospectively. With *concurrent verbal probing*, you ask participant questions as they work. You may have prepared probes in advance to ask about content on each screen, or you may probe spontaneously based on something that happens in the interview. For example, if the participant seems surprised after clicking, you might ask, "What were you expecting to happen when you clicked that button?" Or if a participant sees an unfamiliar button and says, "'Check on friends'...hmmm," you could follow up with, "What does that mean to you?"

To ensure that you do not over-probe during concurrent verbal probing, try counting to five in your head. This practice will give participants time to volunteer what they are thinking or figure something out on their own before you need to intercede.

In *retrospective probing*, you ask probes after the participant has completed all tasks, rather than asking probes during or between tasks. When this technique follows other methods such as CTA or RTA, it is also commonly referred to as a debriefing interview. As with concurrent verbal probing, you may have prepared probes or spontaneous probes. For spontaneous probes, make a note of what happened and then probe the participant at the end of the interview. It may help to print screenshots to facilitate recall.

As with think aloud, there are a number of differences between these two approaches, and the best approach will depend on the goals of your study. Table 6.2 summarizes the key differences between the two approaches.

Table 6.2 Differences between Concurrent and Retrospective Probing	
Concurrent Verbal Probing	**Retrospective Verbal Probing**
<ul><li>Immediate thoughts (good recall) and more detail</li><li>May be biased</li><li>Affects task performance and usability metrics</li><li>Ideal for exploratory tests and cognitive/usability combined tests</li><li>Better for participants with low cognitive ability</li></ul>	<ul><li>Relies on memory (recall failure), less detail</li><li>Less biased</li><li>No effect on task performance or usability metrics</li><li>Can be used in any stage of testing</li></ul>

- *Recall.* The main advantage to concurrent verbal probing is that it allows you to capture participants' immediate thoughts and reactions while the memories are still fresh. For example, when a participant clicks on a link, the moderator may ask, "How well does this page match what you were expecting to find?" Immediately after clicking a button, participants are able to answer that question easily and accurately. If the same question is asked 30 minutes later at the end of the session, their expectations of what a button will do may be tempered by what actually happened. In addition, participants may not recall as much information. Poor recall is the main disadvantage of retrospective probing, particularly for long or complex tasks. Memory is fallible, and participants may not remember everything they were thinking while completing the task. In addition, when participants are ultimately successful, they sometimes downplay any trouble they may have had along the way. As such, retrospective probing is not as reliable.

For example, for a usability test on a web survey for the Census Bureau, Nichols (2016) used a combination of CTA and retrospective probing. To facilitate the latter, she printed out screenshots of the survey in advance, but they did not reflect a last-minute change in the survey that the participant completed. As shown in Fig. 6.3, the screenshot (A) had a different version of the select language item than the tested web survey did (B). Participants shown the screenshot were asked, "Did you see that button at the top?" Even though participants had not seen this version, they said that they had seen it and provided their opinions on it. This example suggests that retrospective probing is subject to memory error in which participants remember differently, even just 10 minutes after the session ends.

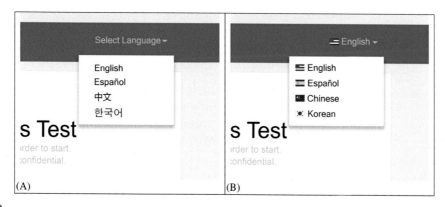

(A)   (B)

FIGURE 6.3

Participants were asked whether they saw the button at the top of (A) when they actually saw the item in (B) during the usability test. Even though participants had not seen the version they were asked about, they indicated that they had and provided their opinions on it. *Reproduced with permission from Nichols, E. (2016). Cognitive probing methods in usability testing—Pros and cons. In Presented at the American Association for Public Opinion Research, Austin, TX.*

- *Bias.* Concurrent probing can interfere with participants' natural thought process and create a heightened sense of awareness as they complete the survey.

- *Interference with task performance.* Participants may need to stop in the middle of a task to answer a moderator's question. Or, the act of answering probes about past tasks may change how participants behave on future tasks. Participants may begin to anticipate probes and interact differently. For example, a participant may think, "I know if I click that link, I'm going to have explain what I was expecting to see. So I just won't click anything unless I really need to."

- *Interference with usability metrics,* such as task accuracy, completion time, or eye tracking. For example, participants may pause while listening to or addressing a moderator's probe. Or even though they continue to complete a task, their attention might be diverted while they respond.

■ *Stage and type of testing.* Retrospective verbal probing can be used at any stage of testing and is frequently combined with either concurrent verbal probing or CTA.

Concurrent verbal probing works particularly well for early-stage, exploratory testing on products that do not yet have clickable or usable features, such as paper prototypes or wireframes. At this stage, task performance is less critical. What is more informative is how people understand the survey's design and intended function.

In later-stage testing, concurrent verbal probing can be useful when you know that something is problematic, but you are not sure why or how to fix it. Verbal probing allows you to delve a little deeper into what a participant is thinking when using your product, which may give you more insight than the verbalizations produced during CTA.

Concurrent verbal probing is frequently used for cognitive interviewing. If you are conducting combined cognitive and usability test interviews, using concurrent verbal probing is reasonable for usability aspects as well. Task performance will already be affected by the cognitive interviewing process.

■ *Participants with low cognitive ability.* Concurrent verbal probing also can be useful for subpopulations with low cognitive ability who may be less skilled at think aloud and have difficulty recalling information for retrospective verbal probing.

Although a keystone for cognitive testing, concurrent verbal probing is rarely used for usability testing due to the increased bias and interference in task performance and usability metrics. Despite these concerns, sometimes the benefits of concurrent verbal probing outweigh the limitations. For example, you may want to know WHY a participant did something. For example, why did participants leave a question blank? Was it because they did not know the answer, they did not see the question, or they thought the question did not apply to them? Was the visual layout of the question distracting? If you wait to ask these probes retrospectively, the participant may not recall their reasons, and it will not yield as useful of information.

In these situations, another option is to use a hybrid approach between concurrent and retrospective probes. Rather than probing as participants are completing tasks, ask immediately after they complete one task but before they start the next. This reduces the effect concurrent probing can have on task performance, while reducing the effect that retrospective probing can have on recall.

COMBINING COGNITIVE AND USABILITY TESTING

Although a survey can be cognitively tested and usability tested separately, both are often done during the same session, particularly in later rounds of testing. In addition to saving time and money, combining can allow you to more efficiently address all potential sources of error than one form of testing can (Romano Bergstrom, Childs, Olmsted-Hawala, & Jurgenson, 2013).

Efficiencies are gained because a survey's design and layout can affect the understanding of a survey question. For example, placing two survey questions on the same screen, instead of separate ones, can affect how respondents answer survey items—but not necessarily in a predictable direction. Several studies found that when items were combined, respondents answered the two questions more consistently (higher inter-item correlation) than questions placed on separate screens (Fuchs, 2001; Tourangeau, Couper, & Conrad, 2004). Other studies found they were answered *less* consistently (lower inter-item correlation) (Garland, 2009; Van Shaik & Ling, 2007).

In these examples, conducting at least some rounds of cognitive interviewing on a programmed instrument may help to evaluate whether the way people use the instrument affects how they understand the instrument.

A methodology commonly used for combined cognitive and usability testing is to use think aloud and verbal probing. Scripted cognitive probes can address potential concerns with question understanding. Spontaneous probes can be used as needed to address cognitive or usability issues.

A challenge, though, is that the level of verbal probing often used for cognitive interviewing may interfere with task performance and affect usability metrics, such as accuracy and efficiency. For example, asking a participant, "How did you come up with your answer?" may make them decide to change the answer. In addition, answering cognitive probes requires participants to start and stop, which may distract or interrupt their focus as they complete a task.

If usability metrics are a priority, then cognitive probes should be asked retrospectively. Alternately, if cognitive interviewing is the priority, then use concurrent probing and rely more on qualitative usability feedback than metrics, such as task accuracy or task completion time.

Selecting and Crafting Probes

Standard Probes

In this section, we provide guidance on developing probes to address your research questions and better understand whether participants can successfully complete a survey.

Verbal probing has been used in cognitive interviewing for decades to assess potential pitfalls in surveys. First, we provide examples of common probes used in cognitive interviewing and then explain how these probes can be adapted to assess usability.

Willis (2005) recommends taking an appraisal-based approach to verbal probing by first reviewing a survey question for features that will keep it from being understood as intended. The next step is to craft probes to address the potential concern in that question. He identified common survey-question pitfalls and associated probes that can be used to evaluate those pitfalls (Fig. 6.4). A survey question may have several problems, and thus you may ask several probes on a question. Other questions may not have any potential pitfalls identified, and thus no probes will be asked.

Although a staple of cognitive interviewing, verbal probing is used far less in usability testing. Extensive probing is rarely necessary for usability testing because we can simply observe participants as they complete a task. This behavioral data, combined with commentary provided during CTA, is often sufficient to identify many usability concerns.

Yet, there may be times when we want more information than can be provided through think aloud and observation. In these situations, you need to (1) know HOW to develop unbiased probes that elicit useful feedback and (2) WHEN to apply these probes, particularly for concurrent verbal probing.

Here are some of the most common usability probes and the goals they support:

- *Obtain participants' immediate thoughts or reactions.* These probes are meant to mimic the types of verbalizations provided in CTA, which have limited moderator-imposed bias:
  - *What are your thoughts on this [screen/page/feature/tool]?*
  - *What are you thinking?*
  - *What are you doing?*
  - *What are you looking at?*
  - *What are you trying to do?*

  We often add the phrase, "Tell me," or "Can you tell me" before any of the questions to keep the probes from sounding too repetitive for the participant. For example, "Can you tell me what you're thinking?" works just as well as "What are you thinking?"

- *Determine whether survey functionality matches participant's expectations.* To make the survey intuitive, the design should match the respondents' mental mode of how the survey should work. To evaluate this, ask participants:
  - *What do you expect to happen when you [click that link/button]?*
  - *What did you expect to happen when you [clicked that link/button]?*
  - *How did you expect that to work?*

- *Understand the user.* We tend to assume that respondents have the same goals that we have, but usability testing often shows us that they have

STEP 1 – READING: Determine whether it is difficult for the interviewers to read the question in the same way to all respondents.	
1a. **WHAT TO READ**: Interviewer may have difficulty determining what *parts* of the question should be read.	PROBE: None. Interviewer should attend to this potential difficulty and note it.
1b. **MISSING INFORMATION**: Information the interviewer needs to administer the question is *not* contained in the question.	PROBE: None. Interviewer should attend to this potential difficulty and note it.
1c. **HOW TO READ**: Question is *not* fully scripted and therefore difficult to read.	PROBE: None. Interviewer should attend to this potential difficulty and note it.
STEP 2 – INSTRUCTIONS: Look for problems with any introductions, instructions, or explanations from the respondent's point of view.	
2a. **CONFLICTING OR INACCURATE INSTRUCTIONS**, introductions, or explanations.	PROBE: [*At the end of a long intro, but before the question itself*] Before I get to the actual question, tell me what this introduction is telling you.
2b. **COMPLICATED INSTRUCTIONS**, introductions, or explanations.	PROBE: Same as above.
STEP 3 – CLARITY: Identify problems related to communicating the *intent or meaning* of the question to the respondent.	
3a. **WORDING**: Question is lengthy, awkward, ungrammatical, or contains complicated syntax.	PROBE: Can you tell me in your own words what that question was asking?
3b. **TECHNICAL TERM(s)** are undefined, unclear, or complex.	PROBE: What does the word [term] mean to you, as it's used in this question?
3c. **VAGUE**: There are multiple ways to interpret the question or to decide what is to be included or excluded.	PROBE: Tell me what you were thinking when I asked about [topic].
3d. **REFERENCE PERIODS** are missing, not well specified, or in conflict.	PROBES: (1) Can you remember what time period the question was asking about? (2) You said [answer]. What time period does that cover?
STEP 4 – ASSUMPTIONS: Determine if there are problems with assumptions made or the underlying logic.	
4a. **INAPPROPRIATE ASSUMPTIONS** are made about the respondent or about his or her living situation.	PROBES: (1) How well does that question apply to you? (2) Can you tell me more about that?
4b. **ASSUMES CONSTANT BEHAVIOR** or experience for situations that vary.	PROBE: Would you say that mostly stays the same, or does it vary or depend?
4c. **DOUBLE-BARRELED**: Contains more than one implicit question.	PROBE: Tell me more about your opinions on that.

FIGURE 6.4

Sources of Error in Survey Questions, with Corresponding Probes. *Reproduced with permission from Willis, G. B. (2005). Cognitive interviewing. A tool for improving questionnaire design. Thousand Oaks, CA: Sage Publications, Inc.*

STEP 5 – KNOWLEDGE/MEMORY: Check whether respondents are likely to *not know* or have trouble *remembering* information.	
5a. **KNOWLEDGE** may not exist: Respondent is unlikely to *know* the answer to a factual question.	PROBE: How much would you say you know about [topic]?
5b. **ATTITUDE** may not exist: Respondent is unlikely to have *formed* the attitude being asked about.	PROBE: How much would thought would have say you've given this?
5c. **RECALL** failure: Respondent may not *remember* the information asked for.	PROBES: (1) How easy or difficult is it to remember [topic]? (2) You said [answer]. How sure are you of that?
5d. **COMPUTATION** problem. The question requires a difficult mental calculation.	PROBE: How did you come up with that answer?
STEP 6: SENSITIVITY/BIAS: Assess questions for sensitive nature or wording, and for bias.	
6a. **SENSITIVE CONTENT** (general): The question asks about a topic that is embarrassing, very private, or that involves illegal behavior.	PROBE: (1) Is this OK to talk about in a survey, or is it uncomfortable? (2) In general, how do you feel about this question?
6b. **SENSITIVE WORDING** (specific): Given that the general topic is sensitive, the wording should be improved to minimize sensitivity.	PROBE: The question uses the word [term]. Does that sound OK to you, or would you choose something different?
6c. **SOCIALLY ACCEPTABLE** response is implied by the question.	PROBES: (1) How did you come up with that answer? (2) Do all the possible answers here seem OK, or did it seem like there's one that's supposed to be the right answer?
STEP 7 – RESPONSE CATEGORIES: Assess the adequacy of the range of responses to be recorded.	
7a. **OPEN-ENDED QUESTION** that is inappropriate or difficult.	PROBE: Was it easy or difficult to decide what answer to give?
7b. **MISMATCH** between question and response categories.	PROBES: (1) How easy or hard was it to find your answer on that list? (2) You said [answer]. How well does that apply to you?
7c. **TECHNICAL TERM(S)** are undefined, unclear, or complex.	PROBE: In this list, what does [term] mean to you?
7d. **VAGUE** response categories are subject to multiple interpretations.	PROBE: Tell me what you were thinking when I asked about [topic]?
7e. **OVERLAPPING** response categories.	PROBES: (1) How easy or hard was it to choose an answer? (2) Tell me why you chose [answer] instead of some other answer on the list.
7f. **MISSING** eligible responses in response categories.	PROBE: How easy or hard was it to choose an answer?
7g. **ILLOGICAL ORDER** of response categories.	PROBE: How was it for you to go through that list? Did that cause any difficulties?
STEP 8 – OTHER PROBLEMS: Look for problems not identified in Steps 1 – 7.	
8. Other problems not previously identified.	PROBE: Can you tell me more about that?

FIGURE 6.4

(Continued)

different or unanticipated goals. For example, imagine a participant is stuck in a loop, unable to proceed. He feels that a specific question does not apply to him, but there is no "Don't Know" option, and a response is required to proceed. He tries backing up and answering questions differently but is not able to get past the question. To evaluate whether the survey supports participants' goals, you can ask:

- *What do you want to accomplish?*
- *Can you describe the steps you are taking now?*
- *How did you feel about that process to [complete task]?*
- *What's going through your mind right now?*

- *Expansive probes.* These probes are often used to elicit more information following a volunteered comment or a response to a verbal probe. The purpose is to get the participant to expound on a topic without needing to ask a specific probe, which might introduce bias.
  - *Can you tell me more about that?*
  - *Tell me more.*

- *Echoing.* Repeating participants' words is a way of showing the participant that you are listening to and interested in what they are saying.

Echoing is different from paraphrasing, which is rephrasing a participant's remarks or trying to interpret them. Echoing is simply repeating, using an upward intonation to imply a question. For example, if a participant remarked, "That was weird." You might reply with "That was weird?" or simply "Weird?"

Scripted, Spontaneous, and Conditional Probes

Verbal probing—both concurrent and retrospective—consists of *scripted* and *spontaneous* probes. As the names suggest, scripted probes are prepared in advance, and spontaneous probes are asked spontaneously, usually as a reaction to something that happened in the interview. To identify as many errors as possible, become adept at both probe types.

Use of scripted probes requires you to carefully consider the tasks to be completed and any potential issues or concerns that may need to be probed during the usability session. As a result, scripted probes tend to be proactive; that is, you seek out potential issues or concerns. Spontaneous probes, on the other hand, tend to be more reactive—asked in reaction to something that has occurred.

Scripted probes are usually not sufficient for evaluating all the potential errors in a survey. You might need multiple spontaneous follow-up probes to determine whether the participant-survey interaction is working as intended. The following example showcases the use of unscripted, spontaneous probes to support scripted probes.

SCRIPTED PROBE:

What did you expect would happen when you clicked the "Help" link?

PARTICIPANT:

That I would be taken to a new page.

SPONTANEOUS PROBE:

What did you expect to find on that new page?

PARTICIPANT:

Oh! I thought it would it would provide definitions for some of the terms used in the survey, but it just provided a phone number and an email address.

During the usability test sessions, unanticipated situations will come up. When they do, you need to understand them. Spontaneous probes can help you explore what happened. Frequently, unanticipated situations identify the biggest flaws in a survey, helping to demonstrate the benefits of pretesting.

Asking spontaneous probes can be more challenging for new moderators because they require quick thinking: You must attend to what participants are saying, while thinking of probes to elicit additional information. While some situations require creating a custom probe, you usually can often just apply a standard probe to a spontaneous situation.

Scripted probes are often asked of all applicable participants even if the participant appears to understand the question or complete an action without difficulty. This is to ensure you collect the same information for all participants in a study—not just the people who had problems. A probe can be helpful for confirmation, even if the participant addressed the issue while thinking aloud. For example, you might say, "I know you already mentioned this, but I just wanted to confirm: ....." However, you must balance that with a desire to avoid fatiguing or boring the participant.

An exception is *conditional probes*. In some cases, a scripted probe applies only to certain participants or in certain conditions. These are called conditional probes (Conrad & Blair, 2004). For example, only participants who use an optional hover-over definition may be asked a probe about that definition.

Table 6.3 provides situations that are likely to occur in a usability test and suggested probes that could be asked conditionally. These can be administered concurrently or retrospectively to match your interviewing approach.

To apply conditional probes retrospectively, note any remarks or reactions—what the participant said and what screen was used—that you want to follow-up on. You then can remind the participant what happened and show screenshots or play back a video of the session to aid in administering the probes.

Table 6.3 Examples of Spontaneous Probes

Situation	Suggested Probe(s)
Participant does an action repeatedly (e.g., clicks the same button a few times)	"Tell me what you are trying to do."
Participant seems surprised	"What just happened?"
	"What were you expecting to happen when you did that?"
	"How does that compare with what you were expecting to happen?"
Participant makes a brief remark but does not explain or elaborate	"Tell me more about that."
Participant says, "I don't like this."	"What did you dislike about this?"
	"Tell me more."
Participant answers a question in a way that is contrary to what you were expecting	"How did you decide what to enter for this question?"
	"Tell me more about what you just did."
Participant uses a certain tool, feature, or function (e.g., hover-over definition or calculate button)	"How helpful or unhelpful is this [tool/feature/function] in completing your task?"
Participant seems frustrated	"You seem frustrated. Can you tell me what happened?"
	"What are you trying to do?"
Participant seems confused by something that happened	"What part of the [question/page/screen] is not very clear?"
Participant says, "I don't know what to do here."	"What do you see as your options?"
	"What would you do if I were not here?"

Guidelines for Crafting Probes

Depending on your research needs, you may need to ask more targeted probes that assess the specific nuances of your survey. When drafting probes, consider the following guidelines for avoiding bias and achieving better results:

- *Avoid "yes" or "no" questions.* These can suffer from acquiescence bias—the cultural tendency for people to answer a question positively because it is viewed as politer to agree than disagree. For example, imagine a task with moderate complexity. Whether you asked participants, "Was this task difficult?" or "Was this task easy?," a majority of participants will say "Yes." This seemingly incongruous response is because there could have been aspects of the task that were easy and other aspects of the task that were difficult. So instead, ask the balanced question, such as "How easy or difficult was this task to complete?"

Similarly, participants might be inclined to answer "Yes" simply to be polite. They do not want to disparage the product or survey, even if you tell them that you did not create it and that your role is to learn from them. Therefore, instead of "Did you like that?" or "Was that feature helpful?," give the participant the opportunity to indicate that they did not like something without appearing rude. For example: "How helpful or unhelpful was that feature?," "What did you like or dislike about this feature?," or "Tell me the best and worst thing about this survey."

"YES" OR "NO" PROBE:

Was this task difficult to complete?

BETTER PROBE:

How easy or difficult was that task to complete?

"YES" OR "NO" PROBE:

Did you like that?

BETTER PROBE:

What did you like or dislike about this feature?

- *Ask open-ended questions.* These questions encourage the respondent to provide insight and explanation, which is useful for understanding potential usability issues. Starting a question with "what" or "how" can often turn a short-answer question into an open-ended one.

  SHORT-ANSWER PROBE:

  Was this [button/link/tool] helpful or unhelpful?

  BETTER PROBE:

  How helpful or unhelpful was this [button/link/tool] in completing your task?

  The "better" probe is likely to generate a little more detail about whether the feature was helpful. You can also add an open-ended follow-up question such as, "In what way was it helpful/unhelpful?"

- *Be careful with "Why" questions.* These questions can be problematic for three reasons. First, they are broad and unlikely to elicit a targeted answer from participants. For example, "Why did you click that link?" might get a generic response such as, "I wanted to see what was on that page." What you really wanted to know, though, was why the person chose that link over the other links on the page. Instead, a better way to ask the question would be, "How did you decide which link to click?" or "How did you decide where to go next?" which will yield a more specific answer.

Second, "why" questions can make participants feel defensive or that they did something wrong. For example, asking "Why did you click that link?" may imply to a participant that clicking that link was an incorrect action. In addition to possibly offending participants, this can make participants second-guess their decisions and possibly change their behavior as they complete a task.

Third, people do not always know why they did something. For example, text might have appeared to be clickable, so they clicked. However, if you ask why they clicked it, they might make up stories to fill in the gaps.

"WHY" PROBE:

Why did you click that link?

BETTER PROBE:

How did you decide which link to click?

- *Focus on what the participant is trying to accomplish, not the specific feature or design itself.* Researchers might want to learn about a specific feature or aspect of the survey, but respondents want to accomplish their goals. As a result, evaluating a specific feature is more meaningful within the context of participants' goals.

PROBE:

What did you think of the glossary?

BETTER PROBE:

How helpful or unhelpful was the glossary when you answered these questions?

- *Use balanced, unbiased questions.* Avoid unbalanced or leading questions, which suggest that one answer is the correct one. For example, the question, "How important is this feature to you?" suggests that the feature is at least somewhat important, making it more likely that participants will indicate that the feature has some importance. A balanced question, on the other-hand makes it clear that either option—being important or unimportant—is reasonable.

BIASED PROBE:

How important is this Calculate Total button to you?

BETTER PROBE:

How important or unimportant was the Calculate Total button in providing your response?

- *Ask general probes before specific probes to avoid bias.* As a researcher, you may want to know specific information about how a participant uses your product. However, specific probes prime participants, so they have the potential to introduce bias. Therefore, begin by asking a general probe to elicit participants' unbiased thoughts, and only ask the targeted probe if needed. In this example, beginning with the specific question could have prevented learning that participants had different ideas about how to print.

GENERAL:

If you wanted to print a copy of this survey for your records, what would you do?

You are testing the survey, not the participants.

SPECIFIC:

What do you expect to happen if you click the "Print Report" button?

- *Avoid probes that have the potential to introduce reactivity.* This occurs when the probe influences participants to complete the task differently than they would if they were not probed (Willis, 2005). For example, by calling attention to a survey feature, such as a hover-over definition, you imply to participants that they should use it. As they complete the rest of the tasks, they may click on the hover-over definition even if they would not have otherwise. So wait until the debriefing interview to ask about specific features that participant did or did not use.

  REACTIVITY-INSPIRING PROBE:

  Did you see the hover-over definition for "first-time student?"

  BETTER PROBE:

  How did you determine who was a "first-time student?"

- *Avoid asking participants if they noticed something.* Researchers want to know whether a participant noticed a particular feature, such as instructions, help menu, hover-over definition, calculate button, or logout button. When participants are asked directly, "Did you notice X?," you've learned they often answer "Yes," even when there was no evidence of their notice. But a "No" response can be equally problematic because it's not clear: Did they not notice it or simply did not need it?

A better solution is to create a task or scenario that will help you evaluate how participants feel about that aspect of the survey. For example, rather than asking participants whether they noticed the logout button, which lets them save their survey responses and resume later, develop a task or scenario to evaluate the button.

You can also use eye tracking to understand the aspects of the survey that attract participants' attention. Eye tracking allows us to passively evaluate if and when people see certain things.

"NOTICE?" PROBE:

Did you notice the logout button?

BETTER:

Assign the participant the following task and scenario: "You got interrupted and had to quit the survey for a while. Later you want to get back to it. How would you quit and resume the survey?"

Confusion is not the participant's fault, but the fault of the survey or product.

- *Do not ask the participant to do your job for you.* When participants point out something they do not like, you may be tempted to ask them what they recommend instead. Do not ask for suggestions for three reasons:

  - They are not design experts.

  - They are there to do a different job—asking them also for design suggestions can cognitively burden them.

  - You might influence their behavior: Eventually participants may stop pointing out problems if you ask them how to fix them.

  If you are considering alternative designs, you can have participants react to those.

  PARTICIPANT:

  The Print Report button label is confusing.

  BURDENSOME PROBE:

  What would you recommend we use instead?

  BETTER PROBE:

  That's helpful to know. Can you tell me more about why it's confusing? Would Print Survey Responses be more or less clear than Print Report?

- *Avoid blaming the participant.* You are testing the survey, not the participant. Therefore, you should not make the participants feel at fault if they do not understand something or cannot complete a task. A participant's confusion may be obvious to you, but questions such as, "Did you find this confusing?" or "Do you understand what to do on this screen?" make it seem that the confusion is the participant's fault. The problem is with the survey or product, not the participant.

  BLAMING PROBE:

  So, you found this confusing?

  BETTER PROBE:

  What part of the [question/page/screen] is not very clear?

- *Avoid test-like questions.* Because you want to make clear that it is the survey being tested, also avoid test-like questions that have a "right" or "wrong" answer. Even without such questions, the fact that you are asking participants to complete tasks can already cause anxiety. Avoiding test-like questions reduces pressure to "perform."

  TEST-LIKE PROBE:

  Do you know what to do here?

  BETTER PROBE:

  What would you do next on this screen?

- *Be clear and specific.* In attempting to ask unbiased probes, researchers can sometimes end up with probes that are too vague.

  VAGUE PROBE:

  What does Print mean to you?

  BETTER PROBE:

  What do you expect to happen when you click the Print button?

- *Be careful of hypothetical questions.* Rather than asking about future behavior (e.g., "Would you use this feature?"), ask more reliable questions about actual experiences instead.

  HYPOTHETICAL PROBE:

  If you got this error message while taking the survey at home, would you quit or try to keep going?

  BETTER PROBE:

  Have you ever taken a survey and received an error message like this? What happened? Did you try to resolve the error or did you quit?

  Avoid particularly unlikely or complicated hypothetical questions (e.g., if you lived out of your car instead of a house, would you . . .).

- *Don't over-probe.* Allow the participant time to think and complete a task without constantly probing, which could interfere with task completion.

CHOOSING A MODERATING TECHNIQUE

Selecting the right moderating technique or mix of techniques for your study depends on several factors, including the testing stage (exploratory, assessment, and verification), the product (e.g., paper prototype, finished product), the project goals, and your comfort with each method.

Table 6.4 summarizes the advantages and disadvantages of each of the moderating techniques. If is often not necessary to choose a single method because multiple methods work well. For example, you can either assign half of your sample to one approach (e.g., CTA) and the other half to another (e.g., RTA). Alternately, you can combine CTA with retrospective verbal probing in the same test.

Table 6.4 Advantages and Disadvantages of Moderating Approaches

Approach	Advantages	Disadvantages
CTA	<ul><li>Feedback in real-time</li><li>Good recall</li><li>Procedural comments</li><li>Shorter session length (vs RTA, concurrent verbal probing)</li><li>Unbiased feedback</li><li>Easy for moderators to learn</li></ul>	<ul><li>Slight effect on task performance (vs RTA)</li><li>May affect usability metrics</li><li>Some interference with eye-tracking data</li><li>Less natural</li><li>Hard for some participants</li></ul>
RTA	<ul><li>Explanatory comments</li><li>No effect on task performance or usability metrics</li><li>Accurate eye-tracking data</li><li>More natural</li><li>Unbiased feedback</li><li>Easy for moderators to learn</li></ul>	<ul><li>Recall failure</li><li>Longer session length (vs CTA)</li><li>Hard for some participants</li><li>Requires heavy cueing</li></ul>
Concurrent verbal probing	<ul><li>Feedback in real-time</li><li>Good recall</li><li>Ask targeted questions</li><li>More detailed comments</li><li>Works well for exploratory tests, cognitive/usability combined tests</li><li>Easiest for participants, especially with low cognitive ability</li></ul>	<ul><li>May introduce bias</li><li>Negative effect on task performance and usability metrics</li><li>Hardest for moderators to learn</li><li>Longest session lengths</li></ul>
Retrospective verbal probing	<ul><li>Less biased (than concurrent verbal probing)</li><li>Ask targeted question</li><li>No effect on task performance or usability metrics</li><li>Can be used in any stage of testing</li><li>Easier for participants (than think-aloud)</li></ul>	<ul><li>Recall failure</li><li>Requires some cueing</li><li>Less detailed comments</li><li>Hard for moderators to learn (vs CTA and RTA)</li></ul>

EXAMPLE: CONCURRENT THINK ALOUD AND CONCURRENT VERBAL PROBING

The following case study (Fig. 6.5) is based on a combined cognitive/usability study conducted to test an early prototype of a mobile application for the 2020 Census. Parts of the usability session have been edited for clarity and redacted to maintain confidentiality.

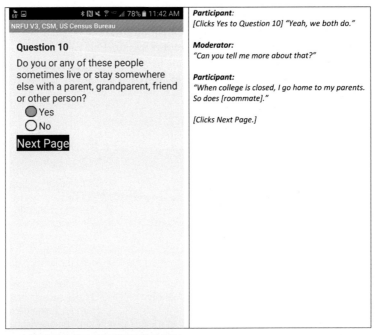

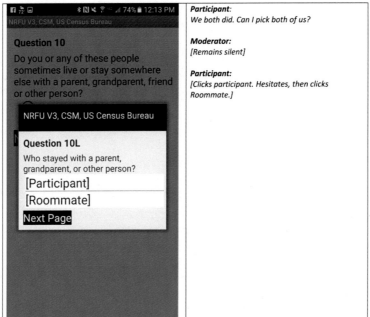

FIGURE 6.5

Example of concurrent think-aloud and verbal probing in a combined cognitive/usability.

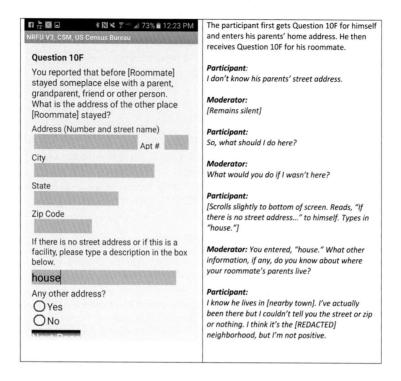

FIGURE 6.5
(Continued)

In this example, the participant needs a reminder to think aloud when he gets to Question 10. Then, the moderator remains silent as the participant completes the questions, letting him figure out whether he can select more than one person on Question 10L. Similarly, the moderator only intervenes on Question 10F when the participant indicates he is stuck. She uses a redirecting probe to help him remain on task.

When the participant answers Question 10F with just "house," the moderator asks a spontaneous probe to determine whether the participant knew any more information. Partial address information, particularly city and state, would be helpful to the Census. Yet, we observed that when participants did not know the city and state, they opted to leave all of the address fields blank rather than enter partial information.

The text below the zip code field, "If there is no street address or if this is a facility ..." was intended to gather supplemental information about a location, but instead many participants used it to type in a description of the location when they did not know the full address.

To improve the address information collected, we recommended that the screen include just the primary address fields. If the address fields were left blank, the survey could provide a prompt asking for partial information such as city and state.

References

Barnum, C. M. (2010). *Usability testing essentials: Ready, set … test!.* Burlington, MA: Elsevier.

Bavelas, B., Coates, L., & Johnson, T. (2000). Listeners as co-narrators. *Journal of Personality and Social Psychology, 79*(6), 941–952.

Bavelas, B., Coates, L., & Johnson, T. (2006). Listener responses as collaborative process: The role of gaze. *Journal of Communication, 52*(3), 566–580.

Bowers, V., & Snyder, H. (1990). Concurrent versus retrospective verbal protocol for comparing window usability. In *Proceedings of the human factors society 34th annual meeting* (pp. 1270–1274).

Capra, M. (2002). Contemporaneous versus retrospective user-reported incidents in usability evaluation. In: *Proceedings of the human factors and ergonomics society 46th annual meeting* (pp. 1973–1977).

Conrad, F., & Blair, J. (2004). Data quality in cognitive interviews: The case for verbal reports. In S. Presser, J. M. Rothgeb, M. P. Couper, J. T. Lessler, E. Martin, J. Martin, & E. Singer (Eds.), *Methods for testing and evaluating survey questionnaires.* Hoboken, NJ: John Wiley and Sons.

Davis, J. N., & Bistodeau, L. (1993). How do L1 and L2 reading differ? Evidence from think aloud protocols. *The Modern Language Journal, 77*(4), 459–472.

Dumas, J. S., & Redish, J. C. (1999). *A practical guide to usability testing.* Norwood, NJ: Ablex, 1994.

Eger, N., Ball, L., Steens, R., & Dodd, J. (2007). *Cueing retrospective verbal reports in usability testing through eye-movement replay. Proceedings of the 21st British HCI group annual conference on people and computers: HCI … but not as we know it-Volume 1, BCS-HCI '07* (pp. 129–137). Swinton: UK British Computer Society.

Ericsson, K., & Simon, H. (1980). Verbal reports as data. *Psychological Review, 87,* 215–251.

Ericsson, K., & Simon, H. (1984). *Protocol analysis: Verbal reports as data.* Cambridge: MIT Press.

Fuchs, M. (2001). Screen design in a web survey. In: *Paper presented at American Association for Public Opinion Research.*

Garland, P. (2009). Alternative question designs outperform traditional grids. Retrieved from <http://www.surveysampling.com/en/news/ssi-research-finds-alternative-question-designs-outperform-traditional-grids>.

Guan, Z., Lee, S., Cuddihy, E., & Ramey, J. (2006). *The validity of the stimulated retrospective think aloud method as measured by eye tracking. Proceedings of the SIGCHI conference on human factors in computer systems, CHI '06* (pp. 1253–1262). New York, NY: ACM Press.

Krahmer, E., & Ummelen, N. (2004). Thinking about thinking aloud: A comparison of two verbal protocols for usability testing. *IEEE Transactions on Professional Communication, 47*(2), 105–117.

Loftus, E. (1984). Protocol analysis of responses to survey recall questions. In T. B. Jabine, M. L. Staf, J. M. Tanur, & R. Tourangeau (Eds.), *Cognitive aspects of survey methodology: Building a bridge between disciplines* (pp. 61–64). Washington, DC: National Academy Press.

Maughan, L., Dodd, J., & Watlers, R. (2003). Video replay of the eye tracking as a cue in retrospective protocol … don't make me think aloud! In *Scandinavian workshop of applied eye tracking, 2003.*

Nichols, E. (2016). Cognitive probing methods in usability testing—Pros and cons. In: *Presented at the American Association for Public Opinion Research, Austin, TX.*

Nielsen, J. (1993). *Usability engineering.* Cambridge, MA: AP Professional.

Norman, K. L., & Murphy, E. (2004). Usability testing of an Internet form for the 2004 overseas enumeration test: A comparison of think aloud and retrospective reports. In: *Proceedings of the Human Factors Society 48th Annual Meeting, Human Factors Society, New Orleans, LA.* Retrieved September 24, 2008, from <http://lap.umd.edu/lap/Papers/Tech_Reports/LAP2004TR04/LAP2004TR04.pdf>.

Ohnemus, K., & Biers, D. (1993). Retrospective versus concurrent thinking-out-loud in usability testing. In *Proceedings of the Human Factors and Ergonomics Society 37th Annual Meeting* (pp. 1127−1131).

Olmsted-Hawala, E., Murphy, E., Hawala, S., & Ashenfelter, K. (2010). *Think aloud Protocols: A comparison of three think aloud protocols for use in testing data dissemination web sites for usability. Proceedings of CHI 2010, ACM conference on human factors in computing systems* (pp. 2381−2390). New York, NY: CSM Press.

Olmsted-Hawala, E. L., & Romano Bergstrom, J. C. (2012). Think aloud protocols. Does age make a difference? In *Proceedings from the society for technical communications summit, May 2012, Chicago, IL.*

Page, C., & Rahimi, M. (1995). Concurrent and retrospective verbal protocols in usability testing: Is there value added in collecting both? In *Proceedings of the Human Factors and Ergonomics Society 39th annual meeting* (pp. 223−227). Santa Monica, CA.

Romano Bergstrom, J., Childs, J. H., Olmsted-Hawala, E., & Jurgenson, N. (2013). *The efficiency of conducting concurrent cognitive interviewing and usability testing on an interviewer-administered survey.*

Romano Bergstrom, J. C., & Olmsted-Hawala, E. L. (2012). Effects of age and think aloud protocol on eye-tracking data and usability measures. In: *Poster presentation at Usability Professionals Association (UPA) conference, Las Vegas, NV, June 2012.*

Rosson, M. B., & Carroll, J. M. (2002). *Usability engineering: Scenario-based development of human-computer interaction.* San Francisco, CA: Morgan Kaufmann Publishers.

Rubin, J., & Chisnell, D. (2008). *Handbook of usability testing: How to plan, design, and conduct effective tests* (2nd ed.). Indianapolis, IN: Wiley Publishing.

Sugirin. (February 1999). Exploring the comprehension strategies of EFL readers: A multi-method study. In *Paper presented at an International Workshop on Written Language Processing at the University of New South Wales, Sydney, Dec. 9, 1998.* (ERIC Document Reproduction Service No. ED 428 548).

Tourangeau, R., Couper, M. P., & Conrad, F. (2004). Spacing, position, and order. Interpretive heuristics for visual features of survey questions. *Public Opinion Quarterly, 68*(3), 368−393.

Van Den Haak, M., De Jong, M., & Schellens, P. (2003). Retrospective vs. concurrent think aloud protocos: Testing the usability of an online library catalogue. *Behavior & Information Technology, 22*(5), 339−351.

Van Den Haak, M., De Jong, M., & Schellens, P. (2004). Employing think aloud protocols and constructive interaction to test the usability of online library catalogues: A methodological comparison. *Interacting With Computers, 16*(6), 1153−1170.

Van Schaik, P., & Ling, J. (2007). Design parameters of rating scales for web sites. *ACM Transactions on Computer-Human Interaction, 14*(1), 35.

Willis, G. B. (2005). *Cognitive interviewing. A tool for improving questionnaire design.* Thousand Oaks, CA: Sage Publications, Inc.

CHAPTER 7

Conducting Usability Sessions

You have determined your research objectives, identified what aspect of the survey you are testing, recruited participants, decided on your testing approach, and developed your moderator's guide. Now you are ready to actually conduct the sessions.

SET UP PROCEDURES

The first time you conduct a usability session, the setup can be daunting. Do not worry though, once you have been through the process a few times, it will become easier.

Remind Participants via Phone/Email

A day before a participant's scheduled session, send participants another reminder. If possible, call the participant, and, if you do not get an answer, leave a message. You may send an email or a text as well, but we find that no-show rates are lower when participants receive a reminder phone call and not just an email.

Prepare Materials

On the day before (or the morning of the usability sessions), prepare all of the materials you will need for the usability tests. Preparation includes:

- Making sure that all testing equipment is fully charged and ready to use
- Printing and organizing all paper materials
- Obtaining incentives, if you will be paying participants.

Checklists are useful for ensuring that you have all the needed materials and are particularly helpful when working with other moderators. Fig. 7.1 includes a sample checklist for a usability study conducted in the field.

163

Usability Testing for Survey Research. DOI: http://dx.doi.org/10.1016/B978-0-12-803656-3.00007-5

Interviewer Checklist: What to take with you to usability interviews

- ☐ Interviewer Folder
    - ☐ This checklist
    - ☐ Screenshots of the survey
    - ☐ Mobile device login procedures
    - ☐ Participant overview form (recruitment criteria met)
    - ☐ Protocol guide – verify correct version
    - ☐ Consent form (2 copies)
    - ☐ Incentive receipt
- ☐ $40 in case (place in folder if desired)
- ☐ Testing device and power cord
- ☐ Laptop and power cord
- ☐ Mobile sled with attached camera, USB cord
- ☐ Driving directions and/or map
- ☐ Coins for parking meter or tolls
- ☐ Your employee ID badge
- ☐ Two working pens or pencils
- ☐ Company brochure (in the event the participant has questions about the organization involved)

FIGURE 7.1
Example interviewer checklist.

Dry Run

A day before the first session—of each round, if you have multiple ones—conduct a dry run to test your procedures and equipment. We cannot stress enough the importance of this step to avoid the risk of your first scheduled session being the dry run.

For example, you may realize that you forgot to bring a mouse. Even worse, you may learn that the survey cannot be accessed from the testing location, which would result in losing the entire session.

To the extent possible, mimic the setup that will be used for the actual sessions. Therefore, if you will be testing in the laboratory, your dry run should also be there. If your usability sessions will be off-site, try to do the same for your dry run. If it is not possible, e.g., if the sessions will be in a participant's home or business, pick a similar location.

If you will be providing laptops or other devices for participants, conduct the dry run on those devices. If testing will be conducted on a participant's laptop or computer, test on a computer that is not connected to your company's network. Surveys and websites that are still in development are often hosted on internal servers that cannot be accessed from a computer outside the network. Therefore a dry run conducted with your computer instead of a test computer may not reveal potential connectivity issues.

We recommend testing the procedures by conducting a dry run from start to finish, including having your dry-run participant complete each task. This process helps ensure you have thought of everything your participants will need, and you can time the session to ensure it does not run over the allotted time. Often, at this step, you will realize that you have forgotten something basic, such as the laptop power cord or a clipboard to assist with note-taking, or something more significant, such as the sled to hold the mobile device.

Use the dry run to verify that that following aspects of your usability session are in working order:

- *Recording equipment.* Practice using the recording equipment to ensure that it is working correctly, that any physical devices (e.g., cameras or digital recorders) are fully charged (and have charged batteries and a charger), and that you know how to use them. Do a test recording and play back the recording after the dry run to verify the audio and picture quality are acceptable. Make sure you have enough free space on your hard drive for the recording, and bring an external drive for backup.

- *Screen-sharing software (if used).* Verify that the screen-sharing software has been installed on the test computer, that the software is working, and that observers can view the shared screen. Send a test link to an observer or colleague to test.

- *Eye-tracking equipment (if used).* Set up the eye-tracking test in the eye-tracking software to determine how the stimuli will be presented and the parameters for the eye tracker to know the dimensions of the stimuli (e.g., for desktop—the dimensions of the whole screen, or for mobile—the screen dimensions of the mobile device). Conduct the eye tracking, including calibrating your dry-run participant, so you are comfortable with it on the day of the actual sessions. Play back the recording to ensure it is working properly.

- *The survey.* Verify the following:
  - People can access the survey.
  - The most recent version is downloaded.
  - Test logins work.

- *Devices.*
  - Hardware, such as a laptop, is fully charged and working correctly, and your survey can be accessed on it.
  - You have a mouse, if using a laptop.

◾ Mobile device, when needed, is fully charged and working. Make sure you know the password to use the device, and bring a charger.

◾ *The printed materials*. Print out all forms, and verify that you have the appropriate ones for the moderator (e.g., screenshots, protocol, consent form, incentive receipt, pre- and post-questionnaire) and any observation forms needed for note-takers and observers. Verify that your printed materials reflect the most recent updates to your survey.

If you are using logging software for noting observations, test this process too, to become familiar with it.

For the dry run, we recommend using a coworker, especially one who is less familiar with the project and survey, rather than an actual user. This person can identify any parts of the process that would be unclear or confusing for the participant.

Once the dry run is complete, you likely will make edits to the protocol and materials. You may decide to change some questions or the order of tasks, incorporate something new, or cut something for the sake of time.

MODERATING THE SESSION

The key logistical steps involved in moderating a usability test session are:

1. Set up testing equipment.
2. Queue up the survey for participant (for testing in the field, do this after you arrive).
3. Greet the participant and escort him or her to the testing room, if applicable.
4. Administer the informed consent form, including permission to record.
5. Read your script:
   a. Introduce participants to any in-person observers, and notify participants of anyone who may be observing via phone or web.
   b. Introduce the purpose of the study and what you will ask them to do.
   c. Provide an example of think aloud, if applicable.
6. Administer the pre-test questionnaires, if applicable.
7. Start audio/video/screen recording and screen sharing (you can also start the recordings before introducing the purpose of the study so that you do not forget).
8. Provide participant with tasks/scenarios.
9. Watch the participant complete tasks, and take copious notes.
10. Administer a post-test questionnaire (e.g., satisfaction), if applicable, before you ask additional questions.

11. Administer retrospective think aloud or verbal probing/debriefing, if applicable.

12. Ask observers whether they have additional questions for the participant.

13. Ask the participant whether he or she has anything to add or ask.

14. End the session, and stop the recording and screen sharing.

15. Provide participant incentive, if applicable. (It is also fine to have provided the incentive at the beginning of the study.)

16. Escort participant out, if applicable.

17. Organize and label paper and electronic notes; save recordings.

18. Record some quick notes about the session, if time allows.

19. Debrief with observers, between participants (if time allows), to discuss what you learned and to assess whether changes should be made to the protocol before the next participant arrives.

20. Prepare for next participant.

Moderator Role and Responsibilities

The moderator is pivotal in obtaining detailed and unbiased information that can be used to answer the research questions. Commonly, usability test moderators also contribute to analyzing the data and reporting the findings.

Build Rapport With Participants

Quality research relies on participants telling you what they think and feel. To provide honest feedback, participants must feel comfortable during the discussion, and they must feel that they can trust you. As a result, one of your main roles is to build that connection with participants and put them at ease.

To do so, always set aside a little time for greetings and formalities. These everyday social graces can put participants at ease. Avoid the temptation to "get down to business" and just begin with the interview as soon as all the paperwork is signed. Treat the participant like a human being and not a test subject or laboratory rat. Recognize that being in this "testing" environment may make the participant feel uncomfortable. They need reassurances that you are a nice, reasonable person who will not be judging and evaluating every move they make (even if you are!).

Although it is called a usability "test," remember that it is the survey that is being tested, not the participant. Remind the participants that they are helping you test the survey, and that you are not testing them.

> Test the survey. Not the participants.

Another way to build rapport is to try to match participants' general attire. To a certain extent, people feel more comfortable with people who are similar to them. For example, if you are conducting sessions with professionals, dress more professionally, in business casual attire. If you are conducting sessions with children, dress more casually.

Although it is not always possible to "match" the moderator to the participants, you can minimize any obvious differences that might be off-putting. For instance, if participants are of low income, you could dress more casually and inexpensively and not wear fancy jewelry.

More important for the moderator than looking similar is being perceived as objective. Participants' perceptions can affect the amount and quality of information they provide. For example, in a focus-group study with breast-feeding women, the participants surprisingly appeared to be a little more hesitant when talking with the female moderators than with the male moderators. During debriefing, the participants revealed they felt less comfortable with the female moderators, because they thought they were being judged. Because of the study's topic, male moderators were perceived as more neutral. If you are uncertain about the effect the moderator will have on participants' comfort, test a few different moderators at the beginning of your study.

During all interactions, the moderator needs to exercise extreme care to avoid introducing bias into the participant's responses and actions. Participants should never be made to feel that certain actions or responses are better than others. This can lead to participants choosing certain behaviors or saying certain things just to please the moderator.

Maintain an Objective Viewpoint

In addition to being perceived as objective, the moderator must actually *be* objective. When a participant criticizes an aspect of the survey, do not become defensive or try to justify or explain the decision. You must be open to all feedback: negative or positive.

Remain Calm, Be Flexible

Be prepared for surprises, and handle them smoothly. Despite lots of planning, usability sessions can sometimes go awry. A good moderator is prepared for these occasions and is flexible and adaptable.

For example, if there is a glitch in the web-based survey, the participant may become extremely frustrated or upset. The moderator needs to remain calm and try to salvage as much of the interview as possible. Have printouts of the screens ready to use in emergency cases like this.

Ask probes related to the survey topic to keep the participant engaged while the survey slowly loads, or give up on the survey and conduct an interview about prior experiences using this survey.

> Have printouts of screens to use in an emergency, such as when your survey is slow to load.

Report Accurately

The ideal moderator must be able to report accurately, even when the results are not what the client or stakeholders want to hear. This can be particularly difficult for individuals who are too close to the project. If you had significant input in designing the survey, hearing about an aspect that does not work well may be difficult.

Moderating Guidelines

In addition to probing skills, you need to know how to handle various situations that you may experience during a usability session. We provide tips for handling these situations in neutral, unbiased ways.

Providing Neutral Feedback

Providing feedback to participants is an essential part of any type of qualitative interviewing. Feedback conveys to the participants that the moderator is listening and that their input is valuable. Boren and Ramey (2000) found that, when using the think-aloud approach during usability testing, some participants needed "a continuous yet unobtrusive stream of acknowledgment" to stay on task and continue providing verbalizations.

- For concurrent think aloud, keep feedback as minimal as possible, using short utterances such as "mm hmm" and "uh huh" to convey that you are listening. These utterances have been found to be most effective at encouraging participants to continue to think aloud without interfering with task completion (Goodwin, 1986).

- Other utterances such as "Oh," "Yeah," and "Ok" have been associated with a shift in speakership from the participant to the moderator (Condon, 1986; Drummond & Hopper, 1993). These utterances are commonly used to indicate transitions, such as the moderator asking a question or giving a command. As a result, the participant may stop talking, assuming that you have something to add.

- In general, do not use "Right" and "Good" because the participant might take these to mean they are doing well and "got the answer right." Then when you do not use the same word after another task, participants may think they got the answer "wrong," or that some of their comments are more useful or valuable than others.

- Avoid nonverbal feedback (even when you are in the same room as the participant), such as head nodding, as participants' eyes are on the screen and not on you.

- In verbal probing, which involves more back and forth between the moderator and the participant, you can use more conversational feedback, such as "Thanks," and "That's helpful."

Provide consistent levels of feedback, regardless of whether the participant made positive or negative comments. If participants' critical comments trigger more moderator feedback than other comments, participants may think that the moderator cares only about problems. That also means they are less likely to point out survey aspects they like.

Boren and Ramey (2000) further noted that in thinking aloud, participants often pause in a task until the moderator has acknowledged them. In verbal probing as well, you may need to instruct the participant to continue by saying, e.g., "Please continue" or "What would you do next?" or by asking another probe.

Probing Further
If a participant makes a vague remark, such as "That's confusing," it may be unclear what the participant finds confusing. Rather than making assumptions— the wording? the layout? the task?—you can probe to get more information.

Other scenarios that may require probing further are when a participant gives a short or inadequate response to an open-ended question or when a participant says something you do not understand. Three generic ways of probing further that will not introduce bias are:

- Use echoing, which is simply repeating the participant's last word or phrase back as a question (e.g., "That's confusing?").

- Ask the participant, "Can you tell me more?"

- Ask the participant to provide an example. "You said that you think this feature would be useful. Can you provide an example of when it would be useful?"

Redirecting

Make sure that participants stay focused on their assigned tasks; redirect if necessary. Sometimes the novelty of the tested product distracts them, and they want to explore aspects unrelated to what you are testing. Certainly this is more likely to happen if they are testing a new Apple iPhone than a survey about iPhones.

Alternatively a participant might start providing opinions on the survey questions, survey topic, or survey sponsor—"I don't know why the government needs to do a Census, the NSA already knows who everyone is."—rather than providing commentary solely on what they are thinking and doing to complete the survey.

Here are some tips on how to redirect:

- *Participants go off task.* If time allows, let the participant pursue these tangents, and then try to bring them back to the assigned task. It can be helpful to learn what catches participants' attention or what distracts them, causing them to abandon a task. Allow time to see whether the participant voluntarily returns to the task. If not, you can say, "That was helpful to get your feedback on X. Now, I am interested in how you would [complete original task]? Can you show me what you would do?" Finally, consider whether the original task is appropriate or should be modified for other participants.

- *Participants talk too much.* In general, we do not worry about participants who talk too much during think aloud, as long as they stay on task and talk about what they are doing and thinking related to completing the survey. However, you need to redirect them if they talk so much that the talking interferes with their ability to complete the task or they are talking about something other than the task. For example, if a participant continually takes his gaze off the computer to talk to you, ask you questions, or share stories, you can give the participant gentle reminders, such as "Continue with [the task]," "You can keep going on [the task]," or you can ask, "What would you do next?" Moderating from a separate room from the participant can reduce this type of issue.

  We sometimes encounter the participant who rambles off-topic. This can be distracting and can eat up time in the interview. Look for a natural break in the participant's rambling to intervene. Say "Ok. I would really like to know your thoughts about [the task]," and then ask probes related to the task as necessary to focus the participant. For example, "Tell me what you think about this screen" or "How did you decide to click X?" can get the participant back on track. The goal is to allow them to keep talking, but make them talk about completing the task instead of another topic.

  You can also stop the participant (during that natural break) and say, "For the sake of time, I am going to move us along, but let's come back to that later." Then you can decide if you want to come back to the topic later, even if it is only as you escort them out at the end of the session. Telling them that you will come back to it later makes them feel like the thought is important; reminding them about the time reminds them that they are there to help you.

- *Participants ask for help.* Knowing that they are being observed can make some participants feel uncomfortable. Rather than do something "wrong," some participants tend to ask for help prematurely. Most of the time, these participants can figure out what to do when they are encouraged to try. Reflect the question back to the participant by asking, "What would you do if I weren't here?" or "What do you see as your possible options?" See the next page for what to do if the participant is actually stuck.

- *Participants ask "Is this right?"* Another consequence of some participants' fear of making a mistake is their need for validation from you that what they do is correct. However, you are as interested in how participants recover from an error as in whether they get it right the first time. So say, "We just want to see how you do it" or "What would you do if I was not here?" The participant may discover an alternate route you had not considered. If they press you, remind them that there is no right or wrong answer and that they are helping you to test the survey.

- *Participants blame themselves.* Sometimes participants with low computer literacy—especially older adults—tend to blame themselves when they are unable to complete a task. Remind the participants that you are not testing them and that their feedback is helpful. If necessary, you can convey that message by saying, "A lot of people have had this problem" or "Your feedback helps us learn what we need to improve." If possible, wait until the end of the session to give this type of feedback so you do not interfere with what would naturally occur if you were not present.

When to Try a New Approach
When the participant does not understand the scenario, task, or probe, clarify the wording. In these situations, it is acceptable to use slightly different wording for one participant than for another. While we try to use the same protocol for all interviews to minimize bias, usability test data are still valid, even with slight changes from one case to another. If you try a new approach and the participant still does not understand, move on. If several participants have the same problem, perhaps the tasks are not appropriate, or you are using jargon, so revise the protocol.

Participant Thinks the Task Is Completed, but It Is Not

When a participant mistakenly thinks that they have finished a task (e.g., only partially answers a question or fails to hit the Submit button), the reason for the misperception can be unclear: Was the problem that the participant did not understand the task? Or was it that he or she did not understand how to complete it? Start by verifying that the participant understood the task. To get the participant's interpretation of what happened, say, "Ok. Before we move on, let's stop here for a second. Tell me what you just did." This will help you to understand the participant's interpretation of what happened—if they think they are done, misunderstood the task, or something else.

If the participant understood the task, the fact that he or she thought it was complete when it was not is informative in itself. It is not necessary to let the person know that they did not actually complete the task. If it must be completed for evaluating the next task, simply instruct them in what to do so that you can give them a new task. For example, "I would like to have you complete another task, but first I need for you to enter your information again and hit the Save button." Another option is to take control of the mouse and finish the task, indicating to the participant that you are setting up for the next task.

Participant Is Stuck

Give participants who appear stuck a chance to resolve the situation. There is no set time for how long you allow a participant to be stuck before intervening, but you want to avoid having them become too frustrated. If participants are happily trying different strategies, you can allow them to continue longer than if they are clearly frustrated. You might ask, "If you were completing this survey on your own at [home/work/other], what would you do?" It can be helpful to see if they would break-off, call to ask for help, or keep trying. When you have determined that a participant is truly stuck, acknowledge that the problem is with the survey or product and move on to a new task by saying: "I see that this part of the survey could use some improvement. That's helpful for us to know. Let's try another task now."

If you can move on to another task without having to complete the previous task, then you should do so. If the participant asks how the task should have been completed, say that you will explain that at the end of the session. That prevents biasing future tasks. But in the case of tasks that build off of each other, you may have no choice but to show the participant how it was done. Once all the tasks are complete, you can revisit the issue with the participant to discuss what happened.

Participant Makes a Mistake/Does Something Incorrectly

When a participant errs, just quietly observe, rather than showing surprise or concern. Often it is helpful to know whether participants can identify and correct the mistake. Many participants adopt a "trial and error" approach and will go back and try something different if their first method does not work. This is helpful for determining the "learnability" of a product.

Participant Is Unfamiliar or Has Difficulty With the Hardware

We often assume that participants who have a computer or smartphone are familiar with how to use one. However, this may not be the case. Of course that lack of familiarity becomes more pronounced and problematic when usability tests use your equipment, rather than the participants'. Even participants who are familiar with the testing device or software you will use for testing may get tripped up by different settings. You may need to provide a brief tutorial on how to use the device. Also, be prepared to help if the participant encounters usability issues with the hardware (as opposed to the survey or app being tested).

If the test will be done on a computer, you may also be able to cut down on problems by providing a mouse, a keyboard, and a real monitor with the resolution adjusted for clarity rather than a laptop.

Salvaging a Task

When participants complete a task in a different way than you intended, allow participants to complete the task their way and then ask them to complete the task again using a different path. For example, you may have wanted the participant to manually enter data so you could test certain screens, but she used the upload feature. Or the participant used the "search" feature instead of clicking through the pages or they used Control-F to find a term rather than scrolling and scanning. In these cases, you can say, "Let's go back to the beginning. If you had to complete this task but could not use the [upload feature/search bar], what would you do?"

To avoid affecting behavior and depending on how the original interaction affects what you are trying to test, you may want to wait until all the tasks are completed before you ask for another go. However, sometimes you cannot wait, and you must redirect them. For example, if a participant says she would leave the survey, go to a search engine to find terms, contact someone for help, and figure out how to upload responses, then you may need to say right away: "This is good information, thank you. For the sake of this study, what would you do using this survey/site?"

Moderating Remote Usability Sessions

One of the biggest challenges with moderating usability sessions remotely is ensuring you are able to observe and record participants successfully. Prepare for things to go wrong. Be ready with workarounds in case equipment does not work or is not available. For example, if the participant's audio does not work through the web conference, you can use the telephone to communicate. If you run into technical difficulties, and you must cut the interview short, you can always reschedule.

Setup

Remote sessions work best when participants simply have to click on a link in an email invitation to join the session. However, some web- and video-conferencing systems require participants to download and install something. Some participants may have difficulty, especially if their company's firewall blocks downloads.

In addition to conducting a dry run of your equipment and recording/streaming setup, ask your participant to do the same. Identify the software your participants will need in each case and ask them to install it before the session. If they have trouble installing, ask them to let you know right away so you can troubleshoot or come up with an alternative. Also allow an additional 10−15 minutes extra time at the start of your interview to deal with any technical difficulties on the participant's end (or yours).

Printing

Do not assume that participants have printers to make hard copies of any materials they will need for the test. Ask whether they need materials mailed to them. If so, follow through right away. Ideally hard copy materials should be sent about a week before the test to ensure enough time for them to arrive, but not so much time that they are misplaced.

Lag Time

Another challenge with remote moderating is a delay between what the participant is doing and what you see on your screen. Depending on the connection, the delay may be negligible or it may be as much as a few seconds. When the delay is long, it can make it difficult to determine whether an error has occurred and when to administer probes.

Think-Aloud Commentary

Participants can be more reluctant to providing think-aloud commentary during remote sessions. Without the moderator physically present, participants may feel uncomfortable talking out loud to themselves. To get feedback, expect to prompt participants even more often than you would in person.

Distractions

In a remote setting, participants are more likely to be distracted and interrupted. And because you typically cannot see facial expressions or body language (unless a web camera is used), you may not even realize when a participant is distracted. However a real respondent will likely experience distractions and interruptions, which may provide useful insight into how someone interacts with the survey in the real world.

Lack of Privacy

Mimicking the real-life settings of actual survey respondents, participants sometimes take the usability test in public locations, such as coffee shops or their cubicles. But lack of privacy may make participants more reluctant to think aloud and respond to questions as thoroughly as when alone. To avoid that challenge, ask participants to work in a quiet place.

Who Makes a Good Moderator?

With the proper training and experience, almost anyone can learn to moderate usability tests. Practice and observation are what make a good moderator. Record and critique yourself. Seek out experienced moderators, and ask if you can watch them at work. Also ask them to observe and critique you.

Basic knowledge and experience in the following areas will also help you to become a skilled moderator:

- *Survey design experience*. Gaining experience with survey design will help you identify potential usability issues, determine when to probe further, determine the priority of problems, and identify strategies for resolving problems without introducing additional error. You will begin to pick up on issues even before participants struggle. To improve your knowledge of survey design, start with the Question Appraisal System (http://appliedresearch.cancer.gov/areas/cognitive/qas99.pdf), which identifies common question pitfalls. To read more about designing survey questions, particularly for the web, see Couper (2008) and Dillman, Smyth, and Christian (2014).

- *Qualitative methods*. Experience in qualitative data-collection methods, such as in-depth interviews, cognitive interviews, or focus groups, will help you understand how to ask unbiased probes and provide neutral feedback. These skills are helpful for encouraging participants to verbalize their thoughts in a neutral manner to minimize the potential for bias. Unbiased moderating is a difficult skill to learn and often

> ## DO COGNITIVE TEST INTERVIEWERS MAKE GOOD USABILITY TEST MODERATORS?
>
> In general, cognitive test interviewers tend to make excellent usability test moderators. Cognitive test interviewers have experience with questionnaire design and qualitative methods, which fit well with conducting usability tests of surveys.
>
> One challenge for cognitive interviewers is that they may want to ask many probes. While cognitive testing and usability testing commonly use the think-aloud approach, usability testing typically requires less detailed verbal probing because we rely more on observation. We can learn a lot by simply watching a participant interact with a survey. Probes are typically reserved for getting additional insight about the observed behaviors. In addition, they are often administered retrospectively.
>
> As long as cognitive test interviewers avoid the temptation to fill silences by observing instead of probing, they should do fine.

requires sufficient practice to excel at it. If you lack qualitative interviewing experience, we recommend observing as many usability tests as possible to see how experienced moderators handle certain situations. It can also be helpful to conduct mock interviews with friends, family, or coworkers before moderating with actual participants. That way, if you hear yourself asking an unbalanced question or giving biasing feedback, you can just stop and try again.

- *Subject matter.* You do not need to be a subject-matter expert to be a moderator. But it helps to have a basic understanding of the content. Become familiar with the survey topic and common jargon and acronyms. This familiarity will help you understand participants' comments, and you will be viewed by participants as credible. It will also help you understand when the responses captured do not match the constructs that are being measured.

- *General usability testing methods.* Someone who has usability tested websites or other products should be able to apply those skills to usability testing surveys. Although the testing focus and concerns are different for surveys, the mechanics of moderating are similar.

Notice that web programming is not a required skill, but you should have the survey web programmer observe the sessions to understand how people interact with the product he or she programmed.

COLLECTING AND RECORDING DATA

Note-Takers

With the use of advanced screen and video recording, a note-taker in the room may not be necessary. Either you or someone else on the team can review the screen recordings after the interview, and note observations as needed. When note-takers are used, they likely will need to review the screen recordings to supplement their notes too. Actively watching the screen and taking detailed notes at the same time is difficult, even for experienced note-takers. However, note-takers still can be useful for the following reasons:

- *Back up*, in the case of a technology failure that prevents the session from being recorded.

- *Quick interview write-up.* When note-takers document much of what they observe during the interview, they can move more quickly through the recordings to fill in gaps.

- *Assistance with analysis/moderating.* By observing all of the interviews, note-takers gain familiarity that can help with analyzing the interview. If they become familiar enough, they might even be capable of trading off with the moderator for back-to-back sessions.

- *Capture of tone, sentiment, and other nonverbal cues.* Understanding and capturing the overall feeling or sentiment from the respondent is easier when observing an interview live than a recording. For example, you may wish to record things such as:

  - Are the participants leaning forward or backward?
  - Gesturing?
  - Clenching their hands?
  - Making harsh movements with the mouse?
  - Are they sighing or make other sounds that might not be picked up easily on the microphone?

These nonverbal cues can be harder to discern when notes and observations are made only from audio- and screen recordings.

Despite these benefits, a dedicated note-taker can add expense, especially if travel is required. So for every usability test, consider whether note-taking's benefits compensate for the expense and fit into your budget.

TIPS FOR AGILE TESTING

Often when you are in a hurry (such as when we have too little time between tests and presenting findings), you must be your own note-taker. In these cases, in particular, speed up your process by using highlighters to color-code your notes. For example, when the participant struggles, highlight (or just dot) your notes with the color, maybe pink, that you use to indicate struggles. Then, say, green could show where the participant has a positive reaction and things go well. And maybe yellow can show anything noteworthy that does not fall into the "problem" or "positive" categories. At the end of the sessions, the colors will help you spot anything you need to share with the team.

Noting Observations

During a usability test, document more than just what went wrong. Also document other observations, such as what the participants found engaging, features they liked, or specific pathways they took through the program.

Also document your inferences—your hypotheses and interpretations of the problem (Dumas & Redish, 1999). Noting them along with the problem provides a more complete picture of what occurred and why. For example, even more helpful than knowing that a participant skipped an item in a grid question is knowing why. Maybe the grid was very long, which required the participant to scroll down to see the bottom half, and the participant accidentally missed a row by scrolling too far.

Sometimes we can draw inferences based on our observations alone; other times we rely on the participants' comments to help explain why a problem occurred. So document both relevant comments by participants and your interpretations/thoughts about your observations. It is best to document these in the moment. If you wait until the end of the session to record your thoughts, you might forget something important.

Even if interviews will be recorded, it is still common to make observation notes during the usability sessions. If there are technical difficulties and you are not able to access the recordings, it will be helpful to have noted key observations from the usability test. Furthermore, if you will administer retrospective verbal probing, your notes will serve as a reminder for what to probe on when the participant completes the task. Similarly, for retrospective think aloud, you will use your observation notes to decide what portions of the usability test to focus on and to replay with your participant. However, it is not necessary to document everything that the participant says and does in real time. You can review the recordings as needed to provide a more detailed account of what occurred and why.

For recording observations and participant comments, we typically prepare either a copy of the moderator protocol with extra spaces for notes or a separate observation form, as shown in Chapter 4, Planning for Usability Testing. Encourage observers to note their interpretation of any problem they identified (i.e., why the problem occurred). Make it easy for observers to follow along by giving them copies of the protocol or observation forms. These forms can be either hard copy or electronic, depending on your and observers' preferences.

You may have identified certain performance measures or usability metrics that you would also like to specifically document for each usability session. These may be common things, like whether the task was completed successfully, the number of clicks to complete a task, or the start and end time to complete the task. It may include observations, such as when the participant asked for help, when they made an error and how they recovered, what/when they used a feature, or when they expressed positive or negative feelings and what those were. These will be used during analysis, along with problem lists and participant comments, to evaluate participants' accuracy, efficiency, and satisfaction with the survey.

Fig. 7.2 displays an example of a protocol that was used in a combined cognitive interview and usability testing session. The protocol includes a screenshot of each survey screen (which usually corresponded to one question). Screenshots are helpful for three reasons:

- They ensure that any documented observations are associated with the correct screen.
- They make it easier for observers—who may be less familiar with the survey—to follow along.
- They allow for circling, drawing, or writing on the image to help convey what happened during a usability session.

If it is not feasible to include screenshots (e.g., it would make the protocol too long), it is helpful to include the key text or information from the screen.

The document in Fig. 7.2 also includes instructions about the sort of performance measurements to document during the interview. This information will be used during the analysis to evaluate how well participants were able to complete the task (in this case, providing the location where a person was living or staying on Census day). The protocol also includes scripted usability/cognitive probes that the moderator asked based on how the participant completed the survey. In this example, the probes were used to assess the cause for issues in completing the address.

You can also use dedicated logging software for documenting participant comments, observations, and usability metrics. Such software allows you to define tasks in advance. Depending on the study, the tasks may be survey questions or tasks, such as logging out and resuming a survey. Before the session, you plug in observation codes such as "C—comment," "H—asking for help," "E—user made an error," or "FC—first click." During the session, using just the code followed by a few details about what happened saves time.

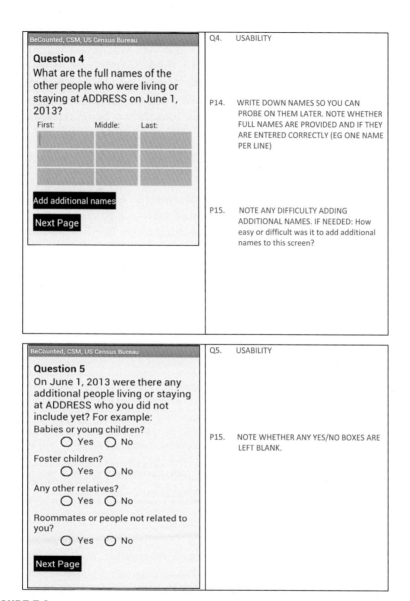

FIGURE 7.2
Example interviewer protocol form that can be used to document participants' verbal comments and usability observations.

Logging software can associate a particular event with the time it occurred in the video, which makes it easy to later find and review the specific clip. For any event (e.g., task start, error), you enter a marker, which becomes associated with a particular timestamp in the video. As you review the recording, you can jump directly to any spot that has a marker. This lets you quickly expand upon your notes. The software also lets you revise your coding scheme retroactively, as needed, if, e.g., you think of additional codes during or after the session that would be helpful. Keep in mind that you (or someone on your team) will later analyze the output. Make sure to provide enough context so your comments make sense when being reviewed days after the session.

Logging software also quickly calculates metrics, such as task-completion times or success rates, for all coded cases.

But despite the benefits of logging software, there is a learning curve. Unless you are doing usability testing frequently or with a large number of participants (over 20), it may be too time consuming to get familiar with the software, learn how to set up the tasks and codes and to log the observations. For infrequent testing, it may be easier to log observations by hand or with word-processing documents or spreadsheets. To be able to find specifics parts of the recordings, you can still include time stamps—simply record the time on the clock.

TIPS FOR AGILE TESTING

Another logging trick is to stream the session to your laptop. Show the live stream along with the logging at the bottom or side of your screen. Record this view. By doing this, you will have the participant's actions along with your notes in one recording, and you can easily fast forward the recording to a specific spot that you see in your notes. Because you are recording notes in real time during the recording, you can fast forward to the part where you are typing those notes. You can see that the notes are being typed, and that is how you know that this is the part of the video where the event of interest is occurring.

Collect only as much information as you will actually use during analysis. For example, how helpful is it to know how many times someone used the glossary or clicked a specific link? Similarly, task-completion times may not matter with concurrent think-aloud or verbal probing. You can always go back later to review the recordings and assess something new, but from the outset, it is best to identify only what you need and record only those things.

A sample output of logged observations is shown in Table 7.1. In this example, observations were logged, time-stamped, and coded in real time. The moderator added the detailed descriptions of the code only after reviewing the recording.

Date/Time	Code	Code Name	Description
Table 7.1 Example of a List of Coded Observations From a Usability Session			
Task 1. Provided updated administrative data on employee personnel			
8/5/2016 10:10	ST	Start task	
8/5/2016 10:12	E	User error	Participant wanted to change his answer to a previous question, but there was no previous button. He used his browser's back button and received an error
8/5/2016 10:21	F	Used feature	Participant used the "calculate total" button to sum the rows in the table. However, he had already manually calculated the sum before he saw the button
8/5/2016 10:28	S	Suggestion	Participant suggested that for the really long grid question, the header rows be repeated on the bottom of the grid so that he would not have to keep scrolling up and down
8/5/2016 10:30	ET	End task	
8/5/2016 10:30	TF	Task successful	Participant had some trouble but was able to complete the task successfully
Task 2. Print a copy of survey responses			
8/5/2016 10:30	ST	Start task	
8/5/2016 10:30	FC	First click	Participant clicked on "Print Survey" immediately
8/5/2016 10:31	ET	End task	
8/5/2016 10:31	TS	Task successful	Participant was able to complete the task easily

GUIDELINES FOR OBSERVERS

Observers in a Different Room

When possible, observers should be in a different room from the participant and moderator, particularly if there will be multiple observers. It can be intimidating for a participant to have a number of people in the room watching and observing them. When observers are in a separate room or observing remotely, it is easier for the participant to forget they are there, and they interact with the survey in a more natural way. The observers can view the participant and the participant's screen, but they can also discuss what they are seeing with each other without disrupting you or the participant.

We recommended having another team member available in the observation room to assist the observers as needed. This team member can assist with the following:

- Providing any necessary background on the project, the usability test, or the participant

- Distributing any materials, such as protocols or observation forms to the observers
- Addressing any questions observers have about the survey, the test, or what has occurred
- Trying to minimize side discussions to ensure that observers watch the entire session. Observers can easily get side-tracked trying to solve the first issue and miss the rest of the session.

You can email guidelines to your observers ahead of time to remind them of their roles and your expectations. For example, some common guidelines include:

- All observers should try to arrive 10 minutes before the session starts.
- When you arrive at a facility where observers and participants use the same entrance, say that you are observing the sessions being conducted by [your moderator's name]. Do not mention your company name to the receptionist or host, if possible.
- In the backroom, please try to keep sideline discussions to a minimum. There will be time either during moderator visits to the backroom or after the session ends to ask questions and share feedback.
- Remember that loud chatter, laughter, or other noise can be heard through one-way glass and are quite distracting to participants. Please be mindful of the noise level in the backroom while participants are in session.
- Take notes throughout the session to record any memorable moments and any questions or feedback you have.

Observers in the Same Room

There may be times when observers cannot be in a separate room such as when you are traveling to participants' homes or offices to conduct interviews. One or two in-room observers are generally not problematic as long as observers follow a few guidelines to avoid disruption or bias:

- *Stay for the entirety of the interview.* Observers must arrive before the session starts and stay for the entire time. Arriving late or leaving early can be disruptive to the interview. Furthermore, leaving early may make the participant think that they were not interesting.
- *Remain silent.* When an observer interjects either to make a comment such as "That's interesting" or to ask the participant questions, the participant may start directing comments to the observer instead of the moderator. Tell observers in advance that if they have questions for

the participant, they should write them down. Plan time at the end of the session (or after each task) to ask whether they have any questions for the participants. Also instruct observers to refrain from talking to each other.

- *Remain neutral.* Also instruct in-room observers to refrain from any reaction, regardless of what the participant does. Not only does this apply to sounds, such as laughing, sighing, or groaning. If observers will be visible to the participant, they should also keep their facial expressions and body language neutral.

Spend some time before the sessions to ensure that all observers are clear on their roles and expectations. Sometimes senior-level stakeholders may think it is ok to chime in and start asking questions, but you need to make it clear that this is not the purpose of their observation. They are there to observe the research to understand how users interact with the product. Provide guidelines ahead of time.

Remote Observation

While it is great to have in-person observers, it is not always feasible or affordable, especially when it requires traveling. With today's technology, it is increasingly easier to facilitate observation from any location. Screen sharing and web conferencing are great options for allowing observers to watch usability sessions live from remote locations (St. Onge, Alvarado, & Stettler, 2014). However, it is important that observers remain muted throughout the interview. Depending on your setup, you may be able to mute observers from your end or they may have to mute themselves on their end. If the conferencing system makes alerts or beeps when members join or drop off, observers should be instructed to join on time and stay online for the entire session to minimize disruptions to the participant.

In addition to live screen sharing or web conferencing, you can make recordings of the usability sessions available for team members to review at their convenience. You can even provide time stamps or abbreviated recordings to highlight specific things that you want stakeholders to see.

Observer Responsibilities

Regardless of whether observers are in the room with the participant, in an observation room or observing remotely, give them materials such as a protocol guide or observation form so they can follow along with the interview. Even if you do not have a specific Observation Form, like the examples in Chapter 4, Planning for Usability Testing, you can provide the moderator's guide with extra spacing to take notes. Instruct observers to write down any notes or observations they have. When observers take notes on the protocol guides and Observation Forms, their commentary is easier to follow because it is clear what screen or question the comment or observation applies to.

DEBRIEFING WITH THE TEAM

After each round of testing, schedule a debriefing meeting with the moderators, note-takers, and any observers. (Note that this is different from the *debriefing interview* conducted with participants.) If you are conducting a lot of usability tests (i.e., more than nine) for one survey, avoid bias toward the most recent tests by scheduling periodic debriefings.

Debriefings should provide a head start on analysis and revision. Collectively, you can diagnose the biggest observed problems and start brainstorming possible solutions. It is unlikely that you will leave the debriefing with a full list of problems and solutions. It is likely that you will need to conduct a close review of the recordings as well, which will identify subtler usability issues that may be just as important as the glaring ones. You will probably need additional time to think through any potential solutions to make sure they are (1) feasible and (2) are not likely to introduce any new problems.

References

Boren, T., & Ramey, J. (2000). Thinking aloud: Reconciling theory and practice. *IEEE Transactions on Professional Communication, 43*(3), 261–278.

Condon, S. (1986). The discourse functions of OK. *Semiotica, 60*(1/2), 73–101.

Couper, M. P. (2008). *Designing effective web surveys.* New York, NY: Cambridge University Press.

Dillman, D. A., Smyth, J. D., & Christian, L. M. (2014). *Internet, phone, mail and mixed-mode surveys: The tailored design method* (4th ed.). Hoboken, NJ: Wiley.

Drummond, K., & Hopper, R. (1993). Back channels revisited: Acknowledgement tokens and speakership incipiency. *Research on Language and Social Interaction, 26*(2), 157–177.

Dumas, J., & Redish, J. (1999). *A practical guide to usability testing.* Portland, OR: Intellect Books.

Goodwin, C. (1986). Between and within: Alternative sequential treatments of continuers and assessments. *Human Studies, 9,* 205–217.

St. Onge, H., Alvarado, H., & Stettler, K. (2014). Using WebEx for usability testing: Considerations for establishment surveys. In *Paper presented at the 2014 Federal computer-assisted survey information collection, Washington, DC.*

CHAPTER 8

Analyzing and Reporting Results

You watched participants as they completed the survey, and you observed and recorded what they did. Now, you need to analyze what you saw, determine what it means for the survey, and then decide how to address the problems. Usability testing does not end with analysis though. You will make changes, and then test the survey again to determine whether the changes addressed the usability issues and whether there are additional problems. Usability testing is an iterative process of zeroing in on the design that will work the best for survey respondents.

Determining what to revise works best after a thorough review and analysis. Avoid the temptation to begin immediately "fixing" problems (beyond typos and program glitches) based on your immediate impressions. Although it is helpful to start thinking about solutions early, it can be advantageous to wait to revise any specific problem until you have summarized all of the findings. Otherwise, you may jump to erroneous conclusions based on what happened in just one interview.

This chapter provides guidance for a measured analysis approach, plus guidelines for addressing usability issues and reporting findings.

DETAILED ANALYSIS APPROACH

In this section, we first present an idealized way of analyzing the results of usability testing. The purpose of this section is to guide you through the full analysis process in a step-by-step fashion. We recommend using this full analysis approach the first few times you analyze usability data or when analyzing the results from a large number of usability tests. We discuss how many of these steps can be simplified when you are analyzing only a handful of cases. As you become more familiar with conducting and analyzing usability tests, you will be able to decide what parts of the analysis can be simplified, conducted in parallel or skipped altogether to save time.

187

Usability Testing for Survey Research. DOI: http://dx.doi.org/10.1016/B978-0-12-803656-3.00008-7

The best way to analyze usability data is to use a technique called *triangulation* (Dumas & Redish, 1999), which combines data from multiple sources (e.g., self-reported, observational, and eye tracking) to identify the usability issues. If instead you rely on first impressions or only part of the available data, you could address only a symptom of the problem instead of the problem itself. Or you could miss certain problems altogether.

Triangulation reveals not just the problem, but also why it was a problem and how big of an impact it could have on the survey. For example, observation might show us what was problematic (e.g., participants did not click on an essential button). We might infer that the button label "advanced solutions" was not clear. However, combining participant comments with our observations might reveal that participants' mental models did not match the survey design (e.g., "I was expecting advanced options to be down here, below the table, and not above the table"). Finally, eye tracking might show that the participant never looked at the area above the table. The fact that participants mentioned "advanced options" but did not click on the "advanced solutions" button indicates a potential problem with the button's location.

> The best way to analyze data is to use a technique called triangulation—it reveals not just the problem, but why it was a problem and how big of an impact it could have.

Quantitative usability metrics (which can be self-reported, observational, or implicit) can provide additional information, e.g., showing how severe a problem was (e.g., although you expected the task to take about 1 minute to complete, it took some participants up to 6 minutes). When we take all the data together, we learn what the true problem is (the location of the button) and potentially how to fix it (move it to a more salient place).

To begin analyzing the data (identify the key problems and diagnose their cause), use a three-step process: (1) compile, (2) summarize, and (3) interpret.

Compiling Data

Below are the main types of data that are typically produced from usability sessions.

- Self-reported
  - Background data from screener or pretest questionnaire
  - Verbalizations: Think-aloud comments, verbal-probe responses, and debriefing interview
  - Satisfaction and difficulty ratings from questionnaires

- Observational
    - Usability metrics, such as completion times, errors, and other performance measures
    - Click patterns
    - Nonverbal observations, such as facial expressions and finger tapping
- Implicit:
    - Eye-tracking data

Also, gather any information that was collected prior to the usability tests such as a literature review, expert review, focus-group data, or cognitive interviews results. Although you do not analyze these as part of the study data, review them for any useful context, background, or benchmarks.

Qualitative Self-Report and Observation Data

Prepare an interview summary or "summary sheet" of both observational and self-reported data collected (e.g., think-aloud commentary, moderator debriefing, responses to probes, click/selection patterns, participant behavior, usability issues). If you have more than five participants, create a separate summary sheet for each participant. For fewer, it might suffice to combine the tests on one sheet.

The summary should capture the participants' main comments and actions during the interview. Although it is primarily qualitative, it can also include key performance measures such as whether the task was successful or any errors encountered. Interview summaries facilitate a triangulated approach: rather than looking at one document for observations, another one for participant comments, and a third for performance metrics, the necessary information is in one place.

If you are not using usability software, create a template for the interview summary, to ensure consistent interview reports. Design the template to correspond to your testing focus and concerns, as well as the usability metrics you plan to capture. For example, you might tailor the template around individual survey questions or on tasks, especially those tasks that span multiple survey questions or screens. If you used usability software to document participant comments, observations, or performance measures, you can typically output a file that includes this information and that will be your interview summary.

To complete the summaries, start with notes or observations you or your team made during the interview and then review the recordings to fill in gaps or add detail about what happened or why you think a problem occurred. When documenting the participant's action in the summary, you may want to provide a detailed description of everything that the participant looked at and clicked on even when no usability issues occurred. Or, you may only be interested in noting problems or errors that the participant had. Similarly, you may include participants' verbatim comments from think aloud and from verbal probes, or you may summarize participant comments.

The level of detail included in your summary depends on the level of analysis you plan to do. The analysis level is often determined by the development stage. For testing conducted late in the cycle, you may be interested only in findings that verify whether changes led to improvements. For early-stage testing or testing with multiple subgroups of participants, you need a more thorough analysis to evaluate the overall design and identify differences by subgroup.

The level of detail may also depend on who will be analyzing the results. If only one person moderates and analyzes all of the interviews, the moderator may record only high-level observations and paraphrase participants' comments in a simplified summary. If multiple people are conducting the usability sessions or the analyst is not the moderator, the summary needs more detail. This ensures that inferences and conclusions are drawn consistently across all interviews.

Deciding what to include or omit in the summary and how to paraphrase comments is a form of analysis in itself. It is subjective. The amount of detail might also depend on your experience with analyzing usability data. If you have less experience, you might prefer the extra processing time that is afforded by recording verbatim comments and detailed observations in the summary sheets, and then summarizing this information later. Others may feel confident summarizing as they prepare the summaries, noting only key findings. If you do this, you should still include some verbatim remarks, which can be useful in reporting findings to let stakeholders "hear" what participants said.

> Include some verbatim remarks in your summary, which can be useful in reporting findings to let stakeholders "hear" what participants said.

When you can, prepare each interview summary immediately after the interview while the case is still fresh in your mind. Doing so will make it easier to provide inferences or hypotheses about what caused a usability issue and how best to address it.

Fig. 8.1 shows a (redacted) interview summary from a cognitive/usability test of the 2020 Census Household form. The test was administered on smartphones. Eight interviewers conducted 67 usability tests in a single round.

CaseID 4-digit number:	XXXX
Instrument (BCA, HHD3, NRFU3, HHD4, NRFU4, GQ):	HHD3
Mode (Tablet, Smartphone):	Smartphone
Interviewer initials:	EMG
Interview length (in minutes):	55
Location (NC, DC, Chicago, San Diego):	NC
Interview date (mm/dd/yyyy):	1/9/2013
Date of summary (mm/dd/yyyy):	1/16/2013
Q1. Please take a look at this calendar. On October 1, 2012 were you living or staying at [ADDRESS]?	Yes
U1. Usability	[None.]
P1. What does "living or staying" mean as it was used in this question?	Who has a residence here or who might just be staying here.
Q2. What is your full name?	
P14. NOTE WHETHER FULL NAME IS PROVIDED AND IF IT IS ENTERED CORRECTLY.	[Yes. R provided his full name: one first name, two middle names, and last name. As R was filling out the form he said, "It's (FIRSTNAME) (MIDDLENAME1) (MIDDLENAME2) (LASTNAME), but I'll just do (FIRSTNAME) (MIDDLE INITIAL 1) (LASTNAME)." He then said, "Well, I'll put them both [middle names] actually." He said he normally just provides his first name and the initial of his first middle name, but that his driver's license and Social Security card have both middle names spelled out. He said it's a long name to spell out all the time. I asked why he decided to include both middle names instead of the initial of his first middle name for this survey. "Because the Census is official."]
Q2a. Was there anyone else living or sleeping at 1234 Home Address on October 1, 2012?	Yes
U2a. Usability	[None.]
P15. What does "living or sleeping" mean to you as it is used in this question? How does that compare to "living or staying?"	It means the same as Question 1. [R went on to explain that some of the individuals in the house are single and may have people who stay the night, but he would not count them. I asked how long someone would have to be living or staying there for him to include. He did not really understand the intention of the probe and said that he would not let just anyone move in.]
Q2F. What are the full names of the other people who were living or sleeping at 1234 Home Address on October 1, 2012? Anyone else?	[R listed his sister (Person 2), his brother-in-law (Person 3), a roommate (Person 4).]
U2F. Usability	[R commented that the question only had space for three names. Because the keyboard was up, he did not see the second question:"Anyone else?" He asked me what he should do. I told him to do what he would do if I were not here. He said that he was just going to list the adults, so he excluded his nephew. When he was done listing the three adults, he hit "done," which removed the keyboard. He then immediately hit the Next button without noticing the "Anyone else?" question.]

FIGURE 8.1

An example of an interview summary for a usability test case shows the survey question text and response, verbal probes and responses, and usability issues the participant experienced.

P16. How did you determine who was living or sleeping here? [Was there anyone you were unsure about including? IF YES: Can you tell me more about that?]	The owners of the home. [R explained that his sister and brother-in-law own the home and they live there with their son (R's nephew). The brother-in-law also has a friend who lives in the loft. The roommate shares the kitchen and living space with everyone else.]
P17. NOTE WHETHER FULL NAME IS PROVIDED AND IF IT IS ENTERED CORRECTLY (E.G. ONE NAME PER LINE).	[For Persons 2-4, R just listed a first name and a last name. During follow-up, I asked about middle names. He said that he just didn't provide them. He then went on to explain that his nephew is actually a junior and has the same full name as his brother-in-law. His brother-in-law goes by his middle name instead of his first name. And so R listed the brother-in-law as MIDDLENAME LASTNAME on the census. R did not include "junior" or "senior" for the nephew or the brother-in-law. R did not know what was on the brother-in-law's license but said that all of his mail is addressed to MIDDLENAME. It wasn't until I probed on what people's middle names were that he even thought about the fact that his brother-in-law did not go by his legal name.]
Q3. Were there any additional people living or staying at 1234 Home Address on October 1, 2012 who you did not include yet? For example: babies, foster children, other relatives or people not related to you?	No
U3. Usability	[None.]
Q4. Was there anyone else staying here on October 1st, 2012 who had no permanent place to live?	Yes
U4. Usability	NA
P22. What does "no permanent place to live" mean as it is used in this question? What were you thinking of?	Somebody staying on the couch, like [Person 4].
Q4F. What are the full names of the people who had no permanent place to live?	NA
U4F. Usability	[R listed Person 4, the roommate, because he had no permanent place of his own and was staying with his brother-in-law until he could find his own place. However, when R entered Person 4's name, he provided the person's nickname and not his full first name. As a result, the survey treated him like he was an additional household member (Person 5), instead of recognizing that he was already listed as Person 4. So he received the follow-up questions for this person twice, which he found very confusing.]
P23. FOR ANY PEOPLE ADDED, PROBE TO UNDERSTAND THEIR RELATIONSHIP TO THE PARTICIPANT AND HOW FREQUENTLY THEY LIVE/STAY THERE.	[Person 4 has been living there for the past 3 months because his wife kicked him out of their house, and he had nowhere else to stay.]
P24. NOTE WHETHER FULL NAME IS PROVIDED AND IF IT IS ENTERED CORRECTLY (E.G. ONE NAME PER LINE)	[R did not list his full first name; he provided a nickname that has one fewer letter than his full first name.]

FIGURE 8.1

(Continued)

The large number of participants was needed to test several survey instruments with slight variations on several subpopulations (e.g., people experiencing homelessness, people with second homes, and people who moved recently) in various locations across the country.

Detailed templates and training in their use allowed the interviewers to summarize the sessions consistently. For example, moderators were instructed to put their own commentary in brackets to distinguish it from verbatim participant remarks. Moderators also learned to append notes they received from observers after the sessions.

The summary form contains five key components that make it particularly useful during analysis:

- *Header (dark gray boxes)*: The header contains basic information such as the case ID, the tested survey version, and the interviewer's initials. It can also include any important background information captured in a screener or pretest questionnaire. Including this information in the summary can help to determine patterns—e.g., perhaps a certain usability issue occurs only with respondents who have children.

- *Survey question text and responses (in bold)*: Including the survey question and the participant's answer saves time and effort during analysis; you do not have to constantly flip back and forth between the write-up and the survey.

- *Usability issues (light gray boxes)*: In this protocol, we only noted usability problems. Depending on the goals of your study, in addition to usability problems, you may also find it useful to capture general information about participants' behavior, such as what they clicked and where they navigated.

- *Probes/Think aloud (white boxes, sentence-case type)*: Because this was a combined cognitive/usability test, we asked a number of scripted, concurrent verbal probes such as, "What does 'living or staying' mean, as it was used in this question?" A usability-only study is likely to contain fewer scripted probes. In that case, you could include a row to capture the participant's think-aloud comments for each question or survey screen.

- *Metrics (white boxes, capitalized type)*: We also included metrics, such as whether a full and complete name was provided, which we can sort or tally during analysis. If you use logging software or Excel to code key metrics, you can either append them to the summary or pull them in separately.

If this study had collected other quantitative data (e.g., satisfaction ratings, task completion times), the template could have included a row for this information for each task or question. Although it is not imperative to include all quantitative data in the summaries, it makes it easier to cross reference the quantitative data with the qualitative data later. However, for simpler projects with less data, it is often sufficient to include only usability observations and participant comments in the interview summary.

The interview summary in Fig. 8.1 was prepared using a template created in Word. The right-hand column of the summary for each participant was then cut and pasted into a spreadsheet so that each participant was a different column as shown in Fig. 8.2. The spreadsheet format permits seeing comments or observations about a specific item for all participants, which facilitates analysis. In this example, we could sort participants based by response to the survey question and mode of device (e.g., tablet vs smartphone).

If you prefer to use qualitative analysis programs to analyze data, these templates can be formatted so that they can be read into this software as well.

Quantitative Self-Report and Observation Data

Although usability data are primarily qualitative, you will likely have collected some self-report and observation data that is quantitative as well. Look at both types of data to understand the whole picture. Presenting and analyzing quantitative data from a small sample can be problematic—presenting them as statistics can be misleading because findings may not be generalizable across the population. The fact that 20% of participants had a specific problem does not mean that 20% of all respondents will have it. That percentage could be much higher or lower. But even with small samples, quantitative data can be useful for understanding usability concerns, as long as the point is not to make inferences about the general population. The goal here is to understand your usability test participants.

> Presenting and analyzing quantitative data from a small sample can be problematic—presenting them as statistics can be misleading because findings may not be generalizable across the population.

Next, we demonstrate how to tabulate quantitative data to facilitate cross referencing with qualitative or other types of data. Table 8.1 shows an example of task-completion times presented in spreadsheet form.

We have calculated the average completion time by task and by participant. For example, it is useful to report that four out of five participants completed Task 1 in 2 minutes or less, whereas one participant took 7.45 minutes to complete the task. (Knowing the average completion time—2.52 minutes—for the task is not so useful.) These values provide more insight when

CaseID 4-digit number:	0001	0002	0003	0004	0005
Instrument (BCA, HHD3, NRFU3, HHD4, NRFU4, GQ):	HHD3	HHD3	NRFU3	NRFU3	NRFU3
Mode (Tablet, Smartphone):	Smartphone	Smartphone	Tablet	Smartphone	Tablet
Interviewer initials:	EMG	DSC	TRK	DSC	BRS
Interview length (in minutes):	55	45	75	54	50
Location (NC, Chicago, San Diego, DC):	NC	Chicago	Chicago	Chicago	San Diego
Interview date (mm/dd/yyyy):	01/9/2013	10/31/2012	12/12/2012	11/16/2012	12/13/2012
Date of summary (mm/dd/yyyy):	01/16/2013	11/5/2012	12/13/2012	11/22/2018	12/21/2012
Q1. Please take a look at this calendar. On October 1, 2012 were you living or staying at	**No**	**No**	**No**	**No**	**No**
U1. Usability	[None.]	[None.]	[R said that having the calendar on the screen is not useful here because it was too small.]	[None.]	[None.]
P1. What does "living or staying" mean as it was used in this question?	Who has a residence here or who might just be staying here.	It means being present at that address, sleeping there, and staying there. Just physical presence.	Either visiting or living there permanently.	[R said your mailing address— "where you eat at most of the time."]	[Living means] the homeowner and or resident. And staying, for me, would be a guest.

FIGURE 8.2

Using an interview-summary template formatted in Word, you can cut and paste each case into a spreadsheet or chart to facilitate analysis.

Table 8.1 Example Task Completion Times by Participant

Task	Participant						Average
	1	**2**	**3**	**4**	**5**	**6**	
Task 1	1.23	1.58	1.92	7.45	2.00	.98	2.52
Task 2	3.12	4.81	6.12	5.21	3.89	5.00	4.69
Task 3	12.10	8.94	10.11	15.12	7.45	8.93	10.44
Task 4	5.01	6.12	5.09	5.98	5.55	6.11	5.64
Total	21.46	21.45	23.24	33.76	18.9	21.02	
Average efficiency	5.37	5.36	5.81	8.44	4.73	5.26	

compared with qualitative data. We can then use other data to evaluate why it took Participant 4 so much longer to complete the task than the other participants. For example, was the participant distracted? Did he have difficulty? If so, what difficulties did he have? We might also learn that Participants 4 and 5 experienced the same usability issue, but only Participant 5 was able to quickly resolve the issue and complete the task. This indicates two issues—the problem encountered as well as difficulty in overcoming it. In this case, even if we are not able to make changes that prevent respondents from making the error, we can help them to recover from and resolve it.

Similarly, descriptive data for task-difficulty ratings also are not terribly meaningful without additional information. Table 8.2 shows that all tasks have a similar *average* difficulty rating. Yet, Task 1 shows that some participants rated Task 1 as very difficult and some rated it as less difficult. Again, we will want to analyze why Participants 4 and 5 found the task less difficult than other participants found it. Did the other participants have difficulty that they could not overcome, and did Participants 4 and 5 overcome similar difficulties? Combining this information with the efficiency data, we see that Participant 4 rated the task as less difficult but took the longest of all participants to complete the task.

Table 8.2 Example Task Difficulty Ratings by Participant (1 = Not Difficult At All, 7 = Very Difficult)

Task	Participant						Average
	1	**2**	**3**	**4**	**5**	**6**	
Task 1	7	7	7	3	4	7	5.83
Task 2	7	6	6	7	6	5	6.17
Task 3	6	6	6	5	6	6	5.83
Task 4	7	6	7	6	6	4	6.00
Average difficulty rating	6.75	6.25	6.50	5.25	5.50	5.50	

In this case, your next move would be to analyze what Participant 4 said during the task and debriefing. For example, you might discover that he actually had lots of difficulty and could not complete the task. But, you also learn, he blamed himself for the issues, which is why he rated the task as less difficult. His rating just reflected his perception of his skills, not usability. By evaluating all of the data, you will be able to identify the usability issues that people encountered.

Quantitative data are also commonly used to determine whether improvements were made between rounds of testing. It may be that in the first round of testing, errors occurred only for respondents in a specific situation, e.g., participants with really large households. The second round may have shown fewer errors only because fewer participants with large households were included in that round. You would need to delve into the qualitative data to determine whether the problems were resolved for those specific participants in the second round (without making the survey more difficult for other participants).

For example, we might check whether metrics such as task-completion times and difficulty ratings are different among different versions. Table 8.3 displays accuracy and satisfaction for novice participants across four rounds of testing (Romano Bergstrom, Olmsted-Hawala, Chen, & Murphy, 2011). In this study, accuracy and satisfaction increased from Round 1 through 3 but decreased in Round 4. Triangulating the data all together—quantitative, observational data, and verbalizations—enabled us to identify the usability issues.

Table 8.3 Quantitative Data: Mean Accuracy and Satisfaction for Novice Participants by Round

	Round 1	Round 2	Round 3	Round 4
Accuracy (%)	40	55	74	52
Satisfaction	4.79	5.49	6.51	5.20

Implicit Data

The most common form of implicit data collected during a usability test is eye tracking. It is useful to examine eye-tracking data along with qualitative and quantitative data to gain additional insights about how people interact with surveys. For example, it is common for participants to say they saw or read the instructions, when eye-tracking data show otherwise (Romano Bergstrom & Strohl, 2013).

What a participant looks at, how long he looks at it, and the movement between areas can be used to obtain a number of measurements that are useful for interpreting usability. Table 8.4 presents some of the key measurements and their interpretations (Olmsted-Hawala, Holland, & Quach, 2014).

Table 8.4 Types of Data Eye Tracking Provides

Eye Tracking Measure	Interpretation
Total Fixation Duration or Length: How long participants spent looking at an AOI (area of—moderator—interest) in total	▪ Longer fixations may indicate either engagement or confusion with AOI
Time Elapsed to First Look: How long it took participants to first fixate an AOI	▪ Longer times may indicate that the AOI is not visually obvious
Time to First Mouse Click: How long it took participants to click after first fixating the clicking spot	▪ If they took a longer time from first fixating to making the click, the link label was not clear or obvious, or there were other distractors
Initial Look: Where participants looked during an initial interaction with a question or screen	▪ What stimuli attracted attention at all ▪ What participants are first attracted to
Number of Fixations to First Click: Number of times participants looked at an AOI before clicking on it	▪ Confusion over the purpose of an AOI ▪ Participant wants to make sure it is the correct link for the task
Movement: Whether and how often participants had to recheck the content they were seeking	▪ Difficulty understanding content ▪ Participants' attraction to the location

Adapted from Olmsted-Hawala, E., Holland, T., & Quach, T. (2014). Usability testing. In J. Romano Bergstrom, & A. Schall (Eds.) Eye tracking in user experience design. Waltham, MA: Morgan Kaufman.

Eye tracking yields detailed quantitative data such as x and y coordinates of eye fixations, fixation counts, and duration in tabular or graphic form. You can export this data by task, as well as by time, such as in the first 10 seconds of interaction. As quantitative eye-tracking data is hard to understand, it is beneficial to create graphics such as heat maps, gaze opacity maps, and gaze plots, to help stakeholders visualize and interpret the quantitative data. Graphics alone, however, do not tell the complete story, and it is often necessary to pair graphics with the quantitative data.

> It is common for participants to say they saw or read the instructions, when eye-tracking data show otherwise.

Fig. 8.3 shows mean fixation eye-tracking data for different age groups during one task (Romano Bergstrom, Olmsted-Hawala, & Bergstrom, 2016). The heat maps and gaze-opacity maps showed that older adults looked only at elements in the center; they did not even look at the left navigation when approaching this site. Younger and middle age adults tended to use elements from the middle as well as the left navigation. This helped to explain older adults' difficulty completing tasks that required the navigation menu.

Table 8.5 displays the quantitative data associated with the visuals. It shows that the difference in the mean fixations of older vs younger adults emerged

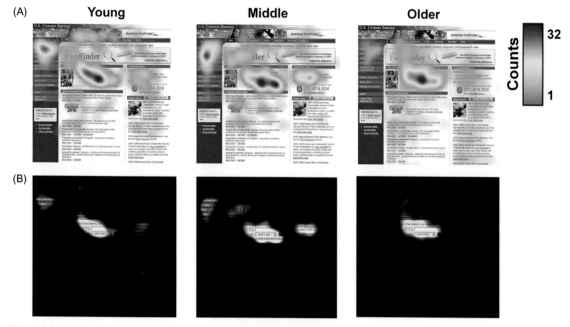

FIGURE 8.3

Mean fixation-count (A) heat maps and (B) gaze-opacity maps for younger (left), middle-aged (center), and older (right) adults. Common areas of attention are in the center of the screen. Differences show up in the left navigation. *Reproduced with permission from Romano Bergstrom, J. C., Olmsted-Hawala, E. L., & Bergstrom, H. C. (2016). Older adults fail to see the periphery during website navigation. Universal Access in the Information Society, 15(2), 261—270.*

Table 8.5 Mean Fixations During the Task and First 10 Seconds of Interaction

	Age Group		
	Young	Middle	Older
Mean fixations during the task			
Left navigation[a]	8.7	6.4	2.8
Top banner[a]	4.4	0.9	1.4
Top navigation[b]	2.4	0.8	1.2
Whole screen[b]	52.6	35.1	43.0
Mean fixations during first 10 s			
Left navigation[a]	4.6	5.2	2.4
Top banner[a]	2.9	1.0	1.2
Top navigation[a]	1.1	0.4	0.5
Whole screen[b]	24.0	20.0	21.0

[a]Significant difference, young vs older; $p \leq .05$.
[b]No significant group differences.
Romano Bergstrom, J. C., Olmsted-Hawala, E. L., & Bergstrom, H. C. (2016). Older adults fail to see the periphery during website navigation. Universal Access in the Information Society, 15(2), 261—270.

in the first 10 seconds of interaction (2.4 vs 4.6, respectively). Examining initial interaction teaches us how people approach products. We can identify any distracting elements, or in this case, any subgroup differences in interaction. In this case, we identified that older adults looked at the center of the screen when first interacting with the website. The visuals showed the overall pattern, and the quantitative data showed when this difference emerged. The findings provided insight into how older adults approached the website and why they had issues completing some tasks (that required the left navigation).

Eye-tracking data is also useful to understand what parts of instructions people actually read. Gaze plots can be used to visualize eye-tracking data at the individual level, which shows where the participants looked, the order in which they looked at various elements, and the duration. Fig. 8.4 (Jarrett & Romano Bergstrom, 2014) shows that the participant scanned the instructions at the top of the page. There she modeled the F-shaped pattern that is common for

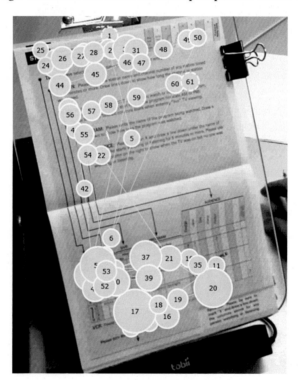

FIGURE 8.4

Gaze plot from one participant. The F-shaped pattern at the top of the page is typical for large blocks of text. It differs from the pattern on the question-and-answer spaces at the bottom of the page.
Reproduced with permission from Jarrett, C., & Romano Bergstrom, J. C. (2014). Forms and surveys. In J. Romano Bergstrom, & A. Schall (Eds.), Eye tracking in user experience design. San Francisco, CA: Morgan Kaufmann.

dense text, where people only scan text. Then the participant more thoroughly read the question-and-answer part at the bottom of the page. We can use this data to improve the design of survey instructions and to evaluate different designs. For example, if certain information is not typically read, but participants are able to complete the survey without difficulty, we can exclude that information. On the contrary, we may need to move more critical instructions to make it more likely they are read.

Summarizing the Data

Creating an Organizational Framework/Outline

The next step after compiling the data is to read through it at least once. This process should reveal some of the themes and patterns and enable you to draft an initial organizational framework or outline. It is useful to organize findings into two main categories: local (related to a specific task or question) and global (applying across tasks and questions) (Dumas & Redish, 1999).

As an example of global findings, if participants tended to have usability issues with any grid question (e.g., accidentally skipping a row or not being able to see the headers for items at the bottom of the grid), it makes sense to analyze these findings across all grid questions. Add a category for grid questions to your framework and summarize the type of usability issues found for that question format. Conducting and observing the sessions may give you a sense of some useful global categories. You will identify more global findings as you get more deeply into the analysis.

Categorizing findings as local versus global will be helpful for determining which issues are a priority. A global finding that affects 20 questions may be a bigger priority to fix than a finding that affects just a single question.

> It is useful to organize findings into two main categories: local (related to a specific task or question) and global (applying across tasks and questions).

Create a flexible framework so you can revise the organization as analysis dictates. Depending on the unfolding data, you may need to remove categories, collapse categories, or add categories. For example, a particular survey question might benefit from subcategories that allow you to summarize each component separately. Alternately, a given question may have multiple types of issues, and you may need to give them more attention in the analysis.

For each local or global finding, analyze differences by participant characteristics or demographics. Differences that are present across a variety of questions could become another global category, such as "Novice vs Experienced Users."

When the mobile version of your survey is substantially different from the desktop or laptop version of the survey, analyze the usability results separately by mode. At the very least, note any key usability differences by mode (e.g., mobile vs desktop/laptop) within each category.

We show an example of organizational framework for analysis. These headings can be used in the findings section of your final report or memo. We find that if observations are sorted by local and global issues, there is usually no need for more complex coding schemes.

Local issues

- Logging in
- Question 1
- Question 2
  - Entering names
  - Adding additional rows
- Question 3
- . . .
- Question 12

Global issues

- Accessing definitions
- Grid questions (Questions 4, 7, and 8)
- Resolving error and warning messages
- New versus experienced users

Reducing Data

You will make it easier to interpret findings if you reduce the data within each category to meaningful chunks: the actionable findings. For example, if three participants had the same problem, discuss that problem only once. Indicate the participants who had the issue so you can easily go back to the participant-level notes, if necessary.

Fig. 8.5 shows an example from a test of the 2020 Census Household form on mobile devices. The screenshots show a series of questions intended to capture a complete listing of household members who lived at the selected address on Census Day, which was October 1, 2012 in this example.

Fig. 8.6 shows participants' answers to question 2F, usability issues observed, and verbalizations made during the session (i.e., think aloud). The interview summaries were cut and pasted into spreadsheets, which allowed us to sort the data easily into the local categories that we identified. Each row is a different participant, and the columns are the local categories, which were individual survey questions (e.g., Q2F) in this example. Organizing observations and participant comments in this way make it easy to quickly read through the data for all participants for Q2F and summarize the usability issues.

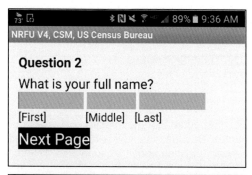

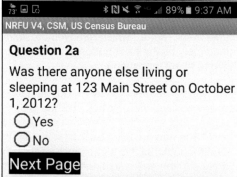

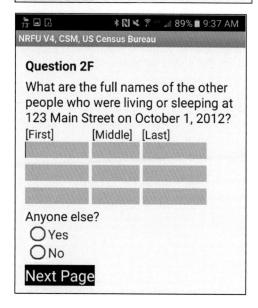

FIGURE 8.5

Screenshots of household roster questions on a test of the 2020 Census Household form conducted on a smartphone.

CaseID	Q2F. What are the full names of the other people who were living or sleeping at 1234 home address on October 1, 2012? Anyone else?	U2F. Usability Issues
0001	[R listed his sister (Person 2), his brother-in-law (Person3), a roommate (Person 4).]	[R commented that the question only had space for three names. Because the keyboard was up, he did not see the second question about "Anyone else?" He asked me what he should do. I told him to do what he would do if I was not here. He said that he was just going to list the adults. Therefore, he excluded his nephew. When he was done listing the three adults, he hit "done," which removed the keyboard. He then immediately hit the Next button without noticing the "Anyone else?" question.]
0002	[R listed her husband (Person 2), their four children (Persons 3-6).]	[R answered the question by giving the names of the other people who lived there. When finished, she reviewed the list of names and said, "My name isn't on there. Why isn't it on there?" She had provided her name in response to Question 2. She thought that this screen included a running list of everyone in the household and was confused that her name was not shown. She then asked if she should enter her name again. The interviewer told her just to do what she would normally do. She decided to add her name again. The survey recognized her name as a duplicate response, and the name did not get added to the roster.]
0003	[R listed a roommate (Person2) and another	[None.]
0004	NA	NA
0005	[R listed his two stepsons as Person 2 and Person 3.]	[R misspelled Person 2's first name, but did not go back to correct it when he noticed. He said he would in a real survey.]
0006	[R's wife (Person 2) and R's sister (Person 3)]	[None.]
0007	[R listed six roommates, Persons 2-7.]	[None.]
0008	[R listed her cousin (Person 2), her nephew (Person 3) and another nephew (Person 4).	[R had some trouble typing and misspelling names due to the length of her fingernails. She did not seem to notice (or care?) that she misspelled names.]

FIGURE 8.6

Example of usability findings grouped by survey question. Observations and responses have been redacted and edited to ensure participant confidentiality.

For each question or category in your study, read through the observations and comments to determine all of the unique usability findings. You might document the findings as you write up your notes or prepare your summary sheets. This list will grow as you review more cases. Or you might wait until all cases have been summarized and identify the findings from all cases at once.

> You will make it easier to interpret findings if you reduce the data within each category to meaningful chunks: the actionable findings.

Findings are anything that affect the survey—respondent interaction in a way that reduces accuracy, efficiency, satisfaction, or ease of use. Findings that affect accuracy typically reflect when the participant's answer to a survey question does not accurately reflect the constructs of the survey. For example, in the 2020 Census study, a participant may have committed an error that led to the omission or duplication of a household member from the roster.

Also note findings that relate to the survey's error tolerance. If a participant makes an error, they may still be able to complete the task accurately if they are able to recover from the error and resolve the problem. However, if participants cannot undo their errors easily or at all, it will affect the accuracy and efficiency of the survey.

Findings related to efficiency or ease of use can include times when the participant was able to answer the question accurately, but the process was unnecessarily complex, not intuitive or time-consuming. For example, the participant was unsure what to do, clicked on the wrong buttons, had to back up or revise an answer, or took a long time to understand and process what needed to be done.

For some surveys, you may be particularly interested in findings related to learnability. As participants repeat the task, are they becoming more efficient, or do they continue to have the same problems? For example, people may look at the navigation button on the left sooner than the one on the right in the beginning of a survey, but they quickly learn that the correct button to proceed through the survey is on the right (Romano Bergstrom, Erdman, & Lakhe, 2016).

Findings related to satisfaction or engagement are often informative. Was the experience positive or did the participant express frustration or confusion? Did they express negative opinions about the design or certain features?

Positive findings should be noted as well. We may observe that a participant enjoyed a particular feature or that a certain aspect of the design made the survey easier for them to use to complete their goal. Knowing what participants liked or enjoyed can be helpful when revising survey aspects that did not improve satisfaction.

Looking again at Fig. 8.6, you can identify three main usability issues that affected accuracy, efficiency, or satisfaction with the survey:

1. Omitted household member:
   a. R did not understand how to add rows for additional household members. The mobile device keyboard blocked part of the screen, making it difficult to see the second part of the question, which may have contributed to the problem (#0001).

2. Names listed incorrectly:
   a. R misspelled Person 2's first name but did not go back to correct it when he noticed. He said he would have in a real survey (#0005).
   b. R had some trouble typing and misspelling names due to the length of her fingernails. She did not seem to notice (or care?) that she misspelled names (#0008).

3. Added name twice:
   a. R did not understand that Question 2F was asking only for other household members (besides herself) and entered her own name again (#0002)

In the summary, the first two findings identified problems with accuracy. The household member's exclusion would lead to an inaccurate count. Incorrect names would make it difficult for the Census Bureau to identify individuals listed at multiple households. The third issue did not lead to an inaccurate roster because the survey was programmed to identify and remove duplicate names. However, it did affect efficiency because the respondent entered her name unnecessarily on the second question.

Continue to summarize the major issues for each survey question, web screen, or task in the same way. Then, note any global issues. For example, the Census study showed that participants were more likely to skip a question or part of a question when more than one question was included on a screen or when a question included multiple parts (Geisen, Olmsted, Goerman, & Lakhe, 2014). We also found that the keyboard blocked the screen, which made multi-question screens with text entry especially problematic. We created global categories for both issues.

Based on the observations and participant comments, we identified the usability problems and as many possible causes for the problems as the data revealed. For example, rather than just noting that a household member was omitted, we explained why, e.g., "R did not understand how to add rows for additional household members." Such causal insights make it easier to address the actual problem, not just its symptoms.

Quantitative data can be used in conjunction with the qualitative data to help to understand the problems. For example, you could contrast the qualitative findings for participants who completed the task successfully with those who failed a task to determine if there are any key differences. Alternatively, you may note that the errors participants made did not affect their task-completion times.

As you summarize the findings, document which participants (by case ID) experienced each problem, rather than just providing a count. Including the IDs is helpful for several reasons:

- Ensures that usability issues are not accidentally double-counted
- Makes it easy to refer back to the interview summary or recordings for context or details
- Facilitates cross referencing the qualitative data with other sources of data, such as background characteristics, performance measures, or eye-tracking data
- Allows you to determine whether problems affected the same set of participants across all questions or affected different participants on different questions.

(Later you may need to remove the IDs for the final report, depending on client preferences and privacy concerns).

Interpreting Data

At this point, you have a summary of the main qualitative findings by question or task as well as a list of global problems. You also have tabulated any quantitative data collected, such as task success or completion times.

The next step is to interpret the findings. What, specifically, was the problem and why was it problematic? When deciding what is a problem, keep in mind the goals of usability testing—to improve data quality and reduce respondent burden. Consequently, not all issues experienced by participants are necessarily problems that affect the capture of high-quality data. For example, with self-administered surveys, yes/no survey questions are likely to generate more yes responses than check all that apply questions (Smyth, Christian, & Dillman, 2008; Smyth, Dillman, Christian, & Stern, 2006). Yet, these surveys often take longer to administer. If a participant said it was tedious to have to check "no" for all questions when only one answer in the list applied, we probably would not consider that a problem. Although answering each question individually is less efficient, the accuracy gains matter more. However, we would probably respond differently if the issue applied to the whole survey.

To identify the cause of the problem, it may help to recall the Usability Model for Surveys (Table 2.2). What part of the survey—respondent interaction did the participant have difficulty with: (1) Interpreting the design, (2) Completing actions and navigating, or (3) Processing feedback?

Interpreting the Design
- Understanding visual design and layout
  - Do participants have difficulty finding the information they need?
  - Do participants misinterpret the visual cues?
- Understanding survey functionality
  - How do participants understand the survey's functionality?
  - Does the way that the survey works match participants' mental models?

Completing Actions and Navigating
- Supporting the ability to complete tasks and goals
  - Can participants complete tasks accurately?
  - How efficiently can participants complete tasks?
- Following navigational cues and instructions
  - Are participants able to navigate through the survey easily?
  - Does the navigational path support participants' goals?

Processing Feedback
- Interpreting and reacting to the feedback provided in response to their actions
  - Do participants know when a selection has been made?
  - Can participants tell when their entries have not been saved?
- Identifying, interpreting, and resolving errors?
  - Do participants know when they have made an error?
  - Do participants know what caused the error?
  - Do participants know how to resolve the error?

Based on the observations in Fig. 8.6, the survey did not support Participant 1's task of listing all of his household members. He did not understand the survey functionality because he did not realize that the survey allowed for additional household members. The screen layout made the method for adding additional members invisible when the keyboard was open. Participant 2 was confused about whether she should list her name. She thought she should list everyone who lives in the household on the same screen. It did not make sense to her to list the other household members separately from herself. The feedback provided by the survey was insufficient in letting her know that she was already included in the roster. Therefore, she added herself again.

AGILE ANALYSIS APPROACH

When you have mastered the detailed analysis approach, you will likely be able to take shortcuts to evaluate usability data more quickly. And sometimes you have to take shortcuts, e.g., when products are tested and revised so quickly that you don't have extensive time to review all the data. Instead, you have only enough time for one quick usability test before the survey launch. In these cases, use an Agile Analysis Approach.

In an Agile Approach, you compile all the necessary data during (or immediately after) the sessions. It may be difficult for novice testers to take sufficient notes and observations while also learning how to moderate, which is why we recommend using the detailed approach at first.

At the end of each session, you quickly and succinctly summarize the findings from your notes. Plan 30–60 minutes between participants to allow time to organize your notes and export recordings, if needed. Do this on a separate sheet of paper or in a Word file. The summaries should include the specific issue and the participant ID (in the event that you have to refer back to the participant-level notes). For example, your summaries might look like this:

Participant #1
- ISSUE: Laughed at branding—branding should be serious.
- ISSUE: Did not read instructions.
- No issues with all questions. Completed all successfully
- ISSUE: Did not click Submit. Thought she was done on Screen 9.

Participant #2
- Likes the branding—reminds her of her children.
- ISSUE: Did not read instructions.
- No issues with all questions.
- Liked having the review at the end because everything is together, and she could recheck answers.

Note how specific the summaries are. At the end of the day, you can scan down your summary and quickly identify issues that recur (such as how the instructions are not read) as well as severe ones that only a few participants may experience (e.g., Participant 1 did not submit the survey). It is helpful to include screenshots in your notes as a reminder and for archiving.

Despite the speed of an Agile Approach, avoid the temptation to interpret findings after each participant. As you have ideas about the issues and their causes, just add them to your notes. You may learn, e.g., that only one person had negative feelings about the branding, whereas the reactions of all other participants were favorable.

> In an Agile Approach, you compile all the necessary data *during* or *immediately after* the sessions.

In an Agile Approach, you can collect as much data as you do in the Detailed Analysis Approach; the difference is the speed at which you summarize and analyze. For example, you probably do not have time to export and analyze quantitative eye-tracking data, but you can export a couple of gaze plots and videos just to illustrate the findings to stakeholders. Similarly, you will look for global and local issues even in the Agile Approach, but you will do so and revise your summary after each participant.

ADDRESSING USABILITY CONCERNS

At this point, you must decide what to do about the problems identified and their causes. Limited time, budget, and resources may make it impossible to fix all of the problems discovered during usability testing, so prioritize the issues. Focus your attention on addressing the highest-priority problems first, and then address lower-priority problems as you are able. However, prior to conducting usability testing, you should carefully consider whether you will have the time and resources to address any identified usability concerns. Building usability testing into the programming schedule will ensure that you have allowed enough time for iterative design and testing. Given the effort and expense of conducting usability testing, you want to make sure that you make the most of your findings.

Determining Priorities

In determining the relative priority of problems, consider two attributes: the problem's effect on data quality and the amount of effort required to fix the problem. As shown in Fig. 8.7, start with problems that both are easy to fix and have a large impact on the data quality. At the other extreme are the problems that will have a small effect on data quality but will be difficult to fix. In between these two extremes, you will address the medium-priority problems as the project's budget and schedule allow.

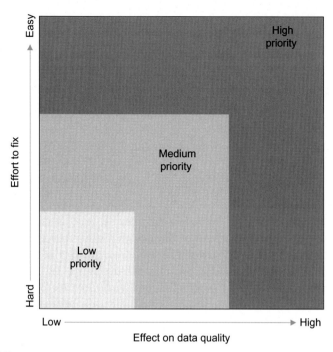

FIGURE 8.7
Priority is determined by the effort required to fix the problem and the potential effect on data quality.

What Types of Problems Have a High Versus Low Impact on Data Quality?

We rarely look at the number of participants who experienced a problem as a determinant of priority. This is because our samples are not representative. Even if an issue affects only one participant in our sample, it could still be a big concern if that participant represents a large portion of respondents or the issue is a showstopper. For example, if even one participant thinks she is finished with the survey and does not submit the survey, that is a big problem that must be addressed. On the other hand are issues that all participants experienced, but they had little or no impact on data quality. Issues that people can easily recover from fall into this category.

Usability issues that will have a high impact on data quality are those that:

- cause missing data (item or unit nonresponse)
- lead to inaccurate responses

- are persistent (i.e., affect a large number of questions)
- most respondents are likely to have
- may cause bias because they affect subgroups differently.

In determining the relative priority of problems, consider two attributes: the problem's effect on data quality and the amount of effort required to fix the problem.

What Types of Problems Are Easy Versus Hard to Fix?

How easy a problem is to fix is a function of both the level of effort involved to fix the problem, and whether there is a clear solution for fixing it.

Level of difficulty also depends on how far along in development the survey is. When usability testing is conducted early in the development process, it is common to use the results to guide the design of the survey. Since less has been programmed, bigger changes can be implemented because programmers have not gone too far down a specific path. For testing that is conducted later in the process, changes are typically limited to those that do not affect the overall design or navigation and that are unlikely to introduce other usability issues.

Generally, it is easiest to fix problems with wording and the order of responses. These changes are also unlikely to affect survey functionality. Moderate effort may be required for other needed changes, such as converting all grid items to individual questions on the mobile version of the survey. Changes that are hardest to make are those that require custom programming (of course) and any aspects that are native to the survey software or to the respondents' device or operating system. Rather than ruling these issues out, though, consider alternate fixes, such as changing survey software.

Revising Surveys

Use these two guidelines for making revisions to surveys:

- Work collaboratively with survey programmers and stakeholders to identify the most parsimonious way to address the problem.
- Consider the impact that a change may have on other aspects of the survey. Will fixing one problem introduce another problem?

The following example demonstrates how usability issues were addressed amid careful consideration for how the changes would affect the rest of the survey.

We conducted usability testing before fielding a large national survey of oncologists. The web survey was designed with a look and feel that is similar to the paper survey. During testing on a desktop computer, we observed that on Question B1 (Fig. 8.8), two participants skipped a row and received a warning message to that effect. The warning message stated, "This question is important to the survey. If you meant to leave it blank, just continue.

B1. How many of your cancer patients received the following multi-marker tumor panels within the **past 12 months**? Please include tests that were ordered by other physicians and tests performed by pathology.

	Not familiar with this test	Familiar with this test, but not used in the past 12 months	1-10 patients in the past 12 months	11-25 patients in the past 12 months	26+ patients in the past 12 months
a. BioSpeciFix (Precision Therapeutics)	○	○	○	○	○
b. DecisionDX (Castle DX)	○	○	○	○	○
c. FoundationOne (Foundation Medicine)	○	○	○	○	○
d. FoundationOne Heme (Foundation Medicine)	○	○	○	○	○
e. Mammaprint (Agendia)	○	○	○	○	○
f. OncoPlex (Diagnostics)	○	○	○	○	○
g. Oncotype DX Breast (Genomic Health)	○	○	○	○	○
h. Oncotype DX Colon (Genomic Health)	○	○	○	○	○
i. Prosigna (NanoString Technologies)	○	○	○	○	○
j. Response DX (Response Genetics)	○	○	○	○	○
k. Solid Tumor Mutation Panel (ARUP)	○	○	○	○	○
l. Suraseq 7500 (Asuragen)	○	○	○	○	○
m. Target Now (Caris Molecular Intelligence)	○	○	○	○	○
n. In-house tumor panel	○	○	○	○	○
o. Other (Please specify):	○	○	○	○	○

FIGURE 8.8

Example of a grid question where respondents received a warning message if a response was skipped. Usability test participants had difficulty when they did not use any other multimarker tumor panels because they were still required to provide a response to the "Other (Please specify):" row.

Otherwise please answer it." Both participants were able to resolve the error easily by providing a response to the missing row. One of these participants received the warning message because he did not select a response for the "Other" category. Unlike the other rows in the table, it is not critical for survey respondents to answer this row so skipping it should not have triggered a warning message. However the survey software would not allow for just some rows to have a warning message if they were skipped.

One solution to the problem for the "other" row would be to deactivate the warning message for the entire question. However, we did not want to do so because it is common to accidentally skip a row in a grid-style question (Couper, Tourangeau, Conrad, & Zhang, 2013; Galesic, Tourangeau, Couper, & Conrad 2007; Kaczmirek, 2011), and eliminating the warning may increase item nonresponse. Instead, we removed the "Other" question from the grid and asked the question separately (Fig. 8.9), which avoided adversely affecting the data quality on other questions.

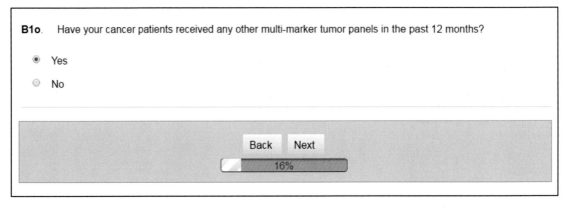

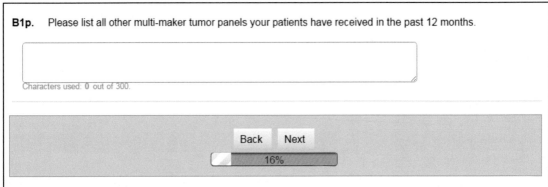

FIGURE 8.9
The "Other (Please, specify):" question item was removed from the grid and asked in a separate question. Respondents who answered "yes" to B1o (top) would then be asked to B1p (bottom).

SPECIAL CONSIDERATIONS FOR MIXED-MODE SURVEYS

Mixed-mode surveys are commonly used to increase coverage, increase response rates, or reduce costs. Achieving equivalent survey data across modes is challenging because different modes support different question design formats. For example, the grid-style questions that work on paper and computer surveys usually do not work well on mobile surveys. Furthermore, the survey mode itself may affect how respondents use and answer survey questions. For example, self-administered surveys may be perceived as more private than interviewer-administered surveys, thus reducing the potential for social-desirability bias.

De Leeuw and Hox (2011) identify three primary strategies that survey researchers use to try to achieve equivalence when designing mixed-mode surveys:

- *Method maximization*. Design questions separately for each mode so that they perform optimally in that mode. The assumption is that the question presented in each mode will measure the same concept, but modes may differ in how accurately the concept is measured.
- *Unimode design*. Use the same question format, text, and structure in all modes. (For a more detailed explanation, see Dillman, Smyth, & Christian, 2014, Chapter 11).
- *Cognitive equivalence*. Produce equivalent responses in each mode by any means, including different question formatting or wording. (For a more detailed explanation, see De Leeuw 2005; De Leeuw & Hox, 2011.)

The mixed-mode approach you choose will affect how usability findings for a given mode are interpreted. Each strategy has pros and cons (see de Leeuw & Hox, 2011 for a more detailed analysis). With a unimode design, usability findings that affect one mode have an impact on all modes. If the usability study reveals problems only with the mobile version, you would need to think of a solution that would work for all versions. And a cognitive equivalence approach requires a more thorough analysis of usability differences by mode.

REPORTING FINDINGS

Throughout this book, we have presented a variety of survey products that can be tested (e.g., paper prototypes, wireframes, mobile, interactive prototypes, finished products), methods (e.g., concurrent vs retrospective, verbal probing vs think aloud), and approaches (e.g., lab, in-the-field, remote). The variability in how usability testing can be done underscores the need to fully document what was done in each project. With time, we can compare the outcomes of different methodologies to better demonstrate what works best. Furthermore, documenting and reporting our findings facilitates transparency and allows us to apply the results we learn to new surveys.

The fast pace of iterative testing often does not allow sufficient time to prepare a full report after each round. So report key findings and recommendations in a brief memo between rounds. Once all rounds of testing are complete, you can prepare a more detailed final report. The sections below show what should be included in the final report.

Final Report Sections

Below is a report outline of the components that should be in every usability test's final report. This outline is based on the Cognitive Interview Report Framework developed by Boeije and Willis (2013) from various checklists used for reporting qualitative research. Given the similarities between cognitive and usability testing, the main framework components apply equally well to usability testing.

1. Introduction
    a. Background
    b. Research Objectives
2. Data Collection Methods
    a. Research Design
    b. Participant Selection and Recruitment
    c. Procedures
    d. Analysis
3. Findings and Recommendations
4. Conclusions
5. Limitations
6. Next Steps

Introduction
This usually includes two sections: the background (what you already know) and the research objectives (what you want to know).

Background
Include general details, such as the survey's purpose, the sponsor/stakeholders and any other relevant background. The section should state the high-level reason for usability testing (e.g., new survey, testing a survey redesign, adding new questions, adding a web mode) and identify and review existing literature

or project work that has been done on the topic. This may include the results from an expert review or the results from any other survey pretesting.

Research Objectives

In addition to high-level goals, this section should also include your testing focus and concerns. For example, was testing conducted specifically to evaluate certain aspects or features of the survey, or to evaluate a finished product?

Data Collection Methods
Research Design

Present an overview of the study's design: e.g., how many rounds of testing and what survey products (e.g., wireframes, prototypes, and mobile) were tested? Note whether the design included any additional methodologies such as cognitive interviewing or eye tracking.

Participant Selection and Recruitment

This section should include information on the following:

- Specific participant subgroups or characteristics that were required for participation (e.g., large households, new employees, low computer-literacy).
- Participant-recruitment methods such as the use of local organizations, online tools such as Craigslist or Facebook, sample lists, participant databases or word of mouth. We commonly reference any recruitment materials used in the appendix.
- Eligibility or screening questions that individuals had to complete to be able to participate. Include the actual screening questions.
- How many total participants were screened, how many were eligible, and how many were recruited for the study.

It can be helpful to include a table that lists the participants along with any relevant demographic or recruitment characteristics. Table 8.6 shows an example of a recruitment table for a study that included questions on alcohol and drug use.

Procedures

Describe in detail exactly what you and the participants did during the sessions. This includes information about informed-consent procedures, session length, and the equipment used to administer and record the sessions. Include the approach, such as think-aloud or verbal probing, and whether concurrent or retrospective. Also include the actual moderator's guide with any scripted probes in the appendix.

Table 8.6 Example Participant Characteristics Table

Case ID	Age	Sex	Race/Ethnicity	Education	Past 12 Month Substance Use
10001	21	Female	White	Some college	Alcohol
10002	33	Female	Black	Some college	Alcohol, marijuana, cocaine
10003	26	Male	White	Some college	Alcohol, marijuana
10004	37	Female	White	Bachelor's degree	Alcohol, marijuana, methamphetamine, cocaine
10005	22	Female	White	Bachelor's degree	Alcohol, marijuana
10006	19	Female	White	Some college	Marijuana
10007	42	Female	Black, Hispanic	High school/GED	Alcohol
10008	18	Male	Black	High school/GED	Alcohol, marijuana
10009	25	Female	Black	Some college	Alcohol, cocaine, heroin
10010	22	Male	Black	Some college	Alcohol, cocaine
100011	16	Male	White, Hispanic	Less than high school	Alcohol, marijuana, cocaine
100012	12	Female	White	Less than high school	Alcohol, marijuana
100013	15	Male	White	Less than high school	Alcohol, marijuana, cocaine, methamphetamine

Data Analysis

Describe what data was collected, such as observations, time on task, task accuracy, and any other metrics that will be used in your analysis. Also describe your general analysis approach and software.

Findings and Recommendations

The section is the meat of your report, where you present your detailed usability findings at the (local) question or task level as well as at the global level. When the recommendations are specific, describe and interpret the findings in the same place that you recommend revisions. This makes it easier for the reader to follow the path from problem to resolution. More general recommendations that apply to multiple questions (e.g., ask only one question on a screen, avoid grid questions, and reduce the amount of text on each screen) can be in a separate section from the findings.

Conclusions

Present your readers with an answer to your research questions. Include a synthesis of the main findings and identify the key takeaways. If applicable, it should also include what the next steps are, such as additional rounds of usability testing, other questionnaire pretesting approaches, or changes that will be made to the survey as a result of testing. We often present the findings to the team before delivering this final report, so we can include the change that will be made as a result of testing.

Limitations

This section should describe any limitations with the design of your study and how it was conducted. You should indicate the extent to which your findings can be generalized to a wider population or not.

As mentioned in the beginning of this book, for usability testing to become a standard pretesting methodology, those of us who do this work need to share our methods, theories, and results in an effort to come to agreement on the best practices. Help this cause by presenting at conferences, publishing in peer-reviewed journals, and documenting your approach and findings in final reports.

References

Boeije, H., & Willis, G. (2013). The cognitive interviewing reporting framework (CIRF): Towards the harmonization of cognitive interviewing reports. *Methodology: European Journal of Research Methods for the Behavioral and Social Sciences, 9*(3), 87−95. Available from http://dx.doi.org/10.1027/1614-2241/a000075.

Couper, M. P., Tourangeau, R., Conrad, F. G., & Zhang, C. (2013). The design of grids in web surveys. *Social Science Computer Review, 31*(3), 322−345.

De Leeuw, E. D. (2005). To mix or not to mix data collection modes in surveys. *Journal of Official Statistics, 21*, 233−255 . Retrieved from <http://www.jos.nu>.

De Leeuw, E. D., & Hox, J. J. (2011). Internet surveys as part of a mixed mode design. In M. Das, P. Ester, & L. Kaczmirek (Eds.), *Social and behavioral research and the Internet: Advances in applied methods and research strategies* (pp. 45−76). New York, NY: Taylor & Francis Group.

Dillman, D. A., Smyth, J. D., & Christian, L. M. (2014). *Internet, phone, mail, and mixed-mode surveys*. New York, NY: Wiley.

Dumas, J. S., & Redish, J. C. (1999). *A practical guide to usability testing* (revised 2nd ed.). Portland, OR: Intellect.

Galesic, M., Tourangeau, R. Couper, M. P., & Conrad, F. G. (2007). Using change to improve navigation in grid questions. In *Paper presented at the General Online Research conference (GOR'07), Leipzig, March*.

Geisen, E., Olmsted, M., Goerman P., & Lakhe, S. (2014). Planning for the future: Usability testing for the 2020 Census. In *Paper presented at the 2014 Federal computer assisted survey information collection, Washington, DC*.

Jarrett, C., & Romano Bergstrom, J. C. (2014). Forms and surveys. In J. Romano Bergstrom, & A. Schall (Eds.), *Eye tracking in user experience design*. San Francisco, CA: Morgan Kaufmann.

Kaczmirek, L. (2011). Attention and usability in internet surveys: Effects of visual feedback in grid questions. In M. Das, P. Ester, & L. Kaczmirek (Eds.), *Social research and the internet* (pp. 191−214). New York: Taylor and Francis.

Olmsted-Hawala, E., Holland, T., & Quach, T. (2014). Usability testing. In J. Romano Bergstrom, & A. Schall (Eds.), *Eye tracking in user experience design*. Waltham, MA: Morgan Kaufman.

Romano Bergstrom, J. C., & Strohl, J. (2013). Improving government websites and surveys with usability testing: A comparison of methodologies. In *Proceedings from the Federal Committee on Statistical Methodology (FCSM) Conference, Nov 2013, Washington, DC.*

Romano Bergstrom, J. C., Erdman, C., & Lakhe, S. (2016). Navigation buttons in web-based surveys: Respondents' preferences revisited in the laboratory. *Survey Practice, 9*(1).

Romano Bergstrom, J. C., Olmsted-Hawala, E. L., & Bergstrom, H. C. (2016). Older adults fail to see the periphery during website navigation. *Universal Access in the Information Society, 15*(2), 261—270.

Romano Bergstrom, J. C., Olmsted-Hawala, E. L., Chen, J. M., & Murphy, E. D. (2011). Conducting iterative usability testing on a Web site: Challenges and benefits. *Journal of Usability Studies, 7,* 9—30.

Smyth, J., Dillman, D., Christian, L., & Stern, M. (2006). Comparing check-all and forced-choice question formats in web surveys. *Public Opinion Quarterly, 70*(1), 66—77.

Smyth, J., Christian, L., & Dillman, D. (2008). Does "yes" or "no" on the telephone mean the same as "checkall-that-apply" on the web. *Public Opinion Quarterly, 72*(1), 103—113.

Glossary

Accuracy A usability metric; the percentage of participants that can successfully complete a task (see also Effectiveness).

Acquiescence The tendency for survey respondents to agree with a question.

Assessment testing Can occur at any point in the survey development cycle; it is usually done in development's early or middle stages, when prototypes exist for at least parts of the survey. It evaluates users' actual behaviors—how well people can actually use the product to complete a goal. It evaluates specific components of the survey and can provide insight on the high-level design or approach as well as a design's implementation. Also known as Summative testing.

Attention A usability metric; what people look at while completing the survey. Best measured implicitly with eye tracking.

Break offs When respondents start a survey, but fail to complete it.

Cognitive interviewing A process that identifies potential problems in survey questions by evaluating the cognitive processes respondents use to answer survey questions. Also known as cognitive testing.

Cognitive testing Identifies potential problems in survey questions by evaluating the cognitive processes respondents use to answer survey questions. Also known as cognitive interviewing.

Computer-assisted interviewing (CAI) An interviewing technique in which the interviewer or respondent uses a computer to answer survey questions.

Concurrent think-aloud (CTA) Participants think aloud as they complete tasks.

Concurrent verbal probing Moderators ask participants targeted questions about their experience completing the survey as they work. Probes may be prepared in advance about content on each screen or probes can be created spontaneously based on something that happens in the interview.

Conditional probes When scripted probes apply only to certain participants or in certain conditions.

Context of use Surveys need to be evaluated for usability in the environment in which they will actually be used (e.g., at a respondent's work place, on a mobile device).

Coverage error Occurs when members of the population we are interested in are not in the sampling frame—the list of individuals, businesses, or households used to select the sample.

Created questions Survey questions in which people must think up responses on the spot. Gaze is on the screen, and attention is elsewhere. Not good for eye tracking.

Ease of use A usability metric: how easy participants perceive the survey to be to use.

Effectiveness Measuring whether users are successfully able to complete specific tasks (see Accuracy).

Efficiency A usability metric; how long it takes participants to complete tasks, the first click, and/or the number of clicks required to complete a task.

Errors of nonobservation Occur when certain members of the target population are not included in the survey. These errors further group into: coverage, sampling, and nonresponse errors.

Errors of observation Occur when the true value is different from the value reported by the respondent, also known as measurement error.

Expert review A usability evaluation conducted by survey methodologists or subject-matter specialists.

Exploratory testing Conducted at the beginning of the survey development process to guide the actual design of the survey. Also known as Formative testing.

Eye-tracking data Data that demonstrates where people look during a usability study.

Formative testing Conducted at the beginning of the survey development process to guide the actual design of the survey. Also known as Exploratory testing.

Gathered questions Survey questions in which the respondent has to get their answer from another source (e.g., look at a receipt, refer to hardcopy materials, perform an online search), and eye-tracking gaze may be intermittently recorded.

Implicit data The most unbiased form of user-experience data. These data measure behavior and physiology that are difficult or impossible for people to be aware of. They include eye tracking, pupil dilation, and electrodermal activity, which users cannot control.

In-the-field usability testing Testing where the participant would complete the survey in their natural environment (e.g., their home or work place) rather than a laboratory setting.

Interviewer error (for interviewer-administered surveys) Occurs when respondents' answers differ due to the ways that interviewers read and administer the survey.

Interviewer-administered survey Survey in which an interviewer asks the questions and records the respondent's responses. Compare to self-administered surveys in which respondents enter their own responses.

Iterative usability testing Several rounds of usability testing are conducted; changes are made to the survey based on the usability testing findings; the survey is tested again, using the same tasks and metrics. Metrics are compared in each round of testing to the previous round, and if usability improves, so do the metrics. This iterative process continues until optimal usability is achieved or a deadline is approached.

Learnability A usability metric; how well participants can learn how to use a survey (typically for interviewer-administered surveys).

Likert-scale questions A series of questions about a given topic in which respondents express their level of agreement or disagreement on a symmetric scale.

Measurement error Occurs when the true value is different from the value reported by the respondent. Also known as Errors of observation.

Mental model The model that participants have in their mind about how a survey should function. It maps onto similar interactions in their environment, such as other web-based surveys, paper surveys, websites, mobile devices, and computers in general.

Metrics for evaluation Data we collect in usability studies, including accuracy, efficiency, satisfaction, ease of use, learnability, attention, and confusion. See Performance measures.

Mobile sled A platform that holds the mobile device and records from a camera above the device.

Mode effects error Occurs when the mode of the survey (e.g., mail, telephone, web) introduces differences in survey results.

Moderator's guide Materials for conducting the usability test, which include the script, tasks/scenarios, the consent form, and the questionnaires. Also known as the usability testing protocol.

Nonresponse error Occurs when survey responders are systematically different than nonresponders on the key concepts the survey is measuring.

Observational data Data that the moderator observes and measures as the participant is completing a usability test. These types of data typically include performance measures (e.g., reaction time, accuracy) and observed behaviors (e.g., click behavior).

Paper prototyping A methodology that consists of creating simple illustrations of the product to facilitate design, development, and testing. Paper prototypes are often used to flesh out a particular design as well as to share ideas among survey designers, programmers, and stakeholders during the user-centered design process.

Performance measures Data we collect in usability studies, including accuracy, efficiency, satisfaction, ease of use, learnability, attention, and confusion (see Metrics for evaluation).

Pilot testing Evaluates how well the survey will work in the "real world" by testing the procedures with a small number of respondents.

Probes Follow-up questions asked of the participant to elicit additional information and feedback as they complete usability tasks.

Product Survey products might include anything from paper surveys to web-based surveys, and self-administered surveys to interviewer-administered surveys.

Question branching Survey questions that "branch" to ask different questions of different respondents.

Remote moderated usability testing Testing where the participant and moderator are not in the same location. The moderator leads the discussion.

Remote unmoderated usability testing Testing where the participant works from their home/ office, and there is no moderator—participant interaction. The researcher receives data once the session is complete.

Remote usability testing Usability testing where the participant works from their home/office (see Remote moderated and Remote unmoderated usability testing).

Respondent error Occurs when differences in respondents' experiences, cognitive ability, and motivation affect responses.

Respondent—survey interaction The way that respondents use and interact with web-based survey to accomplish their goals.

Response formation model A conceptual model that shows the four steps and associated cognitive processes that respondents follow when answering survey questions. Comprised of: Comprehension, Retrieval, Judgment, Response.

Retrospective Think-Aloud (RTA) Participants think aloud or explain what they were doing during the task as they look at screenshots of the survey or a video replay of the usability test.

Retrospective verbal probing The moderator asks probes after the participant has completed all tasks, rather than asking probes during or between tasks (see Concurrent verbal probing). Also commonly referred to as a debriefing interview. Probes may be prepared in advance about content on each screen, or probes are created spontaneously based on something that happens in the interview. It may help to print screenshots to facilitate recall.

Sampling error Occurs because our survey estimates are produced from only a subset of the population we are interested in.

Satisfaction Measuring how satisfied participants are with the task or survey; often self-rated measures or qualitative comments elicited during usability testing.

Satisficing Occurs when respondents are not willing or able to provide the effort (e.g., mouse clicks or movements, or mental calculations) to produce optimal answers to survey questions.

Scenario A real-life situation that you ask participants to put themselves in to test the instrument.

Script A prepared document that guides what the moderator will say to each participant.

Scripted probes Probes that are prepared in advance of the usability test and asked for all participant.

Self-administered surveys Surveys in which respondents enter their own responses. Compare to interviewer-administered surveys, in which an interviewer asks the questions and records the respondent's responses.

Self-report data Data that participants provide, often questionnaire and probe responses as well as think-aloud verbalizations.

Slider questions Survey questions that gather numeric data points from survey respondents in an interactive display, such that the respondent drags a "slider" in order to respond.

Slot-in questions Survey questions that respondents know easily, such as name and date of birth. Respondents' gaze and attention are both at the screen. Good for eye tracking.

Spontaneous probes Probes that asked spontaneously, usually as a reaction to something that happened in the usability test.

Summative testing Can occur at any point in the survey development cycle, it is usually done in development's early or middle stages, when prototypes exist for at least parts of the survey. It evaluates users' actual behaviors—how well people can actually use the product to complete a goal. It evaluates specific components of the survey and can provide insight on the high-level design or approach as well as a design's implementation. Also known as Assessment testing.

Survey software Off-the-shelf survey software packages that allow nonprogrammers the ability to build web-based surveys.

Task Something you want the participant to accomplish.

Think-aloud Participants talk about what they are thinking and doing while completing tasks.

Third-party questions Survey questions in which respondents have to ask someone else for the information. Neither the respondent's gaze nor attention is on the screen, and eye-tracking data cannot be collected.

Usability The extent to which a product can be used by specified users to achieve specified goals with effectiveness, efficiency, and satisfaction in a specified context of use.

Usability Model for Surveys A conceptual model that focuses on how respondent use surveys. Comprised of: interpreting the design, completing actions, and navigating and processing feedback.

Usability testing Watching participants perform tasks to measure the extent to which a product (e.g., survey) can be used by participants to achieve goals (e.g., completing the survey or specific items/tasks) with effectiveness, efficiency, and satisfaction.

User The person using the survey instrument: respondents and/or interviewers.

Validation testing Occurs at the end of the survey development process just before the pilot test or survey launch. At this stage, it is helpful to test the whole survey, from logging in (if required) to completing/submitting the survey. The goal is to ensure the survey is free of any major usability concerns that would cause respondents to break off, or that would provide incorrect data. Also known as Verification testing.

Verbal probing Moderators ask participants targeted questions about their experience completing the survey. Probes may be prepared in advance about content on each screen or probes can be created spontaneously based on something that happens in the interview.

Verification testing Occurs at the end of the survey development process just before the pilot test or survey launch. At this stage, it is helpful to test the whole survey, from logging in (if required) to completing/submitting the survey. The goal is to ensure the survey is free of any major usability concerns that would cause respondents to break off, or that would provide incorrect data. Also known as Validation testing.

Wireframes The skeleton of a web page. Similar to paper prototypes, they are used to lay out the basic structure and design of a website page. Although the wireframe might have headings or labels, it typically does not have actual content or has only limited content. It might have a link, but clicking on the link does not take the user to another location. Wireframes can be shown to participants as a printout or on a computer screen.

Index

Note: Page numbers followed by "*f*", "*t*", and "*b*" refer to figures, tables, and boxes, respectively.

Printed in the United States
By Bookmasters